Certain Change

Certain Change

Social Work Practice in the Future

David Macarov

National Association of Social Workers
Silver Spring, MD 20910

Richard L. Edwards, ACSW, *President*
Mark G. Battle, ACSW, *Executive Director*

Library of Congress Cataloging-in-Publication Data

Macarov, David.
   Certain change : social work practice in the future / David Macarov.
      p. cm.
   Includes bibliographical references and index.
   ISBN 0-87101-191-3 (pbk. : alk. paper)
   1. Social service—United States. 2. Social prediction—United States. I. Title.
HV91.M18   1991
361.3'2'0973—dc20   90-27568
                                                      CIP

Printed in the United States of America

Cover design by Max-Karl Winkler
Interior design by Harper Graphics

Contents

3. Social Work with Tomorrow's Families

4. Responding to the Work World's Evolution

5. Technology's Ongoing Development

6. Social Work and Privatization

7. What Profession Awaits Us?

Acknowledgments

All knowledge is based upon previous knowledge, and every writer owes an enormous and unrepayable debt to everyone who has dealt with the same subject previously. Consequently, I am grateful to my teachers, my students, and my colleagues, as well as to the authors of the items listed in the bibliography and to many authors whose work I read but did not quote.

I would particularly like to thank Bernard Warach, Chana Lerba, and Howard Litwin, who read and commented on various drafts of the chapter on aging; Nina O'Neal, who was good enough to read the chapter on families; Menachem Monnickendam, who made suggestions concerning the chapter on technology; and Howard Karger and Ralph Kramer, who were extremely gracious and helpful with the chapter on privatization. I am also grateful to the Fordham University midtown campus librarians, who extended library privileges to me, and to Sarah Gonen, Netanya Ginsburg, and the other librarians at the Leavitt Library at the Hebrew University, who were invariably helpful.

Special thanks to my wife, Frieda, who not only read and commented on each chapter as it came out of the printer, but who bore the frenzied writing periods and the inevitable fallow periods with equal grace.

Finally, this book is dedicated to my sister, Ruby, who has always been concerned about the future—especially mine.

Introduction

The goal of social work, and the reason for its existence, is to help people live happier, more fulfilling lives. Meeting this goal sometimes requires helping people to overcome current difficulties; sometimes it requires rehabilitation after a previous problem; sometimes it necessitates prevention of possible or anticipated situations; and sometimes social work does not involve problems at all, but requires making available new opportunities, satisfying activities, and meaningful relationships. However, to make sure that any or all of these activities are appropriate, and that they remain effective, it is important for social workers to attempt to foresee what the situation of clients will be in the future. Solutions seen as helpful today may prove dysfunctional in light of future situations. Consequently, projections concerning the future are both helpful and necessary for social work practice, for social welfare planning, and for social work education.

Social work is intimately bound up with the values and the structure of the society in which it takes place. Whether social work is seen as arising from individual needs (Towle, 1965) or whether it is viewed as primarily serving the ends of certain groups, ideologies, or institutions (Macarov, 1978), social work is societally determined and socially sanctioned insofar as goals, activities, and boundaries are concerned.

Consequently, changes that take place in society require new or different functions of social work. For example, the worldwide growth of entitlement programs—from 142 in 1940 (U.S. Department of Health, Education, and Welfare, 1972) to 453 in 1987 (U.S. Department of Health and Human Services, 1989)—relieved social workers of some of their investigative roles. Similarly, the trend toward deinstitutionalization of children, the aged, and the mentally ill has led to a general increase in community services in most countries, and this, in turn, has led to changes in the employment and activities of social workers.

Further, the militancy of certain individuals and groups, peaking in many countries in the 1960s, changed leadership styles and modified the traditional tasks of social group workers and community organizers.

Not only social work activities, but social welfare programs and regulations, reflect changes in society. For example, in the United States, rising divorce and remarriage rates, as well as changing attitudes toward individual freedom, have led to the virtual abandonment of family responsibility laws. An increase in the number of working women in many countries has brought about massive growth in child care facilities. Clients' legally mandated right of access to their social work records has, in some cases, led not only to differences in recording, but to changes in client-worker relationships. It seems certain that future changes in society will continue to affect the roles and tasks assigned to social welfare and to social workers.

This book attempts to envision some of the most probable and important changes destined to take place in Western society during the working lives of current social work graduates, and to draw some conclusions from them in terms of social welfare programs and social work activities. However, it should be clear that each of these changes affects and is affected by each of the others. Consequently, although an effort will be made to depict some of these interrelationships, particularly in the final chapter, these topics are discussed individually purely for heuristic purposes. Indeed, in some places points are deliberately repeated, because they inhere in two or more situations.

Further, the focus of this book is on social work in the Western democracies, with particular emphasis on the United States, although examples will be drawn from other countries when appropriate. In any case, situations in the centrally planned economies (countries formerly called Communist, East Bloc, or Second World) and in the developing, or Third World, countries are not included. This should not denigrate the importance of those areas, nor should it deny the very real impact that they will have on and receive from the industrialized West. That subject requires separate treatment.

The possible future changes mentioned in this book do not exhaust all of the possibilities. One could speculate about many other changes, or possible alternative futures, but it is important that a book like this be based firmly on documented trends; and, further, that the reason for these trends be explained and evaluated. Thus, there are areas of social work practice that are, or are becoming, very important that are not dealt with in this book. For example, the spread of drugs, migration patterns, new diseases such as acquired immune deficiency syndrome, poverty, and homelessness—each of which is a legitimate area for social work activity—are not discussed, because no clear future trends are discernible.

An attempt has been made to avoid pure speculation, as it is irresponsible to call for changes in practice or education for practice on the basis that something "might" happen. Similarly, possible alternative situations should be projected only if the degree of probability of each situation can be deduced. Simply saying, "Let's wait and see which of these happens," is not helpful in planning for change. Consequently, this book on the future of social work deals only with those areas in which there are clear indications as to what the future holds.

Finally, an effort has been made to keep this book from arguing for or against a particular situation or trend (although in some places an unavoidable bias might be discerned). These are changes that seem almost certain to occur during the working lives of present-day social work graduates, whether we like them or not. Because good education involves clarifying questions, rather than giving answers, that is what this book attempts to do.

REFERENCES

Macarov, D. (1978). *The design of social welfare*. New York: Holt, Rinehart & Winston.

Towle, C. (1965). *Common human needs*. New York: National Association of Social Workers.

U.S. Department of Health, Education, and Welfare. (1972). *Social security programs throughout the world, 1970*. Washington, DC: Author.

U.S. Department of Health and Human Services. (1989). Washington, DC: Author.

1

Looking Ahead

Although everyone thinks about the future at some time, the controlled, scholarly, speculative study of probable future social work conditions is relatively recent. There are a number of reasons, some of them compelling, why this type of concern with the future deserves the attention of social workers and social work educators.

WHY STUDY THE FUTURE?

Planning for Survival

Although it is conventional to hold that no one knows what will happen in the future, and therefore that attempts to predict the future are useless, we all predict the future constantly. As we plan what we will do next year, next week, later in the day, or even in a few moments, we are making predictions as to what the situation will be at that future time. To plan, we *must* predict future events or situations.

In addition, it is not true that we cannot accurately predict the future. Jaffe and Froomkin (1968) found that 10-year predictions, at least, are generally reliable, and Ferkiss (1975) pointed out that although unanticipated events may occur, they generally occur in addition to anticipated events—not in place of them.

Sheer Curiosity

At some time, everyone wants to know what to expect in the future. In some cases, this may be mere curiosity, expressed as, "What would happen if . . . ?" or, "What will happen next?" or, "If I did thus and so, what would happen?" Indeed, some of the world's greatest scientific discoveries have resulted from just such curiosity on the part of researchers.

The Need to Know

Sometimes one needs to know the future to be able to plan. The weather forecast, for example, has practical implications, as do class and exam schedules for students. In some cases one needs to know more than or before someone else does, as with changes in the stock market or which team will win the game. In a more serious vein, anyone engaged in planning, whether for an individual, organization, business, or government, needs to know as accurately as possible what the future probably holds. Environmental impact studies are good examples of future planning.

Preparing to Cope with Change

One of the most cogent reasons for social workers, and especially for social work educators, to try to predict the future is to anticipate situations that will require social work intervention, or additions to current practice method repertoires, or efforts to change laws, regulations, or programs.

Lengthening of life expectancy brought about, and will continue to cause, new problems for the aged and their families. If divorce rates continue to rise as they have in the past, problems of children in multiparent families will multiply. As technology creates new work patterns—more leisure time and more unemployment—these in turn will bring about new or aggravated social problems. The spread of acquired immune deficiency syndrome (AIDS); the growing recognition of Alzheimer's disease; the implications of new fertility aids, including mechanical reproduction methods—all require thought about what kinds of help people with these problems will need in the future.

Becoming Sensitive to Change

In addition to anticipating situations, it is important that the social work profession also recognize unanticipated situations when they occur. The profession must not only be sensitive to change but must also be able to identify and measure it.

The profession has not always been distinguished in this area. Although social workers have been dealing with poor people since the beginnings of the profession, poverty became a national issue in the 1960s largely through the publications of non–social workers. In England, clients' rights to see their records came about through a lawsuit *against* a social welfare agency. Many self-help groups, such as the one concerned with Sudden Infant Death Syndrome (SIDS), came into being without the help or notice of social workers. In fact, social work has been only tangentially involved with attempting to predict the future, and there is need for planning and action in this area (Gottschalk, 1974).

Being concerned about future changes that will require social work intervention requires a very long lead time. Marland (1974) estimated that it may take as long as 50 years to get a new idea into the curricula of educational institutions. On the other hand, as Hillard (cited in Abbott, 1978) pointed out, "At the rate at which knowledge is growing, by the time the child born today graduates from college, the amount of knowledge in the world will be four times as great. By the time that same child is 50 years old, it will be 32 times as great, and 97 percent of everything known in the world will have been learned since the time the child was born."

Identifying Cultural Lag

A further aim of future studies is to identify quickly and easily outmoded behaviors, both on the part of clients and of social workers. For example, as employment has become very heavily weighted toward service occupations, research and much social work practice are still oriented toward problems within, and caused by, industrial employment. Family policy is based on a model of a working father, a housewife mother, and two small children in the home—a model that hardly exists anymore. Similarly, in many large cities, the image of homeless people as alcoholic, mentally ill, or deviant, is rapidly becoming obsolete as more people who simply cannot find affordable housing fall into this group. Even the time-honored concept of confidentiality in social work has taken on new dimensions with the advent of computerized records (Macarov, 1990).

There are many reasons, therefore, to attempt prediction. The question is not whether we *do* predict, but to what extent we *can* predict the future accurately. This involves being conscious of the time frame we are using, the instruments being applied, and the subject matter being examined.

Influencing the Future

Without forecasting there is no freedom of decision. Only insofar as we try to influence the direction that the future will take are we exercising choice, rather than resigning ourselves to the inevitable or—to be more precise—to capriciousness. Just as the role of the executive in an organization can be defined not as one who solves problems but as one who anticipates problems and acts to prevent them from arising, social workers, who are committed to preventing social problems where possible and to alleviating those that do occur, require foresight as well. For social workers, prevention means trying to influence individual and social change in a way that creates the least possible human difficulties, or better, that offers the greatest possible potential for human happiness.

In all important societal changes two interacting factors coexist: values and structures. These factors influence each other constantly, either in the same direction or as countervailing forces. Overarching societal change requires that they both be modified.

Defining the Time Frame

Some futurists distinguish between the near or immediate future, by which they mean from one to five years; the middle-range or intermediate future as six to 20 years; the long-range future as 21 to 50 years; and the far future as meaning more than 50 years. Others use the year 2000 because it is convenient, logical, and close enough to seem realistic. However, at the time of this writing, the year 2000 is less than 10 years away, and as a glance back at 1980 will indicate, not many major changes in society take place in so short a time period.

The time frame used in this book is based on different considerations. Students who graduate at age 25 and work until 65 will have 40 years of working life. Therefore, the changes discussed in this book are those expected to take place within the next 40 years—in other words, by approximately the year 2030.

Some of the changes will occur sooner than others. No attempt is made here to predict their order, or even their approximate date. As Simon (1983) pointed out, prediction is easier if we do not attempt to forecast in detail the time path of events, or the exact dates on which they will happen, but instead, focus on the steady state toward which the system is tending. Thus, it is probable at least that at some point in the next 40 years, most, if not all, of the changes mentioned in this book will occur.

CHANGES IN SOCIAL WORK PRACTICE

The changes that are occurring now, or will occur in the future, may require new methods of practicing and of learning to practice social work. Most professions have a tendency toward conservatism, and social work is no exception. Many practitioners continue to use the methods they learned as students—perhaps as long ago as 40 years or more—even when these methods are no longer relevant. For example, the psychoanalytic—or, at least, the therapeutic—approach to dealing with unemployed people may persist even during periods of mass societally induced unemployment, when social action or helping clients to organize as pressure groups is likely to be more effective. The use of computers is another example. Overcoming initial resistance to using computers has been recognized as a problem by software manufacturers, and user-friendly programs have resulted. Whereas new social work graduates tend to be at least computer literate, many old-timers either prefer to continue in ignorance or actively resist the use of computers in social work practice.

New methods of practice also include, or should include, supervising and managing nonprofessional personnel, working with volunteers, designing satisfying leisure-time programs, and helping the very old.

It is impossible to predict every future change that will require new methods of practice. However, one goal of prediction is to create an openness among social workers to participate in ongoing education and continuing education so that they can stay abreast of new situations.

CHANGES IN VALUES AND SOCIETAL STRUCTURE

Values

Although there is a tendency to think of values as deep-seated and long-lasting, changes in values occur in many areas, such as child care, care of the aged, privacy, sex, marriage, and unemployment.

The belief that parental care is more desirable for children than the care available in institutions was a guiding principle among professionals and lay people alike for many years. Every effort was made to keep children in their homes. More recently, as "workfare" programs that require parents receiving welfare to work have gained popularity, extensive child care facilities have become necessary lest welfare parents use child care as an excuse for not working. In fact, the desire of many mothers to work outside the home has made such facilities a growth industry. As a consequence, use of child care provisions outside the home has become not just accepted, but prestigious.

This change brought in its wake a societal value change that holds that contact with other children, even as early as age two or younger, is healthy and that care by professionally trained personnel is preferable to that of amateur mothers. In fact, some now view working mothers as more capable of providing child care than nonworking parents (Raichle, 1980). Thus, the philosophy follows the act, and values become rationalizations for existing situations.

The same process may be observed, in reverse, in the care of elderly and mentally ill people. As institutionalization became more and more expensive, the value of community care began to be touted, and formerly institutionalized people were sent back into the community as a therapeutic measure. The value of community care, although rarely empirically evaluated, now is posited as self-evident.

Again, take the value of privacy. In many countries years ago it would have been unthinkable for all the citizens of a town to agree to have their names and addresses published in a book and thus made available to anyone who wanted to exploit such information. With the invention of the telephone, however, being omitted from the telephone book became a minor tragedy (Brody, Cornoni-Huntley, & Patrick, 1981). Similarly, the invention of automobiles (once referred to as "portable bedrooms") made unmarried sexual activity more accessible to many people and changed their values concerning it. At a later date, the discovery of penicillin and the birth control pill changed sexual mores in one generation (St. George, 1970). Attitudes toward homosexuality were also rapidly moving toward acceptance when the spread of AIDS began to change both sexual attitudes and permissiveness regarding sexual practices. Were preventive or curative methods for AIDS to be developed, sexual mores would again change.

The time-honored concept of marriage as an unbreakable lifetime commitment—"until death us do part"—is being challenged by the fact that more than 50 percent of the first marriages of young adults in the United States today end in divorce, as do 60 percent of second marriages, and that 75 percent of young divorced persons are likely to remarry (Glick, 1984). A new marriage ethic is clearly emerging, if it has not already.

Similarly, when unemployment figures are between 5 and 10 percent, the general assumption is that everyone who wants to work can find a job if he or she just looks hard enough. When the unemployment figure rises to as much as one-third of the labor force, however, as it did during the Great Depression (Bird, 1966), the value put on rugged individualism shifts to a dependence on the government, which is seen as responsible for the situation.

Thus, it is clear that in many cases values arise from, rather than create, situations. Looking to the future, Gordon (1969) held that, "Values change to fit the world which technology presents." Rescher (1969) was more circumspect but nevertheless clear: "Technology acts indirectly, shaping the way in which other forces have their effect on values." Simone Weill (cited by Brugman, 1980) pointed out that human values do not last forever, and Russel (1986) was more specific: "Once conditions are ripe, there often occurs a sudden reversal of opinion that would be quite unimaginable before the fact." It is the relative ease with which values change, despite the mythology of their tenacity, which led St. George (1970) to say, "How shallow are our values."

Current social work values also need rethinking. The concept of absolute confidentiality has been constrained by the courts and is the subject of much discussion in view of the increasing use of computers (Macarov, 1990). Confidentiality also has been widely misused as a rationalization to avoid individual and agency evaluations (Macarov & Rothman, 1977; Meller & Macarov, 1986). With the expected population increase of elderly people, independence as a value will also demand reconceptualization. Similarly, coordination of services—that much-loved goal of administrators and policymakers—is now being questioned as leading to uniformity, lack of initiative, and denial of clients' right to choose.

Consequently, as anticipated future situations require a change in values, social work will have a role to play in determining what those values should be, whereas the values now held to be inherent in social work will require reexamination both by the profession as a whole and by its individual members.

Societal Structure

Values will change, or will need to change, as social structures take on new forms, but structural change needs the support of appropriate values. The two areas are inseparable. For example, as the structure of the family changes, the value placed on the various forms of family will change accordingly. Likewise, as family members' values change (that is, the importance of "doing one's own thing" or "individual freedom"), changes in family structure will result.

Similarly, the drastic reduction in scope of legally defined family responsibility in the United States during the last 20 years was the result of changed values concerning family relationships—a "biological artifact" no longer is considered a sufficient basis for legal responsibility (Eagle, 1960). The growth of universal social welfare programs, beginning in the 1930s, stemmed from the value placed upon equality and the dignity of the individual, among other factors.

Future societal changes will require new structural forms. The growing preponderance of older women versus older men, continued reductions in the need for human labor, and new forms of parenting all will call for new or adapted societal structures.

Social workers can influence the direction change takes, both in the realm of values and of structures, via their expertise and research, their professional and client organizations, the media, and their projections of scenarios for the future.

Thus, there is value in thinking about and planning for the future, because our actions are based more on our images of the future than on our knowledge of the past.

Continuity and Change

Although many things will change in the future, many things will also remain essentially the same. Family structure may change, but parent-infant love will remain. People may work less, but they will use their leisure time for some sort of activity. The relative importance of Maslow's (1954) five types of needs—physiological, security, love, self-esteem, and self-actualization—may change, but the needs themselves will probably remain. There will continue to be unhappiness, mental illness, crime, and probably poverty, but these may arise from different causes, express themselves in changed ways, and be dealt with by means yet to be developed.

On the other hand, nothing is more certain than change. Nothing will remain exactly the same in scope, intensity, shape, or importance. Some changes will be mere details, such as increases or decreases in unemployment compensation. Others will take place in broad strokes, such as a redefinition of work.

For example, technological change may be minor—a new type of walker for the locomotion-impaired, for instance—or sweeping, such as widespread application of superconductivity. It should be noted that change is not uniform. If automobiles had developed from the time of their invention in the same manner that computers have, one could buy a Rolls Royce for $2.75, get more than 3 million miles per gallon, and have enough power to drive the Queen Elizabeth II (Evans, 1979). Likewise, had the airplane advanced at the same pace as computers, the time taken from the Wright brothers' first flight to the advent of the Concorde would have been six months (Freedman, 1983). This raises the question of why some things change, or change more rapidly, and others change slowly or not at all.

DETERMINANTS OF TECHNOLOGICAL CHANGE

There are four major determinants of technological change: scientific feasibility, technical feasibility, economic practicality, and social acceptability.

Scientific Feasibility

There are changes that may be imaginable, but not scientifically possible—at least, not yet. Human beings need oxygen for life. Gravity, at least on the earth's surface, cannot be abolished. Mammals cannot photosynthesize. The examples can be multiplied without end.

In addition, there are many things that, though scientifically possible, have not yet come about. It is possible to put people on far planets through use of replenishable life-support systems, to link parts of the globe through gravity-driven deep underground tubes, to produce a human being through gene-splicing, and to prolong life artificially, to name but a few. These abilities, however, although scientifically feasible, must meet another test: they must be technically feasible.

Technical Feasibility

Superconductivity—the transmission of electricity with virtually no resistance—has been scientifically possible and known for more than 50 years, but its activation only at extremely low temperatures has made it technically possible only in very isolated cases. Recently the technique of combining certain rare elements has made it seem possible to achieve superconductivity at a temperature that is feasible for daily use. Solar energy has been used to turn toy windmills and to perform a few other simple tasks for some time, but a number of new techniques, such as heat-layered pools and absorbent panels and light cells, now make commercial use of solar energy a practical proposition. Many homes in the tropics and semitropics heat water via the sun, and some entire houses are heated the same way. Solar-powered cars, however, although scientifically possible and technically feasible, are not yet available because they do not meet the next criterion: economic practicality.

Economic Practicality

The practicality, and therefore the availability, of solar energy, for example, is directly dependent upon its cost in relation to alternative energy sources. As oil prices rise, or as oil shortages take place, solar energy becomes a more economically viable proposition. As oil prices sink or oil supplies become more available, solar energy compares less favorably. Conversely, the widespread use of small, tough, cheap cars that last for years but need few repairs and undergo no style changes from year to year, while economically worthwhile to the consumer, is impractical for the automobile industry, on which many jobs and much of the rest of the economy depends.

Similarly, it would be possible to eliminate crime almost entirely, but the cost of such measures would be far beyond the economic losses due to crime, and probably beyond the cost governments could afford. It would be scientifically possible to cover an entire city and control its weather, but the cost would far outweigh any advantages to be gained.

Social Acceptability

Many things are possible, feasible, and worthwhile, but are not done because they are socially unacceptable. At the moment, for example, it is not acceptable to produce a human being through gene-splicing, or cloning, although it could possibly be done. Raising children without contact with others could be done, but societal values and mores deem it unhealthy. The question of whether life should be prolonged indefinitely is now a subject of intense debate, including the desirability of continuing life-support systems after brain, nerve, or heart death, or after a certain age (Callahan, 1987).

The question of social acceptability is also dramatically illustrated in the case of replacing human workers with robots. Although robots are not only scientifically possible and technically feasible, as well as cheaper, more accurate, more dependable, and faster than human labor, the social need for work results in opposition to robots.

Thus, for a technological change to come about it must be scientifically possible, technically feasible, economically worthwhile, and socially acceptable.

DETERMINANTS OF SOCIAL CHANGE

Social changes may be related to technological changes, but they may also arise from and be deterred by other sources. Technological forces are one of many kinds that cause societal change. Others include economic changes, people and ideas, and physical changes.

Technological Forces

Societal forms and activities often change as a result of technological diffusion. Families that once were concentrated in the same geographical location for generations in many cases have become far-flung due to the ease of communication and transportation. Education through computer diskettes and videotapes has changed teaching and learning patterns. Narcotics crime increases as new forms of drugs are created, and life is lengthened by improvements in medical technology.

Economic Changes

Large numbers of the unemployed, as during the Great Depression (Bird, 1966), and growth in the number of people in poverty resulted in the Works Progress Administration (WPA) and the Social Security Administration. Similarly, increased costs of welfare engendered programs like the Work Incentive Program (WIN), or workfare, and the Comprehensive Education Training Act (CETA). Agricultural surpluses brought about the food-stamp program. Other economic changes and considerations have been responsible for changes in society and social welfare as well (Macarov, 1978).

People and Ideas

Society is changed by ideas, just as it is by artifacts. MacDonald's 1963 article "Our Invisible Poor" in *The New Yorker* and Harrington's (1963) book *The Other America* were responsible for the War on Poverty during the Johnson administration. Social change is sometimes brought about by an influential or charismatic person. Timothy O'-Leary turned large parts of an entire generation onto so-called consciousness-raising drugs; Carry Nation played an important role in the creation of prohibition in America; Margaret Sanger helped to change laws and customs regarding contraceptives; Rachel Carson triggered the current ecological movement; Dr. Benjamin Spock changed attitudes and actions regarding child care; and Dr. Martin Luther King, Jr., was largely responsible for the civil rights movement.

Physical Changes

Physical catastrophes may cause changes in societal values and structures as well. The eradication of forests in Africa and South America is changing the mode of life there, and potentially throughout the world. The Aswan Dam in Egypt has created both positive and negative changes. The protracted droughts in Ethiopia, Somalia, and other countries are irrevocably changing life-styles, and even the existence of life itself in those areas.

Finally, the eradication of small pox and the virtual elimination of tuberculosis, on the one hand, and the discovery and spread of AIDS, on the other, continue to have deep and lasting effects on the fabric of society.

HOW TO STUDY THE FUTURE

A number of local, national, and international organizations dedicated to studying the future now exist, such as the World Future Society in the United States and Futuribles in France. Through their activities, a set of assumptions, methods, and publications has come into being, and national and international meetings are held at which projections are presented for criticism and discussion. These meetings have resulted in many publications about the future and some consensus concerning methodology.

Several methods are generally used to study the future (Cornish, 1977). One is the use of mathematical models, in which variables are expressed in numbers and given various weights in equations. The solved equation is the result to be expected if these variables perform as anticipated. Another involves using computer simulations, feeding into the computer information on different trends and possible changes and receiving various scenarios of the future, based on how those variables interact.

The method of arriving at a consensus of experts represents another way to study the future. Although there are very formal methods of arriving at such a consensus—for example, the Delphi Method—there also are simple polls, conferences, and interviews that attempt to do the same thing—for example, a recent poll of Nobel laureates (Didsbury, 1990).

Also, analogies can be drawn, as experts look at other societies and compare past and present results. In some cases, analogies involve looking at one subject area (for example, the influence of technology on teaching the sciences) and applying it to another subject (such as the influence of technology on teaching the humanities).

Still another method of predicting the future is through the use of scenarios. Scenarios build a logical picture of a novel situation, offering rational, and sometimes compelling, bases for the differences that exist between the imaginary and the real. Projecting future scenarios is not only a descriptive device, but has prescriptive elements. Many of the futurist scenarios of the past—novels, short stories, plays—did not in themselves change the future, but they inspired people to think of new possibilities and then to begin to work toward achieving them. Of the 136 devices George Orwell mentioned in *1984* (1949), more than 100 are now in use (Rada, 1980). In the case of dystopian scenarios, the result is to stimulate people to try to avoid such futures.

H.G. Wells (1905/1967, 1921) and Jules Verne (1869/1953, 1872/1956) each motivated entire generations of young scientists to try to realize what they had fantasized. Current space programs are an almost direct outcome of such projections. Capek and Capek's *R.U.R. (Rossum's Universal Robots)* (1920/1961) made robots a household word and an industrial goal. On the other hand, *1984* made many people resolve that a world such as Orwell described should not be allowed to come into being and made them act against it. On the level of social welfare, Beveridge's (1943) proposal for insurance for everyone against everything was the forerunner of most current social insurance programs, although the idea was almost entirely visionary when it was published.

Finally, there is the prediction method, which is the principal one used in this book: extrapolation of existing trends. This method takes existing trends and projects their movement into the future. Trend extrapolation is not a tool to be used blindly. It must be blended with analogies, expert opinion, and knowledge of the factors that have caused or are causing the trend. For example, it would be simple to say that a 12-year-old who has grown three inches a year for the last three years and is now five feet tall will be eight feet tall by age 24. However, we know that the growth trend does not continue at that rate and, in fact, levels off at about age 18.

On the other hand, the factors that make for lengthening life expectancy seem destined not only to continue, but to improve. Most trends, however, seem affected by both positive and negative factors. World population growth will be influenced by the move toward Zero Population Growth in some sections and affluence, which makes for smaller families, in others. Additionally, improved dissemination of birth control information and devices and the effects of famine and malnutrition will limit population growth in many parts of the world. Opposing these factors will be growing religious fundamentalism, new methods of overcoming infertility, improved infant health, and lengthened life expectancy.

Trend extrapolation also is subject to fluctuations. Some trends seem to occur in cycles, such as the length of women's hemlines or, on a more serious note, business recession and prosperity. Many economists take very seriously the theory of the Kondratieff Cycle, which mirrors fluctuations in the economy through successive changes in capital investment, depreciation, price changes, and so forth. Finally, there are also theories concerning periods of innovation that ebb and flow. Mensch, for example, wrote in 1982 that the next cluster of basic innovations could be expected about 1989, and it will be some time yet before it becomes obvious whether advances in superconductivity, optical-fiber beams, and other recent developments prove his prediction to be true.

Taking each of these factors into account, one may "grade" trend extrapolations from almost impossible to almost inevitable. In doing so, however, one should consider the importance of the change under discussion. Thus, if something is almost certain to occur, but the results will be trivial, not much energy need be expended in planning for it. Conversely, if something has even a small probability of happening, but the results of such an event would be catastrophic or utopian, then considerable effort would need to be expended to avert the situation or bring it to fruition.

The projections in this book vary in their degree of probability, but the advent of any one of them will bring in its trail such important consequences for society and such enormous challenges for social work that all deserve serious attention from members of the profession, particularly from those responsible for the education of social workers.

REFERENCES

Abbott, W. (1978). Work in the year 2001. In E. Cornish (Ed.), *1999: The world of tomorrow* (pp. 99–101). Bethesda, MD: World Future Society.

Beveridge, W. H. (1943). *The pillars of security*. New York: Macmillan.

Bird, C. (1966). *The invisible scar*. New York: Pocketbooks.

Brody, J. A., Cornoni-Huntley, J. A., & Patrick, C. H. (1981). Research epidemiology as a growth industry at the National Institute of Aging. *Public Health Reports, 96,* 209–273.

Brugman, H. (1980). *Work, Europe and utopia.* Maastricht, Holland: European Centre for Work and Society.

Callahan, D. (1987). *Setting limits: medical goals in an aging society.* New York: Simon & Schuster.

Capek, J., & Capek, K. (1961). *R.U.R. (Rossum's Universal Robots).* Oxford: Oxford University Press. (Originally published in 1920)

Cornish, E. (1977). *The study of the future.* Bethesda, MD: World Future Society.

Didsbury, H. F., Jr. (1990). Beyond mere survival: A report on a poll of Nobel laureates. *Futures Research Quarterly, 6,* 7–34.

Eagle, E. (1960). Charges for care and maintenance in state institutions for the mentally retarded. *American Journal of Mental Deficiency, 65,* 199.

Evans, E. (1979). *The micro-millenium.* New York: Washington Square Press.

Ferkiss, V. C. (1975). Technological man. In J. A. Inciardi & H. A. Siegal (Eds.), *Emerging social issues: A sociological perspective.* New York: Praeger.

Freedman, D. H. (1983). Seeking a broader approach to employment and worklife in industrialized market economy countries. *Labour and Society, 8,* 107–112.

Glick, P. C. (1984). Marriage, divorce and living arrangements. *Journal of Family Issues, 5,* 7–26.

Gordon, T. J. (1969). The feedback between technology and values. In K. Baier & N. Rescher (Eds.), *Values and the future: The impact of technological change on American values.* New York: Free Press.

Gottschalk, S. S. (1974). Futurism, social work and public welfare. *Journal of Social Welfare, 2,* 84–92.

Harrington, M. (1963). *The other America.* New York: Macmillan.

Jaffe, A. J., & Froomkin, J. (1968). *Technology and jobs: Automation in perspective.* New York: Praeger.

Macarov, D. (1978). *The design of social welfare.* New York: Holt, Rinehart, & Winston.

Macarov, D. (1990). Confidentiality in the human services. *International Journal of Sociology and Social Policy, 10* (6/7/8), 65–81.

Macarov, D., & Rothman, B. (1977). Confidentiality: A constraint on research? *Social Work Research & Abstracts, 13,* 11–16.

MacDonald, D. (1963, January 19). Our invisible poor. *The New Yorker.*

Marland, S. P. (1974). *Career education: A proposal for reform.* New York: McGraw-Hill.

Maslow, A. H. (1954). *Motivation and personality.* New York: Harper & Row.

Meller, Y., & Macarov, D. (1986). Social workers' satisfactions: Methodological notes and substantive findings. *Journal of Sociology and Social Welfare, 13,* 740–760.

Mensch, G. (1982). The co-evolution of technology and work organization.

In G. Mensch & R. J. Niehaus (Eds.), *Work, organization and technological change*. New York: Plenum.

Orwell, G. (1949). *1984*. New York: Harcourt Brace.

Rada, M. (1980). *The impact of micro-electronics*. Geneva: International Labour Office.

Raichle, D. R. (1980). The future of the family. In F. Feather (Ed.), *Through the 80s: Thinking globally, acting locally*. Bethesda, MD: World Future Society.

Rescher, N. (1969). A questionnaire study of American values. In K. Baier & N. Rescher (Eds.), *Values and the future: The impact of technological change on American values*. New York: Free Press.

Russel, R. A. (1986). *Winning the future*. New York: Carroll & Graf.

Simon, H. A. (1983). What computers mean for man and society. In T. Forester (Ed.), *The microelectronics revolution*. Cambridge, MA: MIT Press.

St. George, A. (1970). *The crazy ape*. New York: Philosophical Library.

Verne, J. (1953). *Twenty thousand leagues beneath the sea*. New York: Dutton. (Originally published in 1869)

Verne, J. (1956). *Around the world in eighty days*. New York: Dutton. (Originally published in 1872)

Wells, H. G. (1921). *The salvaging of civilization: The probable future of mankind*. New York: Macmillan.

Wells, H. G. (1967). *A modern utopia*. Lincoln: University of Nebraska Press. (Originally published in 1905)

2

The Outlook on Aging

SOCIAL WORK WITH ELDERLY PEOPLE

Definitions and Conceptions of the Aged

Although some object to it, age is usually defined in chronological terms. The point at which one is considered to be "aged," or "beginning to age," is implicitly linked to life expectancy. In Sierra Leone and Ethiopia, for example, where life expectancy for men is 40 years, the concept of "elderly" is obviously different from that in Japan, where life expectancy for men is 75 years (United Nations, 1989).

When Chancellor Bismarck instituted one of the world's first comprehensive social insurance programs in Germany between 1883 and 1889, he chose age 65 as the point at which pensions would begin to be paid, probably because relatively few workers lived that long. With very few exceptions, every western country instituting social insurance since then has used 65 for men, and 62 or 60 for women as pensionable ages. From this has flowed the almost universal categorization of old age as beginning at age 65.

With the lengthening of life expectancy, the term "aged" or "elderly" has begun to be qualified, with the added categories of "young old," "very old," "old old," "oldest old," and the "frail elderly," among others, being used. One set of rather flippant descriptions based on physical condition distinguishes between the go-go, the go-slow, the slow-slow, and the no-go aged. A set of circumlocutions has also evolved, including golden agers, senior citizens, third agers, pensioners, and retirees. None of these designations indicates a generally agreed-upon age range or a beginning point. For example, the United States Age Discrimination in Employment Act begins at age 40 (Wolfbein, 1988), and the American Association of Retired Persons accepts members beginning at age 50. More generally, in both popular and professional parlance, a man who has retired from work (unless he is obviously a very early retiree) or who has reached age 65 is referred to as elderly or aged. The view of women retirees is more diffuse, because many women are eligible for pensions or Social Security payments at age 60 or 62, depending on the country of which they are citizens.

Although for brevity and clarity it is sometimes necessary to refer to elderly people as though they were one homogeneous entity, it should be kept in mind that this is one of the most heterogeneous groups in the population, with differences in gender, age, physical ability, economic status, life situation, ethnicity, religion, geographical location, and many other variables. Despite the generalities that refer to all, or most, of the aged, in social work practice the need to distinguish between individual clients, families, and groups, among other things, is and will remain just as great regarding the elderly as it remains with any other category of clients.

Engagement with Elderly People

The social work profession has been involved with the aged since its inception. "The aged, the widow, and the orphan" have been, since biblical days, the objects of community concern. The almshouse was established as an institution in England in the 1800s to house people unable to work, including the aged (deSchweinitz, 1943; Woodrofe, 1962). In those days, however, although social workers did yeoman's work among this stratum of the population, the aged were rather marginal in the community as a whole. Since then, social workers have of necessity increasingly dealt with the aged—in their homes, in institutions, and in the community; as part of their work with families; in medical settings; as pensioners; and as volunteers. This need for service has been growing continually, and there is little question that in the future much more of social welfare's concern, and social workers' activities, will center on this group.

POPULATION TRENDS AND PROJECTIONS

Population Growth and Life Expectancy

Among the many changes the future seems to hold for western civilization, one seems almost inevitable—a massive increase in the number and proportion of elderly people. In most countries, the proportion of elderly people will be affected by birth rates, and in some countries, like Israel, by the amount and kind of immigration and emigration occurring, but the total number of the elderly will almost certainly grow.

In nearly all European countries (Ireland is one exception), the aged population in 2020 will be more than 50 percent larger than it was in 1960. England, for example, will have experienced growth in the number of the aged from 11.7 percent of the population in 1960 to 17.8 percent in 2020—a growth of 52 percent. In many European countries the proportion of the aged will have doubled since 1960 (European Centre for Social Welfare Training and Research, 1987).

A major factor in this projected increase is the lengthening of life expectancy because of progress in sanitation, public health measures, housing, nutrition, medicine, and prenatal and postnatal care. This increase in life expectancy shows no sign of ending or even of slackening. At the start of the 20th century, average life expectancy throughout the world was 48 years. It is now 72 years (Cetron & O'Toole, 1982), or 76 years in the developed countries (*Jerusalem Post*, 1985).

In the United States, life expectancy for men in 1920 was 54 years, and for women, 55 years; in 1986 this had increased to 75 for men and 78 for women (U.S. Department of Commerce, 1987). A white male born in the United States in 1900 could have expected to live for 46.6 years, compared with 71.9 years in 1985. A black female born in 1900 had a life expectancy of 33.5 years, compared with 62.7 years for a black female born in 1980 and 73.5 years in 1985 (U.S. Department of Health and Human Services, 1988). Without regard for race, a female born in America in 1986 can expect to live to age 78.5 and a male to 71.5 (United Nations, 1989), and it is predicted that by the year 2000, the average life span will be 82 for women and 75 for men (*Daily Telegraph*, 1987). Most experts believe the maximum age attainable is approximately 115 to 120 years, although they do not predict when this will come about (U.S. Department of Health and Human Services, n.d.).

Nor is the observed and expected lengthening of life expectancy simply a statistical artifact based upon lowered infant mortality. When life expectancy at age 30 is examined (thus neutralizing the effect of infant death rates), continual lengthening remains a fact. For example, life expectancy in the United States at age 30 in 1900 was 36 more years for women and 34 more for men (United Nations, 1989); in 1985, these expectancies were 50 and 45 more years, respectively (U.S. Department of Commerce, 1987).

Primarily as a result of such increases in longevity, the proportion of those over age 65 in the United States rose from 4 percent in 1900 to 11 percent in 1984; it is estimated that by the year 2030, the proportion of elderly people in the United States will be 21.2 percent (American Association of Retired Persons, 1985). Between 1980 and 2030, the under-60 age group is expected to grow 25 percent, whereas the over-60 group will at least double. Put differently, in 1900, one person in 16 in the United States was over age 60; now one in six is. In 2030, it will be one in four (Fowles, 1983).

The "Very Old"

Even more striking and important will be the growth of the very old population. Although definitions of "very old" vary from 70 and older, 75 and older (Silverstone & Burack-Weiss, 1983), 80 and older (Siegel & Hoover, 1982), and 85 and older (Joint Distribution Committee—Israel, n.d.; Lerba, 1986; U.S. Department of Health, Education, and Welfare, 1975), the proportionate growth at the higher end of the aging spectrum will be disproportionately greater than the general rise. In fact, the very old group will be the most rapidly growing segment of the American population (Rosenwacke, 1985).

In the United States in 1984, the 65-to-74 age group was more than seven times larger than it was in 1900, but the 75-to-84 group was 11 times larger, and the 85 and older group 21 times larger (American Association of Retired Persons, 1985). At present, a quarter of the U.S. elderly population is over 75; by 2030 that proportion will have grown to a third (Fowles, 1986). It is estimated that the current 85 and older group will have grown by 83 percent by the year 2000 (Fowles, 1983). This group numbered 2.3 million in 1980, will total 4.9 million in the year 2000, and will grow to 13 million in 2040 (U.S. Department of Health and Human Services, 1987). In 1985, people reaching 85 could expect to live another six years (U.S. Department of Commerce, 1987). According to Fowles (1986), in 1986, one in 16 people was 85 years old or more, and in 2030, one in 11 will be. In short, not only will the future see larger and larger proportions of elderly people within the general population, but among these, the number living to age 80, 85, or beyond will grow more rapidly.

Consequently, unless there is a stagnation or reversal of trends toward better health, housing, sanitation, and so forth, life expectancy can be expected to continue to rise—at least during the working lives of current social work graduates—creating a larger aged population and a much larger very old group. Needless to say, this growth has many implications for social workers.

PROBLEMS WITH INCOME

Reductions in Pay

For a great number of the aged, income may become a pressing problem. Most pensioners suffer substantial income reductions when they retire. In the United States, Social Security payments to single

retirees average between 46 percent and 60 percent of their preretirement income, and family incomes are between 62 percent and 74
percent (Grad, 1990). The 65-to-74 age group and the 75-and-over
age group have a lower median pretax income than any other age
group except the youngest—those under 18 (Radner, 1990). They
also constitute the largest age group within the poverty population,
except, again, the youngest (U.S. Department of Health and Human
Services, 1989).

Some argue that this drop in income is commensurate with lowered
financial needs of older people (Meier, Dittman, & Toyle, 1980), who
presumably own their homes, cars, appliances, and so on, and are
no longer supporting children. On the other hand, most elderly peo-
ples' fixed expenses probably diminished a number of years before
they retired, and they have been accustomed to decades at their preretirement standard of living. In addition, many aged parents continue
to support their children and grandchildren. For example, aged parents have been found to be the most crucial support for widowed
daughters (Bankoff, 1983).

Consequently, retirement involves a sudden sharp drop in income
level for many, not only resulting in stress, anxiety, and readjustments, but in a continuing lower standard of living. In addition, many
elderly people are subject to increased expenses for medical costs,
security systems, home helpers, and eventually some sort of community or institutional care. A Blue Cross/Blue Shield study found that
if older people must stay in nursing homes for three months, it will
force into poverty two-thirds of older single people and one-third of
married older people. A Harvard Medical School study found that half
of people 75 and older who enter nursing homes will have exhausted
their finances within three months (*American Association of Retired
Persons [AARP] Bulletin*, 1985a). Many elderly people who were little
concerned about money and savings throughout their lives become
anxious, and even frantic, as they reach old age. As a consequence,
many seek work, but unsuccessfully. For those who do find work, it
tends only to be part-time. Although part-time work results in an
average 46-percent increase in income (Soumerai & Avorn, 1983),
this is more indicative of the low level of prework income than of high
salaries from part-time work.

Poverty and Pension Limitations

As a result of the relatively low rate of retirement income, in most
countries, elderly people have a higher poverty rate than any other
group and make up a large part of the poverty class, constituting 57
percent of the poor population in England, 40 percent in Australia,
and 36 percent in Israel (Macarov, 1987a). Although indexing of Social
Security payments in the United States has kept elderly people closer

to the bulk of the population in terms of income, nevertheless, one survey found that 22.5 percent of people over 60 were below or close to the poverty line (Fowles, 1983). Another study put this figure at 37 percent (Silverstone & Burack-Weiss, 1983), as compared with 18.7 percent of nonelderly people (Fowles, 1983). Elderly households in the United States are about 65 percent as large as nonelderly households, but the median household income of elderly households is less than half that of nonelderly households. In 1983, nearly 43 percent of U.S. households headed by older persons had total incomes below $10,000, compared with only 17 percent of nonelderly households (*AARP Bulletin*, 1985b).

Although income reduction is generally a concomitant of retirement throughout western countries, the poverty and near-poverty of many elderly people often is countered by the argument that they continue to work, or have other sufficient income. The first of these caveats ignores both the limitation on additional earnings imposed by Social Security, as well as the well-documented difficulty that persons over 60 or 65 have in finding employment (Regan, 1989). Concerning the second, it should be sufficient to point out that in 1979, 50 percent of working men and 70 percent of working women were not covered by any pension plan other than Social Security (Rogers, 1980), and only 34 percent of all aged people received private pensions, government pensions, or both (Chen, 1985). Projections are that in the year 2000, Social Security will pay 54 percent of the preretirement year's wage to low earners, 42 percent to average earners, and 28 percent to maximum earners (Chen, 1985). Consequently, reaching retirement age means financial readjustments for most of the aged, and wrenching changes for some.

The financial outlook for elderly people is not reassuring, because no current pension plan (governmental, business, union, or private) is actuarially based on the great numbers of people living 25 to 35 years past retirement age. Although the financial structure of American Social Security has been revised in an effort to provide liquidity during the next few decades, continued lengthening of life expectancy may soon make these revisions obsolete. As Habib (1985) noted, the literature on the economics of aging has barely begun to come to terms with the implications of this phenomenon.

Attempts to adjust pension programs to the new reality of increasing life expectancy will place an ever-increasing burden on the younger, working population—a burden that may be resisted or overthrown. Indeed, the shrinking ratio of working-to-nonworking people may become one of the most difficult problems social and economic planners will face in the coming years (Hardcastle, 1978).

This ratio will become a problem both on the micro and macro levels. In business, the ratio of employees to retirees will shrink—in one study, from five active employees to one retiree in 1975, to 1.8 employees to each retiree in 1985 (Longman, 1988). Before East and West Germany united, 22.4 million West German workers supported 12 million pensioners, and by 2030 it was expected that 14.4 million workers would have to support 15 million pensioners (Goodhart, 1989). In such a situation, proposals to increase individual pension payments will meet with strong opposition, and plans to raise premiums for this purpose will face even stronger resistance. Consequently, the social work task of helping pensioners cope with greatly reduced incomes or find additional income may become greatly exacerbated.

HEALTH

The same factors that have led to lengthened life expectancy will lead to better health among the elderly population in general. Two-thirds of elderly people in the United States have been found to be in good health and functioning adequately (Fowles, 1983).

However, disability rises steadily with age. Consequently, among the growing elderly population there will be an ever-larger number of people requiring medical and social care. Even among the relatively healthy, health-related problems will undoubtedly arise. Complicating matters is the fact that because most welfare systems have well-developed medical sectors, as compared with social services, many elderly people see the former as the only available source of help and therefore turn to medical services even with what are, in some cases, social or emotional problems (Evers & Lagergren, 1987). In Israel, for example, where the costs of necessary home care for certain categories of illness are covered by the equivalent of the Social Security Administration, it is not uncommon to find nurses and social workers attempting to define what are essentially social problems in terms of medical causes, to ensure that the clients receive the mandated home care.

Conversely, to the extent that members of the medical establishment are incapable of or uninterested in caring for increasing numbers of elderly people with ailments, they tend to refer them to social workers and related agencies. Many bodily conditions that cannot be corrected easily and inexpensively or cured by the medical profession (joint ailments, back pains, decreased vision, impaired hearing, and the like) are "relabeled" a lack of mobility, an inability to shop or keep house, or a problem of behavior. In some sense, they then become social, rather than medical, problems. As Boyd (1981) put it, "Medical problems in the elderly present [themselves] in the guise of social problems, and social workers . . . are left to cope with what, in reality, are medical problems." Whether because of medical or social problems, it has been determined that 10 to 20 percent of the aged population are in need of some form of care at home, in the community, or in institutions (Rice, 1985). Although only 5 percent of the total 65 and older group need such help, 31 percent of the 85 and older group do (Fowles, 1983).

We can also expect an increase in the number of chronically ill people, who will remain in their situations for much longer periods than previously. These, and others incapacitated for a variety of reasons, will constitute a growing problem. A person becoming ill or incapacitated at age 60 or 65 may need care for more than 20 years—a situation that rarely existed even a few decades ago. Further, elderly people are among the most expensive consumers of health services—their costs are eight times higher than the 16-to-64 age group's (Judge & Knapp, 1985). When elderly people represent 10 percent of the total population, they account for 29 percent of total personal health care (Silverstone & Burack-Weiss, 1983). As a result of such increasing costs, there have been proposals—violently debated—to eliminate life-extending care for most people over the age of 75 (Callahan, 1987).

Besides the physical havoc they wreak, such long periods of illness—often with no hope of recovery—can strain resources, relationships, and psyches. Social workers will need to help both elderly sick people and their families in coping with their feelings. In particular, the emotional, physical, and financial burdens placed upon the families of victims of progressively deteriorative diseases, such as Alzheimer's disease, will require social workers to be conversant with and active in the field known as psychogeriatrics, which includes, among other conditions, mental illness of functional and psychological origin. Social workers will need to know how to offer or acquire both individual and group support, as well as knowledge of relevant legal instruments such as conservatorships, wills, guardianships, and powers-of-attorney (Cohen, 1985).

Moral and ethical questions will challenge elderly people and their families and the professionals and institutions caring for the aged; they may need help and support with such questions as the "right to die" and euthanasia, as well as with the implications of living wills, organ transplants, and so forth (Hooyman & Lustbader, 1986). Litigation about such matters as signing over one's home as a precondition for entering a home for the aged (as some of them require) may strain family relationships, requiring that social workers know the relevant regulations and have the skills necessary for dealing with the emotions involved and for enlisting the help of other professionals and institutions.

RETIREMENT

Patterns of Development

Although the number of elderly people needing assistance in living will grow in absolute numbers and will grow relative to the total population, most of the aged in the future will probably remain in good health to a much more advanced age than is common today. This means that masses of people considered elderly today, and whose life-styles are affected by that fact, will want and be able to continue their previous activities for much longer periods than are now possible. This will bring to the forefront a congeries of questions and dilemmas concerning retirement.

When Bismarck picked 65 as the beginning age for pensions, he not only inadvertently defined old age, he also set an example for other countries. Since that time, the great majority of the world's nations have adopted 65 as the beginning age for retirement pensions. In addition, the opportunity given working people to draw pensions is almost invariably transformed by employers into mandatory retirement ages. In the United States it is now illegal to dismiss an employee only because of age, but the issue of retirement—voluntary and involuntary—nevertheless continues to affect great masses of elderly people there and throughout the West.

Although there is a widespread mythology that most people resent and resist retirement, miss their work when forced to retire, develop illnesses, and die earlier, little evidence exists to support such beliefs. There *are* problems connected with the reduced income occasioned by retirement, as mentioned above, and there certainly are some people for whom their work, or their work routine, is very important, but when lack of money and lack of work are examined separately, it is the former that creates problems for the great bulk of those reporting difficulties, not the latter.

Retirees who have enough money on which to live decently generally report themselves as happy in their retirement, glad they retired, and sorry they had not retired earlier (Atchley, 1976; Parnes, 1983; Stagner, 1978). Unexpected involuntary retirement does create problems, possibly akin to those connected with job loss, but in one study, men who retired close to their expected retirement age did not differ significantly in their reported happiness from those who continued working (Beck, 1982). Indeed, even without regard to retirement, most people over 65 say they are satisfied with their lives (*Ageing International*, 1988). One-third of them call the later years the best years of their lives, only a quarter report their situations as ''dreary,'' and just 13 percent say they are lonely (Fowles, 1983).

Retirement does not necessarily lead to physical deterioration either. Although 10 percent of blue-collar retirees polled indicated that their health declined after retirement (which may have been purely a function of advancing age or other factors), 25 percent reported actual improvement (Eisdorfer & Cohen, 1983; Parnes, 1983). In a later study, *all* the retirees who had suffered from ill health noted an improvement upon retiring (*Ageing International*, 1988).

Finally, far from resisting retirement, workers have been taking voluntary early retirement in increasingly greater numbers. Men in the United States, given the choice of retiring at age 65 on Social Security and full pension, or retiring at 62 with 80 percent of the pension, are choosing to forgo three more years of salary plus 20 percent of their pensions and a limitation on additional earned income for the rest of their lives. In 1989, 68 percent of all Old Age, Survivors, Disability, and Health Insurance (OASDHI) beneficiaries were receiving reduced payments because of early retirement, compared with 45 percent in 1940 (*Social Security Bulletin*, 1990). Indeed, in 1989, 59.3 percent of people retiring did so at age 62, and 83 percent retired before age 65 (U.S. Department of Health and Human Services, 1989). Even younger men are choosing to leave work—in 1984 one-third of men between 55 and 64 chose to retire (*U.S. News & World Report*, 1984). Only one in 35 men (and a smaller proportion of women) aged 60 and over say they want to continue to work (Rones, 1980).

Due to the financial difficulties current retirees face, agitation by those who do want to continue working, the work ethic as an ideology, and the desire to give people choices concerning their own lives, we can expect continuing pressure on governments to raise the age at which pensions are paid, which has become almost synonymous with retirement. These pressures will be especially strong if old-age pensions remain far below the wage level or if pension payments threaten the liquidity of insurance plans. Such action would relieve financial strains on social insurance programs, as well as on future retirees themselves.

However, proposals to raise the retirement age run head-on into one of western society's most intractable and long-standing problems: unemployment. Unemployment rates have been kept from rising explosively only through constantly *reducing* work time (hours, weeks, years, and lifetimes at work) and through maintaining unnecessary jobs and allowing unproductive work time to grow, as well as through the use of statistical and definitional artifacts, as will be shown in chapter 4. Raising the retirement age would aggravate the current unemployment situation enormously in every western country, canceling out heroic, if unsuccessful, efforts to provide enough jobs for everyone below present retirement age (Taggart, 1977). It would also deny younger workers advancement opportunities, which many fear would feed into the alienation and malaise believed to affect large portions of the present work force (Yankelovich, 1981). It is partly for this reason, perhaps—to make room for young doctors—that a suggestion has been made in Britain to retire all GPs over 65 (*Report of the Royal Commission on the National Health Service*, 1979).

As a consequence of the fears of unemployment, there has been a general move to *reduce* the age of retirement in many countries. France, for example, has reduced retirement age to 60 for men and has eliminated pension increases for delayed retirement. Other countries make early retirement attractive through a variety of incentives. Only in the United States has the opposite trend manifested itself, and then in a very minor way. Due to anticipated liquidity problems in the Social Security system, it has been decided that in the year 2009 the age at which maximum retirement payments are made will rise from 65 to 66, and in 2027 to 67. By positioning this change so far in the future, immediate opposition and political reactions were avoided. In addition, this change presupposes that growth in the unemployment rate will not require a retraction. It is probable, as will be discussed in more detail later, that continuing technological advances will wipe out more jobs. Consequently, it seems that the continuing and difficult task facing governments—that of providing more jobs while needing less human labor—will militate against any drastic reduction in current retirement ages. Thus, the great bulk of the work force will probably continue to retire (or be retired) in their 60s.

In most cases retirement is not simply a "cessation of employment" but also a change in activities, time structure, social status, and self-image. Retirement is more than a rite of passage. It is, in Strauss's (1962) terms, a transformation of identity. As such, retirement may require professional social work to adjust to the changes it causes. These changes may require systematic, planned help, as does any other transition period. Preretirement planning and postretirement programs are already in effect in a growing number of industries and government offices. In particular, occupational social workers are active in preretirement and retirement planning, and the entire role of social workers in this area is growing (Wolpert, 1988).

Leisure Time

Despite the general satisfaction with older age and retirement noted above, a number of people will find either or both of these conditions problematic. These include workers who are involuntarily retired, those with postretirement financial problems, and those who find life dreary or lonely. For many of them, the question of what to do with their greatly increased leisure time may become compelling. Kaplan (1975) held that during weekends, holidays, and vacations, people experiment with and decide upon the activities they find satisfying, thus easing the transition to full-time leisure. It is certainly true that at present, work life begins at a later age and ends sooner, and brings with it more holidays, longer vacations, and shorter workdays than in previous eras.

These changes pale into virtual insignificance, though, when compared with the many additional years of nonwork time that lengthened life expectancy will afford. Periods of 25 to 30 years or more of generally healthy living after retirement present a potential for creativity and happiness, on the one hand, and the danger of sterile, unsatisfying, "time-killing" activities on the other.

There will be a need for activities that are visible, easily accessible, inexpensive, attractive, and satisfying for older people. In planning such activities, social workers will have to take into consideration the fact that within the next two or three decades the aged will be the most educated aged population group ever (Sarasohn, 1977). To meet this challenge, there may have to be a strengthening of social group work and community work to encourage and to help people engage in joint and cooperative activities, political and voluntary efforts, sports, trips, music, parlor and table games, and so forth—roles rarely undertaken today by most social workers. Unless social work chooses to abandon this field to others, leisure-time activities generally (and for the aged in particular) should become a growth area in social work education and practice.

AVENUES OF ASSISTANCE

Women's Employment and Aging

In addition to the influence of retirement, other aspects of the work world will affect the aged. One of these is the growing number of women entering the work force (discussed in more detail in chapters 3 and 4). In the United States, the proportion of women working outside the home rose from 27 percent in 1940 to 55 percent in 1987 (U.S. Department of Commerce, 1987). Continuation of this trend probably will result in fewer family members being available to spend time with older family members, or in their being available only for short periods.

In spite of the growth of equality between the sexes, throughout the West it is still the female member of the family, usually the daughter, who most often supports and cares for elderly relatives. Additionally, it has been estimated that half of those over 80 living at home need help (Bond, 1984). Increases in the number of women working will make providing such support more difficult, necessitating increased use of home helpers, day care centers, institutions, and, where possible, volunteers, including other aged people. Trade-off considerations may result in polarization of women's work, with the better educated and skilled getting higher paid jobs and thus being able to hire home helpers, and the less educated being forced to assume some of the latter jobs.

However, because much of the growth in women's employment consists of part-time work, the situation may be made easier by judicious juggling of time. A current phenomenon in the area of work is the growth of "flexitime" arrangements that make it possible to put in the assigned number of hours in a variety of ways. Thus, family members with responsibility for older people can plan their schedules so they are available when needed, or they can rotate with other family members so that someone is always available. Not as well known are "flexiplace" arrangements in which work can be done at home or close to home. The latter is made possible as a result of advanced tele-communications facilities used by typists, accountants, real estate and insurance personnel, and others. This trend may grow in the future with the perfection of and increase in rooftop satellite receivers.

On balance, however, at least in the short run, the increasing entry of women into the labor force will probably create more problems concerning care of elderly people than it solves. Increased arrangements for nonfamily members to care for the aged will be needed. The role of social workers in helping locate and provide that needed help and, more importantly, in supervising and evaluating nonprofessionals and volunteers, will grow.

Technology

The same technology that makes early retirement, flexitime, and flexiplace possible also affects the amount and kind of help needed. Technological innovations that have aided elderly people in the past included such items as the walker, artificial joints, voice-activated household accessories, two-way video communication systems, electronically controlled wheelchairs, and mechanical aids ranging from garbage disposal units to microwave ovens (*World of Work Report*, 1984). One can confidently expect further technological advances that will give the older person more independence in performing daily tasks and that will relieve human helpers of some of their current activities and anxieties. Social workers' roles will not be limited to recognizing, recommending, locating, and teaching the use of such technological aids but in inventing and proposing others.

THE EVOLVING ROLES OF FAMILY MEMBERS

New and Altered Relationships

With lengthened life expectancy, four-generation families will become commonplace and there will be a growing number of five-generation families (Butler & Lewis, 1977). This will require new perspectives regarding family-member roles and relationships (discussed in more detail in chapter 3) both on the part of family members themselves and on the part of social workers. The place of the healthy, active great-grandparent, in relation to the grandparents, parents, and children, will require new conceptualization. One prediction is that the ambiguity, powerlessness, and ineffectuality that characterized the role of grandparents during the last century will give way to the grandparent becoming the focal person in family relationships (*Ageing International*, 1984). Meanwhile, however, the dual role of middle-aged people being both parent and child—sometimes referred to as the "sandwiched" generation (Hooyman & Lustbader, 1986)—will continue for much longer than at present; responsibilities to parents and children will become more complex and more confusing. Another prediction holds that there will be growing physical and social distance, accompanied by alienation and anomie, as generations are added to the nuclear family (B. Warach, Director, Jewish Association for Services to the Aged, New York, personal communication, 1987). In either case, the role of the social worker gains importance.

The implications of becoming a grandparent (or great-grandparent) have been neglected in social work literature and practice. Grandparenthood is also a transformation of identity—nowadays often taking place in middle-age—comparable in certain respects to marriage, parenthood, or retirement, but has been a somewhat neglected phase of individuals' lives (Cunningham-Burley, 1986). As one of Cunningham's (1984) respondents pointed out, one is not usually given a choice as to whether one wants to be a grandparent or not; on the other hand, those who are not may be subjected to embarrassment or ridicule—"What, not a grandmother yet?" Adapting to the role might involve difficulty either with having one's age revealed, or accepting one's real age, leading to denial or resentment. The traditional role of grandparent may be exaggerated or rejected. Each of these reactions requires social work's attention (Matthew & Sprey, 1985).

Lengthening life expectancy means that children will be older when their parents die (Jennings, 1987). Although there are agencies and services to help young children accept and adjust to the death of parents, this attention seems to fade as the children become older. There is also the phenomenon of adult children (sometimes elderly themselves) dying before their parents (Lesher & Berger, 1989). Gorer (1965) said that "the most distressing and long-lasting of all griefs . . . is that for the loss of a grown child." Nevertheless, one of the neglected areas of social work practice—at least in the literature— concerns the loss of adult siblings or children; and even less attention has been focused on the losses of one's friends (Osterweis, 1985), each loss constituting a crisis in the daily life of the aged person.

Finally, there is the crisis caused by the death of a spouse. There are 800,000 new widows and widowers annually in the United States, and according to Osterweis (1985), 80,000 to 160,000 will suffer true depression. Dealing with reaction to death is a classic social work role but, again, more common when confined to younger people.

Problems of Responsibility

The growing number of older people, as well as the additional years of life now granted them, creates new problems in regard to legal and moral responsibilities. In some countries, the legal responsibility of grandparents for other members of the family, and family members' responsibility for grandparents, is very specific. In other countries, it is specific but unenforced. In still others, the concept of family responsibility has been practically erased from the law. Nevertheless, in most countries, a normative aspect of responsibility remains, which holds families to be the first and most important resource for the welfare of their aged relatives.

The changing structure of the family (discussed in more detail in chapter 3) may weaken family members' sense of responsibility for assorted parents and grandparents and highlights an ideological question as to the extent to which the government, as opposed to relatives, should provide financial and other forms of support. In Denmark, for example, elderly people are completely financially independent of their children because of the welfare structure (Butler & Lewis, 1977). In Israel, family responsibility is legally defined, although not often enforced, to include all adult children and their spouses, one's own and one's spouse's brothers and sisters, one's own and one's spouse's parents, grandchildren, and grandparents (Macarov, 1978). As many social workers have learned, however, enforcing family responsibility can cause more strains and tensions than it resolves.

This responsibility has become more and more complex. Although in 1900 the chance that one white American child in 10 would have all four grandparents alive was only one in 90, in 1972 it was one in 14. Middle-aged people nowadays may have as many as four living parents and eight living grandparents, with all that this involves regarding mutual responsibility (Butler & Lewis, 1977).

Then there is the problem of aged children of very old parents. In the United States, for example, about one in 10 older persons has a child over age 65; the children of octogenarians and nonogenarians are themselves often 60 and even 70 (Boyd, 1981). The aforementioned phenomenon of such children dying before their parents is a growing one; Abrams (1978) found that 35 percent of his respondents over age 75 in Surrey had no surviving children. In the United States, about 10 percent of elderly people never had children, and 10 percent have no living children (B. Warach, personal communication, 1987). However, 79 percent of older people in the United States have living grandchildren and 32 percent have great-grandchildren (Butler & Lewis, 1977). Responsibility for aged relatives may thus pass to the grandchildren—and sometimes the reverse. Obviously, the question of relatives' moral and legal responsibility in such families is a dynamic one, needing both study and redefinition, and is one that may give rise to many familial strains and tensions that will require the help of social workers.

Marriage and Remarriage

Family responsibility for the aged becomes even more complicated in the face of multiple marriages. The role of children-in-law, grand-children-in-law, and perhaps later, great-grandchildren-in-law, when the biological offspring of the older person are deceased, divorced, or remarried (perhaps more than once, with children from each spouse), must be reconsidered and reconceptualized. In the United States, for example (as will be elucidated in chapter 3), about half of all first marriages now end in divorce. In 1976, nearly one-third of all marriages in the United States were remarriages of one or both partners (Stevenson, 1981), and by 1984, this had increased to 46 percent (U.S. Department of Commerce, 1987). Divorce rates among remarried couples are much higher than among those married only once (Stevenson, 1981). This continuing increase in divorce and remarriage means that grandchildren may grow up hardly knowing their grandparents, if at all, resulting in calls for better conceptualization of grandparent-grandchild ties (Matthew & Sprey, 1985).

The visitation rights of grandparents, which are rarely considered in divorce settlements and which tend to be denied by subsequent parental remarriages, already have become the subject of lawsuits in the United States (*Ageing International*, 1984). Social workers dealing with family problems will have to take the needs and rights of grand-parents into account to a much greater extent in the future.

There is also the opposite trend to be considered. As people live longer, the number of times they marry may increase. The widow (or, less often, the widower) who outlives two or three spouses is becoming more and more common today. The repeated crises caused by death and by new living arrangements may become an integral focus for the social worker's professional experience. Take, for example, the widow who nursed her husband through a long bout of cancer, which ended in his death, and who remarries a few years later only to be faced with a similar situation shortly thereafter.

The quest for a new mate may be as strong in the life of a bereaved or divorced older person as it is in the lives of younger people. Many social workers, even those dealing with the aged, are neither cogni-zant of, nor emotionally equipped to deal with, the sexual needs and abilities of elderly people. The same situation persists in institutions for the elderly, such as homes for the aged, sheltered housing, group homes, and so on. In some institutions, there are arrangements and rules concerning contact between the sexes that seem to be modeled on those of institutions for adolescents, or of the previous century.

When the subject of sex is addressed, it often is handled in a patronizing or joking fashion. Thienbaus, Conter, and Rosmann (1986) noted that "sexuality . . . is still neglected in the study and practice of geriatrics . . . [and] gerontological issues are only infrequently addressed in the discussions of human sexuality."

Yet, perhaps as a result of better health and nutrition, the percentage of elderly people who are sexually active seems to be growing (Thienbaus et al., 1986). This aspect of so-called golden aged, or senior citizen, clubs, centers, and activities is important for the participants but often overlooked by social workers who see the groups purely in terms of recreation. Such groups are often "singles' clubs" in every meaning of the term, despite the fact that women members tend to greatly outnumber the men.

The fact that women outnumber men complicates sex and marriage among elderly people. In developed countries, women tend to outlive men by approximately nine years (Hooyman & Lustbader, 1986), creating a dearth of eligible elderly men. In 1970, 37 percent of women and 9 percent of men in the 65-to-69 age group were widowed; in the 75-to-79 group, 61 percent were widows and 21 percent widowers (Blank, 1977). This gap seems to be a concomitant of industrialization, because in the less developed countries men outlive women (Lopez, 1984). Thus, as development continues, these gaps increase.

In 1980 there were 6 million more older women than men in the United States; in 2030 there will be 12 million more women than men. In 1980 there were 116 women for every 100 men between 60 and 64 (Fowles, 1983), 147 women for every 100 men over 65 (Silverstone & Burack-Weiss, 1983), and 220 to 229 women for every 100 men 85 and older (Fowles, 1983; Silverstone & Burack-Weiss, 1983). There are three marriages per 1,000 women over 65 and 17 per 1,000 for men (Bulcroft, Bulcroft, Hatch, & Borgotta, 1989). In the 75-and-older age bracket, 70 percent of women are widows and 70 percent of men are married (Silverstone & Burack-Weiss, 1983). As the proportion and number of older women continues to exceed men, problems related to social and sexual needs will become more complex. There may be pressure to consider new, socially sanctioned, forms of relationships: two or more women living with one man; group living; groups of women living together; and an extension of the present custom of unmarried older people living together (a custom made economically sensible by social insurance regulations). Accepting, helping, encouraging, or initiating such arrangements may require sharp value changes on the part of many social workers.

Finally, as regards family structure, modern families tend to be smaller than in the past, so that the burden of responsibility, financial or otherwise, falls on fewer people (Boyd, 1981). Eversly (1982) estimated that adequate noninstitutional care requires three nonworking female relatives living within reach of the elderly person. He states that a couple married in 1920 and still alive in 1980 would have 42 female relatives alive, of whom 14 would not be working, providing an ample cushion for care. However, a couple married in 1950 and still alive in 2005 will have only 11 female relatives alive, only three of whom will not be working.

ABUSE OF ELDERLY PEOPLE

Abuse by Others

With the number of the aged growing, there is a danger that abuse of elderly people too may grow. Given insufficient numbers of staff, lack of resources, and workers who have not been inculcated with professional values (Chamberlain, Hayes, Kerswell, Martin, & Landsberg, 1982), inadequate screening, job stress, and faulty supervision may result in both inadvertent and deliberate abuse by caregivers. Given the stress and problems that the presence or introduction of an aged member might create for families, abuse by relatives also will rise in proportion to the increase in such arrangements.

There is no generally accepted definition of abuse of elderly people (Hall, 1989), although Abrams (1978) distinguished among physical, psychological, financial, and other types. Sengstock and Hwalek (1987) spoke of physical abuse and physical neglect, psychological abuse and psychological neglect, material abuse, and violation of rights. Others characterize the aged as subject to victimization (Katz-Shiban, 1989) or fraud (Lehman, 1989).

Thus, abuse of the aged can be seen as a continuum from physical abuse and murder to deliberate neglect, fraud, and verbal abuse, to placing a television set too far away for easy viewing, or refusing or neglecting to hand the elderly person eyeglasses from a nearby piece of furniture. That which is seen as abuse by elderly people may not be viewed the same way by the caregiver, and sometimes the definition of abuse hangs on motivation—in the case of the eyeglasses mentioned above, was the caregiver too busy, simply negligent, deliberately punishing the aged person, or engaging in a planned program to decrease dependency?

Further, there may be abuse on the part of the caregiver, but it may also be on the part of those who are not giving any service—family members, relatives, visitors, or outsiders such as businesspeople, repair personnel, sales clerks, or maintenance workers. There is even "structural" abuse, including curbstones too tall to negotiate, traffic lights that change too rapidly, elevators in which doors close quickly and powerfully, and buildings without ramps.

On a more empirical basis, from 500,000 to 2.5 million cases of elderly abuse occur in the United States every year (Cash & Valentine,

1987), representing up to 5 percent (Poertner, 1986) or 10 to 15 percent (Zborowsky, 1985) of the elderly population. Even these are probably gross underestimates, because reports of abuse tend to come mostly from the elderly themselves, many of whom make no such reports for a variety of understandable reasons. Further, of the 44 percent of the 65-and-older age group who live with caregiving relatives, 10 percent of these (Eastman & Sutton, 1982) are said to be at risk of abuse. Insofar as the hospitalized elderly are concerned, a widespread study found that very few social workers had not come across physical abuse of elderly people. When those who seemed to be abusing the elderly were questioned as to their motivation, more than 80 percent cited the stress they were under as the cause of their behavior (Eastman, 1984; Wolf & Bergman, 1989). It seems that too many patients, too much to do, increasing and repeated demands on the part of some patients, and insufficient time and resources put the caregiving staff under excess stress, some of which gets passed on to patients or causes abusive behavior.

An interesting part of Eastman's (1984) study is the fact that although the social workers involved were aware of patient abuse, the directors of the departments studied said that no incidents of abuse had been reported to them. In another study, only 2 percent of abuse cases were reported by doctors, and only 7 percent by hospitals (Cash & Valentine, 1987). Even after making allowances for the distortions that plague survey research (Kelman, 1968), it seems evident that abuse of elderly people is not reported or documented to the same extent as child abuse, for example. There may be many reasons why the social workers in the institutions studied did not report such abuse, or why their reports did not reach the directors (O'Brien, 1989), including the fact that only a few states make such reporting mandatory. However, it is clear that preventing and ameliorating such abuse will become an important part of the task of the social worker who aids elderly people.

Self-abuse

It is estimated that 2 to 10 percent of all elderly people in the United States have alcohol-related problems. Hospitals report alcohol-related problems in 18 to 56 percent of the elderly men admitted, and psychiatric hospitals report 23 percent are similarly troubled (Zimberg, 1984). Additionally, the number of older alcoholics is expected to increase during the coming decades (Mayer, 1979).

One school of thought holds that social workers should focus their attention on identification and diagnosis of elderly alcoholics and on seeking effective methods of treatment (Kola, Kosberg, & Wegner-Burch, 1980). This approach may stem from the fact that formal psychotherapy is rarely used with elderly people, both because of the shortage of trained professionals and the lack of clinical interest in geriatric patients (Chien, 1971; Chien, Stotsky, & Cole, 1973).

Another point of view holds that social workers should cease trying to "rehabilitate" the elderly alcoholic and instead begin to offer constructive and sympathetic maintenance (Van de Vyvere, Hughes, & Fish, 1976). One controlled study found that heavy social drinking by the aged was not associated with any adverse psychological, social, or cognitive attributes (Goodwin et al., 1987). In a nursing home, "beer sociotherapy" appeared to be effective as a practical treatment for improved relations (Chien, 1971; Chien et al., 1973), and it has been found that small amounts of alcohol may retard coronary difficulties (*New York Times*, 1989). In any case, alcoholism among the aged does not appear to have its roots in the stress or relaxation that accompanies old age; alcohol abuse among elderly people rather seems to be a continuation of pre-aging patterns (Linett, 1989).

HOME, INSTITUTION, AND COMMUNITY

Living with Children

Although most elderly people live independently, and the number of those doing so will grow (Okraku, 1987), 18 percent of them live with their children. Of the elderly people without spouses, 25 percent live with their children (Berman, 1987). These tend to be aged females, because only 37 percent of women aged 65 and over are married, as compared to 77 percent of men (Hooyman & Lustbader, 1986). The great bulk of families in which elderly people live probably do not and will not ask for or need social work intervention, working out whatever inconveniences that exist among themselves, at least until the problems exhaust and threaten to overwhelm them (Osterkamp, 1988; Silverstone & Burack-Weiss, 1983). However, with the expected growth in the number of the elderly, the cases in which such arrangements result in emotional, financial, and even physical difficulties is bound to increase. This is especially true as life lengthens and the "live-in" parent is present for 20, 30, or even 40 years, becoming more frail, ill, or disabled, and as the structure and situation of the families inevitably change with the passage of time.

This problem can be more difficult when the requirement or decision to live together is a sudden one. As Berman (1987) pointed out, it is not unusual for adult children to be suddenly confronted with having to make a place in their home for aged parents and for the parents to be confronted with adjusting to sudden change. Even when not sudden, this arrangement usually results in loss of freedom on both sides, possibly leading to some resentment, overt or covert.

Further, an inequality of power may become apparent: the parent is no longer more powerful—or even as powerful—in the home as the children. Decisions may be made for or around the parent, when previously the parent was the dominant voice in decision making. This loss of independence can lead to resentment on both sides. In addition, there is the psychological factor termed an "irredeemable obligation"—no matter how much the child does for the parent, it never can equal what the parent presumably did for the child (Berman, 1987). The children never can reach a point where they can think or say that they have equaled the parent's contribution to their life. Theirs is an open-ended obligation that no amount of care or concern can erase, and with this there may remain a residue of guilt. On the other hand, from the parents' point of view, contact with their children is not always a positive experience. Many parents see this as evidence of undesired dependence on their part, or believe the children view it as such (Allan, 1988).

Finally, living with one's children may involve a geographical change entailing irreplaceable losses of friends and a change of community in both the physical and psychological sense. Familiar sights are gone, and adjustment to new life-space arrangements must be made—a situation that has been found to increase mortality rates (House, Landis, & Umberson, 1988).

Living Alone

Another group requiring help will be those elderly people who live alone. In 1960, 17 percent of elderly people lived alone; by 1982 this figure had grown to 26 percent. Moreover, the number of aged living alone probably will continue to rise (Fowles, 1983), particularly among the more affluent group who move to retirement villages and other forms of sheltered housing. Most of the elderly living alone have relatives, and good contact is maintained between them in what has been called "intimacy at a distance."

Living alone does not necessarily involve loneliness or an inability to remain independent. The great bulk of those living alone will do so without help. However, the need for help increases with age, and much of it can be subsumed under the rubric ADL (activities of daily living) and sometimes IADL (instrumental activities of daily living). This help may be as simple as tying shoelaces or dialing a telephone, but inability to have these tasks performed can lead to inconvenience, or even danger, as well as feelings of frustration and dependence. In addition, many of those who live alone will need help, particularly when ill, with shopping, transportation, house repairs, recreation, health services, housekeeping, and—increasingly—security provisions. Few agencies provide comprehensive assistance, covering all of the needs of elderly people. The role of the social worker therefore becomes one of case manager, finding, soliciting, coordinating, evaluating, and occasionally initiating the needed help. This also involves keeping track of elderly people as they move from home to community to institution, and from the auspices of one agency to another.

Although a number of studies have found that most aged people live reasonably close to their families (Hooyman & Lustbader, 1986), increasing occupational mobility of the labor force, on the one hand, and the continuing move of older people to warmer climes, on the other, will lead to larger numbers of people being geographically distant from their families and friends. In any case, the need of the elderly person for emotional support, or even to feel respected by others, may be as compelling as the provision of material items or services (Depner & Ingersoll-Dayton, 1985). For those living alone involuntarily through loss of a spouse, children or other relatives, or previous living quarters, or because of personal or family economic problems, counseling services may be extremely important during the crisis period. This need for help with the activities of daily living continues, however, even after the crisis has been contained.

Living in Institutions

Finally, there are the 5 percent of the aged 65 and over who are in institutions of various kinds. About 1 percent of Americans 65 to 74 years old were confined to institutions in 1985, but for those 85 years and older, the figure was 22 percent. In 1985, there were 3 million nursing home residents at least 65 years old, an increase of 200,000 from 1977 (U.S. Department of Health and Human Services, 1988). The size of this group in no way indicates the extent of need, however. Most such institutions have long waiting lists, often requiring years of temporary arrangements that too often become permanent. One role of the social worker in such settings is to assess the needs of many clients for the very few places available.

Social workers in institutions seem to play many roles—as caseworkers dealing with the feelings of residents and their families, as group workers arranging activities, and as community workers seeking and marshaling existing and needed services. In many cases, however, due to other staff shortages, social workers perform tasks that may not be strictly defined as professional, such as helping residents move, dress, and eat. Increasingly, as will be detailed later, social workers will need to supervise others.

In addition, ombudsmen have been federally mandated in nursing homes, and in some cases this role is filled by a social worker. In other cases, ombudsmen are other professionals, or lay volunteers. The growing use of ombudsmen offers social workers in institutions an opportunity to improve services through the use of this official, and sometimes through assuming the role themselves. However, as Litwin (1985) pointed out, the social worker as ombudsman may also find himself or herself the nursing home executive's chief adversary. With the spread of the ombudsmen idea to other areas—child care, for example—the role of social workers in relating to this person will become more important, especially because this role can be exploited to improve the condition of clients.

In each of the situations outlined above—living with family, living alone, or living in an institution—the bulk of the unpaid help that elderly people receive will be from members of their own families, augmented somewhat by help from friends or neighbors. Locating or creating natural helping networks, and strengthening them where necessary, will be one of the social worker's tasks. Traditionally, morally, and legally, the family has always been considered the solution of first instance for problems of the elderly—a "moral unit" (Allan, 1988)—and both custom and economic necessity will cause it to remain so.

Consequently, family relationships, social arrangements, time scheduling, and other factors may require help from skilled professionals if exacerbated feelings and damage to one or another family member is to be avoided. Social work counseling in such cases will become increasingly important (Csillag, 1989), as will knowledge of helpful services—respite centers, day care centers, trips, camps, friendly visitors, part-time and temporary helpers, technical devices and their sources, peer groups, support groups, and so on. Skilled professional help also may be needed—regardless of living arrangements—in adjusting to changes such as widowhood, temporary illness, chronic illness, loss of a child, or changes in location.

The Community

Despite the pressing need for more places in homes for the aged, group care homes, sheltered housing, and health care facilities, there is very little chance of achieving any significant increase in the number of such institutions. It has been estimated that even to keep pace with the present growth of the aged population for the next 15 years, 300 to 600 new 100-bed nursing homes are needed (Fowles, 1986). An official British report says, "It is difficult to find any firm evidence of an easing of the pressure on residential places despite the development of community-based services" (Department of Health and Social Services, 1981).

It has also been estimated that for even 1 percent of the very frail in England who require 24-hour-a-day care by their families to move to institutions would require a 25-percent increase in institutional provisions (Darton & Knapp, 1984)—an eventuality that is not even remotely possible on a scale sufficient to make a difference. It is likely, therefore, that the gap between the need and the provision of community facilities to aid elderly people living alone or with relatives will not only continue, but become wider.

This scarcity of community resources obviously will have an impact on social workers dealing with the aged. In a study of social workers' satisfaction and dissatisfaction, one of the major reasons given for the latter was a "lack of resources" (Meller & Macarov, 1985). In the future, social workers may have to learn to handle growing frustration arising from inadequate or lack of necessary services for elderly people, a deficiency that will probably become more severe as the numbers of the aged increase. Working with elderly people may have other occupational consequences, too. For example, the feelings of loss experienced by health care workers at the death of elderly clients in a geriatric ward have been found to be great enough to lead to recommendations for bereavement counseling for health care workers (Lerea, 1982).

Community services, even when ostensibly geared to the elderly population, do not always meet their needs. For example, plans to use adolescents to help elderly people are sometimes based more on a desire to keep the adolescents out of trouble than on the needs of elderly people. Similarly, a survey of activities for elderly people in Israeli community centers found that most such activities were offered in the morning. When queried as to the rationale for this practice, center personnel said they felt that in the morning, when the children went to school and the parents to work, the aged were lonely. An informal inquiry among the aged, however, found that when the children went to school and the parents to work, elderly people did not mind being at home, but when they all returned, the elderly people preferred to get out of the way. In short, events for the elderly were held in the morning to keep the center full of activities when it would otherwise be empty and to release the facilities for adults and children in the afternoon and evening. The needs of the center, rather than the needs of the elderly, were what were being served. Social workers thus will need to be in the forefront in creating suitable and sufficient community facilities for the aged.

Political Action

The growth in the number of the aged gives them the possibility to become an increasingly potent factor in politics and government. In some cases this may take the form of organized action concerning some bill or law. In others, it might be a permanent lobby. There may also be occasions for demonstrations, petitions, and so forth. In some places, the aged have already organized into political parties. In Italy, there is a National Pensioners' Party, which captured 1.4 percent of the total vote in a recent election. In the United States, the American Association of Retired Persons and the National Council of Senior

Citizens have political clout, but usually in regard to specific issues concerning the aged, rather than as nascent political groupings. "Gray Power" is being increasingly taken into consideration by social planners and policymakers.

There is an obvious role for social workers in helping the elderly to organize as a special-interest group, whether on the neighborhood, local, state, or national level. Many of their problems are structural in nature and cannot be alleviated or overcome on an individual basis. Social action for the benefit of the aged, and social action by the aged themselves, are legitimate focal points for social work activity.

THE CAREGIVERS

The changes predicted in the numbers and situations of older people, as outlined above, indicate that in the aggregate, a great deal more care will have to be provided to allow elderly people to live decently and with respect. This means that, in addition to the mechanical aids that certainly will multiply, much more help from people will be required.

The most widespread and general help given to elderly people remains family members, and when one is present, the spouse is the resource of first instance. Because men tend to marry younger women, however, women are more likely to live alone after age 75 and more likely to take care of a disabled spouse (Hooyman & Lustbader, 1986). When no spouse is present, and often when one is, the responsibility for giving care falls to a daughter—usually the eldest daughter, often helped, or at least supported, by her husband—or upon a daughter-in-law (Brody, 1981). For those children without spouses, the burden is obviously heavier. Simon (1987) studied 50 never-married women taking care of elderly parents and found that most of them described prolonged periods of exhaustion, resentment, anger, depression, and guilt in the course of their caregiving. Eighteen of these women developed ulcers, colitis, back trouble, and heart conditions. As time goes on, the demands of eldercare may seriously interfere in the caregiver's own plans, career, and life-style. The caregiver will need help with his or her own feelings, behavior, and situations, as well as help in giving care (Csillag, 1989.)

Taking care of the needs of an elderly relative—even one who is not ill or incapacitated—can be a grueling and trying job. Although most families try to keep the aged person at home and care for him or her, they often need help with specified tasks. Help with homemaking and health care become the major requests (Hooyman & Lustbader, 1986), but emotional and material support for the caring relative will be a growing demand on social work too. In fact, giving help to caregivers will be one of the major jobs facing social workers in the future.

Social Workers

The rapid growth in the number of the aged expected during the next 40 years will require an enormous increase in the number of caregivers at home, in the community, and in institutions. It is highly improbable that schools of social work will be able to graduate social workers in sufficient numbers for all of the planning and administrative tasks involved in this growth, because even now "most social workers spend most of their time not in face-to-face contact with the client but in doing things for and about the client" (Stevenson, 1981).

The numerical lack of social work graduates is not the only reason for insufficient services to the aged. Social workers do not seem to want to work with the aged. Although this disinclination may be overcome by pay and other elements (Yarrow, Marcus, & MacLean, 1981), the initial disinclination seems to be an important factor. When other variables, such as pay, hours, and supervision, are held constant, social workers generally prefer to work with other groups of clients. Several studies of the preferences of social work students and experienced social workers concerning client groups and problems show that elderly people consistently fall among the least-desired groups (Aviram & Katan, 1987; Macarov, 1987b; Rubin, Johnson, & De-Weaver, 1984).

Most observers seem to agree that social workers see work with elderly people as "a poor investment for effort and skill, devalued by society, too set in their ways to be responsive to social work techniques, and of low priority" (Norman, 1982). Whereas work with delinquents, children with problems, clients needing rehabilitation, and those with marital problems, for instance, can result in problems being solved and the situation being returned to the normative, the elderly continue to get older, more feeble, and more dependent. Long-term success becomes hard to measure and harder to attain. There is some support for this thesis in the fact that one of the primary sources of work satisfaction reported by social workers consists of achieving results (Meller & Macarov, 1985)—a satisfaction difficult to attain as the infirmities of age continue.

Further, social workers, like nurses, are said to hold an unattractive image of the aged (Bergman, Eckerling, Golander, Sharon, & Tomer, 1983). They may be seen as crotchety, stubborn, senile, talkative, and dependent. Monk (1985) held that providers of human services hold negative societal images of the aged, including disvaluation, marginalization, internalization, and normativity. Although Geiger (1978) found that most social workers had little knowledge either about the aging process or about the elderly, it is unclear whether more knowledge would lead to more or less readiness to work with them. In many schools of social work, the study of aging is offered as an optional course, at best. Even in courses in human development, aging is dealt with in a cursory fashion. Blanchette (1980) pointed out that little or no experience in gerontology or geriatrics is required in medical training, and few medical schools even offer elective opportunities for such training. Human behavioral courses usually ignore old age, and life-cycle classes are taught as though human development continues only until adulthood or middle age.

There is also the possibility that current attitudes derive from fears of the future, that relatively young people do not want to acknowledge that they themselves will eventually be among the aging. There may also be cases where social workers see (or fear to see) in old people images of their own parents and grandparents. Finally, it may be that current education for social work deals with the area of aging in an inappropriate manner. In any case, it seems clear from both empirical and anecdotal material that the aged as a client group are not given high priority by social workers.

For both the quantitative and the qualitative reasons discussed above, there seems little likelihood of graduate social workers being able to provide all of the personal services needed by elderly people. It is equally unlikely that other helping professionals—nurses, geriatricians, occupational therapists, physiotherapists, psychologists, and so forth—will be able to meet the numerical need in their fields.

In addition, the unavailability of most community resources in the amounts needed, such as sheltered housing, day care centers and the like, as well as their economic costs, has led to and will continue to lead to wide-scale use of part-time and live-in home care workers as the cheapest and most easily available community resource. Some of these are homemakers, some housekeepers, health aides, social work aides, nursing aides, visitors, and others. Together, these individuals are generally spoken of as volunteers and paraprofessionals. In some cases, they are employed and made available by social welfare agencies (governmental, voluntary, and private); in others, by for-profit organizations; and in still others, directly by the elderly or their families.

Volunteers

Although it is conventional to speak of volunteers and paraprofessionals in one category, as distinguished from social workers, the differences between volunteers and paid workers in terms of motivation, rewards, continuity, and willingness and ability to assume certain tasks may be very great. Among professionals who work with the aged at present, there is some feeling that volunteers are more willing and suited for certain tasks than for others. There are many examples of volunteers serving as visitors in nursing homes, assistants in senior centers, and visitors in their own neighborhoods and among their own ethnic groups. Indeed, if a monetary value were to be placed on volunteers' activities, the aggregate amount would be immense. It is even impossible to make a comprehensive list of everything that volunteers do for elderly people. Many settings would not be able to function, or to function adequately, were it not for the help of volunteers (Gidron, 1978).

There is much that is not yet known about volunteering—for example, why some people volunteer and others, under the same conditions, do not. Abrams (1985) held that volunteering comes either from altruism—the roots of which also are little known—or a desire for reciprocity. It is questionable, however, whether volunteers actually expect to receive in return the same kind of help they offer—and certainly not from those whom they are helping. Consequently, Cahn (1986) suggested that the government establish a service bank, where people could receive credit for volunteering, to be repaid by service given them in times of need.

Despite this lack of information, enough knowledge can be drawn from the activities of volunteers and those who work with them to derive some principles for how to make use of and deal with such caregivers. Unfortunately, very little of this information is taught in schools of social work. Darvil and Munday (1984), for example, said that information concerning professional-volunteer collaboration is in a rudimentary stage. They claimed part of the reason for this is that reports concerning volunteer activity are almost always written from the social worker's point of view and rarely from that of the volunteer. Most social workers, even those thrown into contact with volunteers, have little grounded knowledge as to how to work with volunteers. There is even less awareness of how to recruit, motivate, orient, enable, supervise, evaluate, reward, and—when necessary—dispense with volunteers. Nor has much attention been paid to the need to volunteer as a human need.

In cases where volunteers have been used extensively (not exclusively with the aged), questions have arisen concerning accountability, liability, malpractice, and sometimes the eventual desire of the volunteer to be paid, especially when he or she seems to be doing the same thing as paid staff. This has led to a designation of "paid volunteers" in some cases.

In any case, whether or not planned, desired, or prepared for, the use of volunteers for specific tasks will become indispensable as the need for service to the aged increases. It follows, therefore, that working with volunteers will be one of the important jobs of social workers in the future. In some cases, social workers will be the supervisors or administrators of volunteer staff; in others, colleagues or team members; still in others, employees of volunteer organizations.

Paraprofessionals

Despite the positive contributions made, and to be made, by volunteers, the use of paid nonprofessional or semiprofessional personnel will be essential if services to the elderly are to be anywhere nearly commensurate with the need. Not only is there some skepticism about the use of "unpaid labor" as a basis for future planning (Graycar, 1983), but quantitatively, the pool from which paid workers are drawn is immeasurably wider than the pool of volunteers (Schindler & Brawley, 1987). Compared with that of paid workers, the work of volunteers is a "small-scale operation" (Darvil & Munday, 1984). In addition, and more importantly, only paid workers can be persuaded to do the routine, unglamorous, dirty, difficult, and dangerous jobs that are required on a sustained basis. These are the workers who empty bedpans, push wheelchairs, prepare and serve food, clean the floors, change the linen, and undertake the other "dirty, dead-end jobs" (Gans, 1967). It is doubtful whether social workers or other professionals will or should perform these jobs. Indeed, Goldberg (1969) found that professionals tend to push "uncomfortable" jobs onto lesser-trained personnel. However, with the exception of rewards, paraprofessionals present the same challenge to social workers as do volunteers, in terms of recruitment, orientation, supervision, evaluation, and continuation.

The problem facing social work in the massive use of nonprofessional help that the future seems to hold is one that has been met before—that is, distinguishing between the proper tasks of the social worker and those of the semiprofessional, paraprofessional, or nonprofessional. The same question arose with the decision to accredit bachelor degree graduates as well as master degree graduates as professional social workers, and to recognize social work aides. Basically, the question is whether persons with different levels of education and training do different jobs or whether nonprofessionals do the same jobs up to a certain level of complexity or skill. If nonprofessionals are to work alongside or under the supervision of social workers, the role of the latter as practitioners vis-à-vis the other caregivers must be clarified or changed (Brawley & Schindler, 1989).

Insofar as paid nonprofessionals or paraprofessionals are concerned, questions and problems are raised concerning salary, social benefits, tax deductions, and unionization. These are problems that social workers serving as supervisors or managers must become trained and equipped to handle. Indeed, training social workers to relate to paraprofessionals, in whatever capacities, has been badly neglected by most schools of social work (Kestenbaum & Shebar, 1984).

POTENTIAL RESTRUCTURING OF THE HUMAN-SERVICES PROFESSIONS

The explosive growth in the aged population, coupled with efforts to meet their needs, has resulted in a proliferation of agencies and services dealing with the elderly population. This growth has led to battles for "turf" on the one hand and a blurring of professional boundaries on the other (Monk, 1985). The growth of the elderly population may result in different patterns, each of which will have implications for social work practice and education.

The Free-Market Model

One pattern that may develop would entail a sharpening of professional distinctions, such as those between social workers, geriatric nurses, therapists, psychologists, and others, with different professions offering core services to different populations, geographical areas, client groups, or individuals, using other professionals as auxiliary help. This could be seen as the free-market, or "catch-as-catch-can" model.

The Divided-Pie Model

The second possibility is that there will be a sharing of professional knowledge and skills—teamwork—with each profession staking out and keeping within its boundaries. This divided-pie model will require clear definitions and protocols and a mechanism for resolving interprofessional disputes. Given the structure and nature of the various professions involved, this would require constant communication, negotiation, and agreement (Gross & Gross, 1986) with the ever-present danger of the client's needs being forgotten or neglected in the process.

The Family-Feud Model

In the absence of continuing communication and goodwill, disputes over professional perquisites and responsibilities may grow and continue, especially because everyone usually wants to be the coordinator and no one wants to be coordinated. The problems of interagency collaboration have been well documented (Stevenson, 1989). Conversely, the disputes might not be based on a desire to give the service, but because of a lack of resources, on a desire to foist the responsibility for the service onto others. In either case, this situation might degenerate into what one could term the family-feud model.

The Guerilla Warfare Model

The fourth possibility involves professional boundaries becoming more permeable. In the profession's desire to dominate the field or to give better service, each profession could try to widen its competence. Nurses would engage in family counseling; social workers would take temperatures and blood pressures; doctors would help families prepare their homes to receive a hospitalized aged parent; and everyone would engage in diet planning, budgeting, and other heretofore excluded activities. Although it would be desirable that such professional blurring, if it comes about, be done through agreement and cooperation, it will probably be done in a highly competitive manner, with each profession seeking dominance. This would be the guerilla warfare model.

The Mutation Model

Finally, it is possible that the scope and variety of services demanded for good care of elderly people will require the emergence of a new profession—one that contains elements of many present disciplines and activities related to the aged. Such a model would be resisted by existing professions and would have to surmount the difficulties of education and licensure that would arise. Nor is it to be conceded a priori that such practitioners would be more effective than those in the previously described models. However, were it to come into being, this could be called the mutation model.

SUMMARY

The future of the aged in most western countries can be summed up as one characterized by longer life expectancy, resulting in growth in numbers generally, and proportionately faster growth in the number of the very old, or "frail elderly." The aged person's health will be better, but many minor chronic health conditions will become problems of coping and therefore social work problems. Both minor ailments and more serious illnesses will continue for much longer periods than at present, and there will be an increase in the number of people suffering from long-term degenerative diseases.

Institutionalization of all elderly people needing outside help will be economically unfeasible, and therefore the bulk of the care will be provided by family members, who will need increasing help from community resources, particularly as more of the traditional caregivers—female relatives in general and daughters in particular—enter the labor force or move farther away.

Massive increases will be needed in the number of home care workers to care for the aged in their own households, and due to lack of numbers and expressed disinterest in working with elderly people on the part of social workers, the bulk of such helpers will be para-professionals or nonprofessionals, with some help from volunteers. Despite advances in technology, which might make life easier and solve some problems for the aged, it is probable that the amount of care available will still fall short of the amount needed, thus bringing with it the danger of an increase in both deliberate and inadvertent abuse of the elderly.

Although the health and education of most of the aged will be improved, their economic condition may be no better than at present, if not worse. For many older people, questions of family relationships and responsibility will loom large, whereas repeated losses of spouses, relatives, and friends, and the desire for remarriage, or at least for continued sexual activity, will present personal problems. Family members throughout the world tend to live at greater distances from each other. This distance tends to increase the isolation of the aged, diminish family responsibility, both legal and normative, and increase dependency on community resources, including social work.

Retirement and its attendant increase in leisure time will pose problems of adjustment, which might be aggravated by geographical distance from children, relatives, or friends. As structural problems of the aged continue or increase in the form of insufficient income and services, age discrimination, and physical barriers, the need for organization and social action will become important, as will improving public images of the aging. All of these have implications for social workers.

IMPLICATIONS FOR SOCIAL WORK

Tyler's 1950 categorization for the implications for social work is still appropriate today. Implications can be divided into knowledge, attitudes, and skills.

Knowledge

In addition to the knowledge base generally contained in education for social work today, social workers will need more knowledge concerning physiological, psychological, and social aspects of the later years of life. They will have to disassociate widespread societal assumptions about aging from fact, including, for example, the myths that aging is adolescence in reverse, that learning ability diminishes with age, that memory loss is inevitable in the aged, and that sexual desires and abilities disappear.

Social workers will have to become much more conversant with the legal implications of assignment of living quarters, conservatorships, powers-of-attorney, and other aspects that arise from the growing incapacity of some of the aged to handle their own affairs. The definition of elder abuse, regulations about reporting it, and the recourse available will have to be part of social workers' knowledge. Social workers will have to be well informed concerning the availability and sources of various kinds of help for the elderly, perhaps through use of information-retrieval technology. They will need to be aware of the boundaries of the social work profession, if and when those boundaries can be transgressed, and the role of other helping professions.

Social workers with the elderly may need information about budgeting; knowledgeable purchasing; and sources of additional income, such as Supplemental Security Income (SSI) and food stamps. They also will need to know about the existence of various leisure-time activities and their proper use by elderly people.

Attitudes

If social workers are to help elderly people, in both quantitative and qualitative terms, their own attitudes toward this group of clients must be at least neutral, if not positive. If they cannot control their own feelings, they must adopt an approach so professional that their relationships with the clients are not affected—a situation that is possible (Macarov, 1987b). Social workers must guard against the tendency, on their own part and that of others, to view or treat elderly people as incompetent, dependent, or childlike, and try to enable them to achieve the same sort of choice and self-direction people of other ages exercise.

Social workers must be sensitive to abuse of elderly people, especially unintended, on their own part and by others. Further, social workers must see the goal of "adding life to years" as equally important as solving current problems. Finally, dealing with death, loss, and grief may be more prevalent when working with the elderly population than with most other client groups, and social workers must learn to deal with their own feelings when loss occurs so that they can be as helpful as possible to clients and their families.

Skills

In addition to sharpening their present counseling skills to deal with elderly clients, social workers in the future will need to develop an important new skill—managing paraprofessionals and, to a lesser extent, volunteers. Given the massive increase in the personal social services that will result from the growth of the aged group, the most effective role for social workers will be recruiting nonprofessional staff, preparing them for their tasks, and supervising them in their work. This will require skills in management, staff development, record keeping, supervision, and evaluation, among others. At the same time, the social worker will need to deal with those situations beyond the competence or legal limits of the nonprofessional.

Given the multiplicity of agencies and institutions dealing with the elderly population, the social worker will need to become a case manager, marshaling, articulating, and coordinating services for the good of the client. Case management will also require specific, learnable skills.

In short, the massive need for caregivers to serve the elderly population will require social workers in this area to be both managers and specialized practitioners. If social workers do not undertake the role of directing the work of the nonprofessional staff, it will be taken over by other professionals. Relinquishing this role would severely limit the scope of the social work profession in dealing with elderly people, probably to the detriment of the client.

CONCLUSION

The progressive growth of the number of the aged in the population will not be a simple linear matter, requiring more of the same of social work and social welfare. The profession will be called upon to redefine its goals and methods in working with the aged, taking into consideration changes within the group, its heterogeneity, and changes affecting the group. This redefinition process will require a great deal of flexibility on the part of the social work establishment and much thought concerning the redesign of social work education for work with the elderly population.

REFERENCES

Abrams, M. (1978). *Beyond three-score and ten: A first report on a survey of the elderly*. Mitcham, Surrey, England: Age Concern.

Abrams, P. (1985). Policies to promote informal social care: Some reflections on voluntary action, neighbourhood involvement, and neighbourhood care. *Ageing and Society, 5,* 1–18.

Ageing International. (1984). *11,* 5–6.

Ageing International. (1988). *15,* 15–16, 42–43.

Allan, G. (1988). Kinship, responsibility and care for elderly people. *Ageing and Society, 8,* 249–268.

American Association of Retired Persons. (1985). *A profile of older Americans 1985*. Washington, DC: Author.

American Association of Retired Persons (AARP) Bulletin. (1985a). *26,* 5.

American Association of Retired Persons (AARP) Bulletin. (1985b). *26,* 6.

Atchley, R. C. (1976). *The sociology of retirement*. New York: Schenkman.

Aviram, U., & Katan, J. (1987). *Integration of social work graduates into the profession and its relationship with their demographic-socioeconomic background and educational experiences.* Ramat Aviv: University of Tel Aviv. (Hebrew)

Bankoff, E. A. (1983). Aged parents and their widowed daughters: A support relationship. *Journal of Gerontology, 38,* 226–230.

Beck, S. H. (1982). Adjustment to and satisfaction with retirement. *Journal of Gerontology, 37,* 616–624.

Bergman, R., Eckerling, S., Golander, H., Sharon, R., & Tomer, A. (1983). *Nursing the aged: Institutional and personal factors influencing the work of nursing personnel in long-term care institutions.* Jerusalem: Brookdale Institute.

Berman, H. J. (1987). Adult children and their parents: Irredeemable obligation and irreplaceable loss. *Journal of Gerontological Social Work, 10,* 21–34.

Blanchette, P. A. L. (1980). Medical students and geriatrics. In *Perspectives on geriatric medicine.* Washington, DC: U.S. Department of Health and Human Services.

Blank, M. L. (1977). Meeting the needs of the aged: The social worker in the community center. *Public Health Reports, 92,* 39–42.

Bond, J. (1984). Abstracts: Sociology and social policy. *Ageing and Society, 4,* 205–213.

Boyd, R. V. (1981). What is a 'social problem' in geriatrics? In T. Arie (Ed.), *Health care of the elderly* (pp. 158–171). London: Croom Helm.

Brawley, A. B., & Schindler, R. (1989). Professional-paraprofessional relationships in four countries: A comparative analysis. *International Social Work, 32,* 91–106.

Brody, E. M. (1981). Women in the middle and family help to older people. *The Gerontologist, 21,* 471–480.

Bulcroft, K., Bulcroft, R., Hatch, L., & Borgotta, E. F. (1989). Antecedents and consequences of remarriages in later life. *Research on Aging, 11,* 821–906.

Butler, R. N., & Lewis, M. I. (1977). *Aging and mental health.* St. Louis: Mosby.

Cahn, E. S. (1986). *Service credits: A new currency for the welfare state.* Jerusalem: Brookdale Institute.

Callahan, D. (1987). *Setting limits: Setting goals in an aging society.* New York: Simon & Schuster.

Cash, T., & Valentine, D. (1987). A decade of adult protective services: Case characteristics. *Journal of Gerontological Social Work, 10,* 47–60.

Cetron, M., & O'Toole, T. (1982). *Encounters with the future: A forecast of life into the 21st century.* New York: McGraw-Hill.

Chamberlain, E., Hayes, L., Kerswell, G., Martin, D., & Landsberg, A. (1982). Transmitting social work values to non–social work staff: Practice into theory. *Australian Social Work, 35,* 7–31.

Chen, Y-P. (1985). Economic status of the aging. In R. H. Binstock & E. Shanas

(Eds.), *The handbook of aging and the social sciences*. New York: Van Nostrand Reinhold.

Chien, C-P. (1971). Psychiatric treatment for geriatric patients: 'Pub' or drug? *American Journal of Psychiatry, 127,* 110–115.

Chien, C-P., Stotsky, B. A., & Cole, J. O. (1973). Psychiatric treatment for nursing home patients: Drug, alcohol and milieu. *American Journal of Psychiatry, 130,* 543–548.

Cohen, E. S. (1985). Protective services. In A. Monk (Ed.), *Handbook of gerontological services*. New York: Van Nostrand Reinhold.

Csillag, D. (1989). Training families in care provision: A demonstration project. In R. S. Wolf & S. Bergman (Eds.), *Stress, conflict and abuse of the elderly*. Jerusalem: Brookdale Institute.

Cunningham, S. (1984). On telling the news: Grandparenthood as an announceable event. *International Journal of Sociology and Social Policy, 4,* 52–69.

Cunningham-Burley, S. (1986). Becoming a grandparent. *Ageing and Society, 6,* 453–470.

Daily Telegraph (London). (1987, March 10). p. 9.

Darton, R., & Knapp, M. (1984). The cost of residential care for the elderly: The effects of dependency, design and social environment. *Ageing and Society, 4,* 157–183.

Darvil, G., & Munday, B. (1984). *Volunteers in the personal social services*. London: Tavistock.

Department of Health and Social Services. (1981). *Report of a study on community care*. London: Her Majesty's Stationery Office.

Depner, C. E., & Ingersoll-Dayton, B. (1985). Conjugal social support: Patterns in later life. *Journal of Gerontology, 40,* 760–766.

deSchweinitz, K. (1943). *England's road to social security*. Philadelphia: University of Pennsylvania Press.

Eastman, M. (1984, February 2). At most just picking up the pieces. *Community Care*, pp. 20–22.

Eastman, M., & Sutton, M. (1982, November). Granny battering. *Geriatric Medicine*, pp. 11–15.

Eisdorfer C., & Cohen, D. (1983). Health and retirement: Retirement and health: Background and future directions. In H. S. Parnes (Ed.), *Policy issues in work and retirement*. Kalamazoo, MI: Upjohn.

European Centre for Social Welfare Training and Research. (1987). *Social policies beyond the 1980s in the European region*. Vienna: Author.

Evers, A., & Lagergren, M. (1987). Report on Vienna dialogue II— towards better links and balances between social and health services in care for the elderly. *Eurosocial Newsletter, 47–48,* 34–40.

Eversly, D. (1982). Some new aspects of aging in Britain. In K. Hareven (Ed.), *Aging and life course transitions: An interdisciplinary perspective*. New York: Guilford.

Fowles, D. (1983). The changing older population. *Aging, 339,* 6–11.

Fowles, D. (1986) Discovering the older market. *Aging, 352,* 36–37.

Gans, H. (1967, Winter). Income grants and 'dirty work.' *Public Interest,* 110.

Geiger, D. L. (1978). How future professionals view the elderly: A comparative analysis of social work, law and medical students' perceptions. *Gerontologist, 18,* 591–594.

Gidron, B. (1978) Volunteer work and its rewards. *Volunteer Administration, 11,* 18–32.

Goldberg, G. S. (1969). Nonprofessionals in human services. In C. G. Grosser, W. E. Henry, & J. G. Kelly (Eds.), *Nonprofessionals in the human services.* San Francisco: Jossey-Bass.

Goodhart, D. (1989, June 10). Bonn tackles pension bulge. *Jerusalem Post,* p. 6.

Goodwin, J. S., Sanchez, C. J., Thomas, P., Hunt, C., Garry, J., & Goodwin, J. M. (1987). Alcohol intake in a healthy elderly population. *American Journal of Public Health, 77,* 173–177.

Gorer, G. (1965). *Death, grief and mourning.* New York: Doubleday.

Grad, S. (1990). Income change at retirement. *Social Security Bulletin,* 53(1), 2–10.

Graycar, A. (1983). Informal, voluntary and statutory services: The complex relationship. *British Journal of Social Work, 13,* 379–393.

Gross, A. M., & Gross, J. (1986). Can physicians and social workers collaborate? *World Health Forum, 7,* 261–266.

Habib, J. (1985). The economy and the aged. In R. H. Binstock & E. Shanas (Eds.), *Handbook of aging and social sciences.* New York: Van Nostrand Reinhold.

Hall, P. A. (1989). Elder maltreatment items, subgroups and types: Policy and practice implications. *International Journal of Aging and Human Development, 28,* 191–205.

Hardcastle, D. A. (1978). Aging now and in the future. *Journal of Social Welfare, 5,* 41–49.

Hooyman, N. R., & Lustbader, W. (1986). *Taking care: Supporting older people and their families.* New York: Free Press.

House, J. S., Landis, K. R., & Umberson, D. (1988, July 29). Social relationships and health. *Science,* pp. 540–545.

Jennings, J. (1987). Elderly parents as caregivers for their adult dependent children. *Social Work, 32,* 430–433.

Jerusalem Post. (1985, March 6). p. 5.

Joint Distribution Committee–Israel. (n.d.) *A word about the elderly in Israel.* Jerusalem: Author.

Judge, K., & Knapp, M. (1985). Efficiency in the production of welfare: The public and private sectors compared. In R. Klein & M. O'Higgins (Eds.), *The future of welfare.* Oxford: Basil Blackwell.

Kaplan, M. (1975). *Leisure: Theory and policy.* New York: John Wiley & Sons.

Katz-Shiban, B. (1989). The impact of victimization on the elderly in Israel: Acquisition of the victim role in three profiles of elderly victims. In R. S.

Wolf & S. Bergman (Eds.), *Stress, conflict and abuse of the elderly*. Jerusalem: Brookdale Institute.

Kelman, H. C. (1968). *A time to speak: On human values and social research*. San Francisco: Jossey-Bass.

Kestenbaum, S. E., & Shebar, V. (1984). The social work-paraprofessional partnership: A direction for the eighties. *Social Development Issues*, 8, 136–143.

Kola, L. A., Kosberg, J. I., & Wegner-Burch, K. (1980). Perceptions of the treatment responsibilities for the alcoholic elderly client. *Social Work in Health Care*, 6, 69–76.

Lehman, H. (1989). Fraud and abuse of the elderly. In R. Wolf & S. Bergman (Eds.), *Stress, conflict and abuse of the elderly*. Jerusalem: Brookdale Institute.

Lerba, C. (1986). *Research findings on the survey of Jews in Sydney aged 80 years and more living at home*. Sydney, Australia: Sydney Jewish Centre on Ageing, Health, Lifestyles and Home Supports.

Lerea, L. E. (1982). Grief among healthcare workers: A comparative study. *Journal of Gerontology*, 37, 604–608.

Lesher, E. L., & Berger, K. J. (1989). Bereaved mothers: Changes in health, functional activities, family cohesion, and psychological well-being. *International Journal of Aging and Human Development*, 28, 191–205.

Linett, V. Z. (1989). *Driving while intoxicated: A comparative study of aged and non-aged offenders*. Unpublished master's thesis, Southern Connecticut State University, New Haven.

Litwin, H. (1985). Ombudsman services. In A. Monk (Ed.), *Handbook of gerontological services*. New York: Van Nostrand Reinhold.

Longman, P. (1988). The challenge of an aging society. *The Futurist*, 22, 33–37.

Lopez, A. D. (1984). Sex differentials in mortality. *WHO Chronicle*, 38, 217–224.

Macarov, D. (1978). *The design of social welfare*. New York: Holt, Rinehart, & Winston.

Macarov, D. (1987a) Social work with the aged: Some future projections. *Social Work and Social Policy in Israel*, 1, 7–24.

Macarov, D. (1987b). *Social workers' attitudes toward work with the aged*. Paper delivered at European Regional Group Meeting, International Association of Schools of Social Work, Sitges, Spain.

Matthew, S. H., & Sprey, J. (1985). Adolescents' relationships with grandparents: An empirical contribution to conceptual clarification. *Journal of Gerontology*, 40, 621–626.

Mayer, M. J. (1979). Alcohol and the elderly: A review. *Health and Social Work*, 4, 128–143.

Meier, E. L., Dittman, C. C., & Toyle, B. B. (1980). *Retirement income goals*. Washington, DC: President's Commission on Pension Policy.

Meller, Y., & Macarov, D. (1985). Studying satisfactions in human service organizations. *International Journal of Sociology and Social Policy, 5,* 1–15.

Monk, A. (1985). *Handbook of gerontological services.* New York: Van Nostrand Reinhold.

New York Times. (1989, June 13). p. C5.

Norman, A. (1982). *Mental illness in old age: Meeting the challenge.* London: Center for Policy on Ageing.

O'Brien, J. (1989). Elder abuse and the physician: Factors impeding recognition and intervention. In R. S. Wolf & S. Bergman (Eds.), *Stress, conflict and abuse of the elderly.* Jerusalem: Brookdale Institute.

Okraku, I. O. (1987). Age and attitudes toward multigenerational residence. *Journal of Gerontology, 42.*

Osterkamp, L. (1988). Family caregivers: America's primary long-term care resource. *Aging, 358,* 2–5.

Osterweis, M. (1985). Bereavement and the elderly. *Aging, 348,* 8–13, 41.

Parnes, H. S. (Ed.). (1983). *Policy issues in work and retirement.* Kalamazoo, MI: Upjohn.

Poertner, J. (1986). Estimating the incidence of abused older persons. *Journal of Gerontological Social Work, 9,* 3–15.

Radner, D. B. (1990). Assessing the economic status of the aged and nonaged using alternative income-wealth means. *Social Security Bulletin, 53*(3), 2–14.

Regan, P. (1989). Unemployment in Lancaster and Morecambe. *International Journal of Manpower, 10,* 20–23.

Report of the royal commission on the national health service. (1979). London: Her Majesty's Stationery Office.

Rice, D. P. (1985). Report of the expert group meeting on long-term care of the elderly or disabled organized by the international social security association. In L. Reif & B. Trager (Eds.), *International perspectives on long-term care.* New York: Haworth.

Rogers, G. (1980). *Pension coverage and vesting among private wage and salary workers in 1979.* Washington, DC: Office of Research and Statistics, Social Security Administration.

Rones, P. L. (1980). The retirement decision: A question of opportunity? *Monthly Labor Review, 103,* 14–17.

Rosenwacke, I. (1985). A demographic portrait of the oldest old. *Milbank Memorial Fund Quarterly, 63,* 182–205.

Rubin, A., Johnson, P. J., & DeWeaver, K. L. (1984). Direct practice interests of MSW students: Changes from entry to graduation. *Journal of Education for Social Work, 20,* 5–16.

Sarasohn, S. B. (1977). *Work, aging and social change: Professionals and the one life–one career imperative.* New York: Free Press.

Schindler, R., & Brawley, E. A. (1987). *Social care at the front line: A worldwide study of paraprofessionals.* London: Tavistock.

Sengstock, M. C., & Hwalek, M. (1987). A review and analysis of measures for the identification of elder abuse. *Journal of Gerontological Social Work, 10*, 21–36.

Siegel, J. S., & Hoover, S. L. (1982). Demographic aspects of the health of the elderly to the year 2000 and beyond. *World Health Statistical Study, 35*, 133–202.

Silverstone, B., & Burack-Weiss, A. (1983). *Social work practice with the frail elderly and their families*. Springfield, IL: Charles C Thomas.

Simon, B. (1987). *Never married women*. Philadelphia: Temple University Press.

Social Security Bulletin. (1990). *53*(3), 60.

Soumerai, B., & Avorn, J. (1983). Perceived health, life satisfaction, and activity in urban elderly: A controlled study of the impact of part-time work. *Journal of Gerontology, 38*, 356–362.

Stagner, R. (1978). The affluent society versus early retirement. *Aging and Work, 1*, 25–31.

Stevenson, O. (1981). The frail elderly: A social worker's perspective. In T. Arie (Ed.), *Health care of the elderly* (pp. 158–171). London: Croom Helm.

Stevenson, O. (1989). The challenge of inter-agency collaboration. *Adoption and Fostering, 13*, 31–42.

Strauss, A. (1962). Transformations of identity. In A. M. Rose (Ed.), *Human behavior and social processes*. Boston: Houghton Mifflin.

Taggart, R. (Ed.). (1977). *Job creation: What works?* Salt Lake City: Olympus.

Thienbaus, O. J., Conter, E. A., & Rosmann, H. B. (1986). Sexuality and ageing. *Ageing and Society, 6*, 39–54.

Tyler, R. W. (1950). *Basic principles of curriculum and instruction*. Chicago: University of Chicago Press.

United Nations. (1989). *Demographic yearbook 1987*. New York: Author.

U.S. Department of Commerce, Bureau of the Census. (1987). *Statistical abstract of the United States 1988*. Washington, DC: Author.

U.S. Department of Health and Human Services. (n.d.). *Answers about aging: New pieces to an old puzzle*. Washington, DC: Author.

U.S. Department of Health and Human Services. (1987). *Research advances in aging, 1984–1986*. Washington, DC: Author.

U.S. Department of Health and Human Services. (1988). *Health United States 1987*. Washington, DC: Author.

U.S. Department of Health and Human Services. (1989). *Social Security bulletin annual statistical supplement 1989*. Washington, DC: Author.

U.S. Department of Health, Education, and Welfare. (1975). *Statistical memo #31*. Washington, DC: Author.

U.S. News & World Report. (1984, July 2). p. 69.

Van de Vyvere, B., Hughes, M., & Fish, D. G. (1976). The elderly chronic alcoholic: A practical approach. *Canadian Welfare, 52*, 9–13.

Wolf, R. S., & Bergman, S. (Eds.). (1989). *Stress, conflict and abuse of the elderly*. Jerusalem: Brookdale Institute.

Wolfbein, S. L. (1988). The new labour force. *International Journal of Manpower, 9*, 3–9.

Wolpert, D. S. (1988). *Retirement, preretirement planning and employment/ unemployment*. Paper delivered at the North American Conference on Employment and Underemployment, Adelphi University, Garden City, NY.

Woodrofe, K. (1962). *From charity to social work in England and the United States*. Toronto: University of Toronto Press.

World of Work Report. (1984). *9*, 8.

Yankelovich, D. (1981). *New rules: Searching for fulfillment in a world turned upside down*. New York: Random House.

Yarrow, P., Marcus, L., & MacLean, M. J. (1981). Marriage and the elderly: A literature review. *Canadian Journal of Social Work Education, 7*, 65–79.

Zborowsky, E. (1985). Developments in protective services: A challenge for social workers. In G. S. Getzel & M. J. Meller (Eds.), *Gerontological social work practice in the community*. New York: Haworth.

Zimberg, S. (1984). The extent of problem drinking. *Alcohol Health and Research World, 8*, 5–6.

3

Social Work with Tomorrow's Families

Extrapolating current trends to predict what will happen in the future is more helpful when applied to numerical items, such as population figures or employment rates, than when trying to anticipate changes that will occur in family structure and activities. However, because many of the changes within the family will be the result of changes in other areas, it is useful to examine some of the latter with a view toward estimating their probable effects on families, and thus their future impact on family-focused social work.

To begin, it is worthwhile to note that the image of the family on which most social policy and social planning are based—a wife and two or more children at home, with the husband the only breadwinner—now represents only 6 percent of all American households (*Wellness Letter*, 1989). A majority of the 65.1 million U.S. families have no children under age 18 living at home, and there are now more families without children at home than families with them. This change has come about only during the last 10 years (*The Futurist*, 1989). Thus, the bulk of American families are kaleidoscopic in their variety—multigenerational families, two-earner families, single-parent families, unmarried cohabitating partners with and without families, childless families, families with remarried spouses, and more. As is the case with every other client group, social workers must be careful to make distinctions and to individualize within pertinent generalities.

WOMEN IN THE WORK FORCE

One of the most salient trends affecting families today is the entry of women into the labor force. Actually, women have always worked.

In primitive societies, women engaged in agriculture and, to a lesser degree, in herding, although they probably did not hunt as often as men. Even today, there are parts of the world in which large areas of trade and commerce are dominated by women, for example, the so-called "mammy wagons" and market stalls in parts of Africa, where the entire agricultural transportation and selling system is controlled by women.

The entry of women into the world of paid employment, however, dates back to the impetus given by the Industrial Revolution. The primarily textile factories of England drew young girls and boys from the farms to the big cities to operate machines. Measures to protect these girls (and, to a lesser extent, the boys) gave rise to what today would be termed social work activities. Matrons and wardens in boarding houses acted as surrogate parents, both monitoring and socializing the young people under their charge. Centers for wholesome recreation, development of useful skills, and moral education were established, of which Toynbee Hall is often cited as the prototype (Pimlott, 1935). In all of these cases, however, the expectation was that the woman would stop working when she got married, if possible, or, at least, when there were children to care for. Thus, the family with the working father and nonworking mother became the norm for most western societies. This norm was reinforced by child labor laws, which prohibited children from working along with their mothers, and by minimum wage laws, which barred many women from jobs, because they were seen as less productive.

Women's work took another turn with the establishment of the piecework system, in which work could be done at home, thus circumventing child labor laws and minimum wage laws, as well as obviating union organizing. Literature is replete with accounts of entire families working night and day to achieve a livable income or to get ahead financially. In this situation, too, it was implicit that the wife or mother remain at home, whether undertaking paid work there, engaging in the traditional unpaid work of raising a family, or both.

The move toward married women and mothers working outside the home had its roots in the feminist movement. Among the movement's goals have been the right to hold any job, to receive equal pay for equal work, to be free of sexual harassment at work, and to prohibit advertisements that claim applicants of one sex are more valuable or desirable than another. The result has been raised consciousness on the part of many women as to their rights.

Partly due to this change in attitude, the proportion of women in the labor forces of the western industrialized countries has been rising constantly. In 1930, women constituted 22 percent of the American labor force; in 1960, 33 percent; and in 1988, 45 percent (Lingg, 1990). It is estimated that by 1995 at least 60 percent, or three in five, of all women will be working (Conference Board, 1985). By 1998, the labor force participation of married women will equal that of married men (Davis, 1984).

One result of more women working has been a rise in family income. Whereas 20 years ago only a quarter of American families earned more than $25,000 a year, today this bracket, adjusted for inflation, includes 46 percent of all families. It is estimated that in the United States today, about half of women with children under 18 work, 50 percent of mothers of children under six work (Conference Board, 1985), and 55 percent of mothers of children under three work (U.S. Department of Commerce, 1987). From 20 to 30 percent of employed mothers indicate that they would prefer not to work, however.

Reasons for Working

Asked why they work, most mothers—two-thirds, according to one survey—give income as their main reason (Moss & Fonda, 1980). Yet, some women also work to gain the psychological lift that they have acquired by being independent, or less dependent, and in achieving a career. Some seek the creativity a career can afford and the network of relationships found in the workplace. There are also those whose major motivation is that working is more interesting than staying home, or that it allows physical separation, for limited periods, from parents, children, and spouse.

These gains also may involve costs, however. Working may be more difficult, or more boring, than staying home, but financially necessary or attractive. There is some evidence in the data on work satisfaction that women express more satisfaction than do men, but the explanation usually found for this is that the women are happier at having the opportunity to work, or at having found work, but not more satisfied than men with the actual work they perform (Andrisani, 1978). As noted, between 20 and 30 percent of mothers working would rather not. How many nonmothers are working against their wishes is unknown, but undoubtedly there are women who enjoy housework, cooking, and related activities more than their work outside the home. Many women continue to bear responsibility for both sets of tasks.

Clarifying Parental Roles and Capabilities

The number of two-earner families has been steadily rising. In 1977, 52 percent of couples had two salaries; by 1987 this had risen to 67 percent (Morrison, 1990). The strains that might arise from being a working wife or mother are well documented (Howe, 1977; Staines & Pleck, 1983). Not only might the rearrangement of domestic schedules and responsibilities cause tension, but changes in self-images and perceptions about others may also arise. The mother may feel guilty, thinking she is neglecting her husband and children. Conversely, guilt feelings on the part of the husband that his wife is working, or must work, or that he is not undertaking a full share of the responsibilities might occur. It has been noted that when the woman's career surpasses that of the husband—either financially or status-wise—additional strains might result. Ladewig and White (1980), for example, distinguished between the results of being a "dual-career" family as differentiated from a "dual-worker" family, within the general designation of "dual-earner" families. Insofar as the woman continues to bear the responsibility for the house and family, one might want to add the category "dual-job" woman.

Arriving at role clarity, mutually agreeable arrangements, and peace of mind for both husband and wife may require considerable social work help and a high level of professional skill on the part of the helper. When the decision of the woman to go to work aggravates previously existing problems and tensions or is an attempt to solve such problems, the need for help becomes even more pressing and more professionally challenging.

Another possible cost regarding working women concerns the well-being of any children in the family. Child care arrangements range from latchkey children who let themselves into the house after school and fend for themselves, to care by relatives, friends, or neighbors; paid maids or nursemaids; group care arrangements; and prenursery schools, nursery schools, and kindergartens. In all of these cases, the question arises of whether the fact that the mother works affects her children's well-being.

Theories in this regard have shifted several times. At one time social workers were generally convinced that even a "poor" natural parent was more desirable for the child than any institution, even one known as a "good" institution. The one-to-one relationship and the "natural" love between mother and child were cited, among other reasons, as to why an institution could not supplant a parent. With the steady increase in parents working, however, and particularly under heavy societal pressure to force female welfare recipients to go to work by removing the excuse of child caring duties from them, the question began to be raised as to whether the fact of giving birth makes one a desirable parent. The emerging theory that it is better for the child if the parents work is sometimes based on the premise that increased income makes it possible for the mother to compensate her children in other (more or better) ways for the reduction in time together and the loss of interaction that may ensue. The trained professional in the child care setting is said to be more helpful to the child—at least in terms of socialization—than the untrained mother. Raichle (1980) took this argument further, in somewhat loaded terms: "Women with outside interests may be far better capable of coping with child rearing than those who are sheltered from the outside world."

Questions concerning parental competence, coupled with observations based on socioeconomic conditions, have led to the creation of a number of programs designed to help parents become more competent, such as Israel's Mother-and-Child Stations; programs to stimulate and enrich the child's home environment, such as outgrowths of the Head Start program; and programs to provide financial help based on the child's need. Almost every industrialized country in the world, except the United States, and many nonindustrialized countries, has a system of children's or family allowances. In the United States, income tax deductions based on the number of dependents serve somewhat the same purpose, but only for those whose income is large enough to be taxed.

Nonfamily Child Care

All of these measures to help children be cared for at home have been overtaken, however, by the growth of child care agencies. Surveying the extent to which local authorities in England provide services in line with government guidelines, George and Wilding (1984) noted that only in the case of "day centre" classes does the provision of services meet the mandated norm—and, in fact, exceed it. In the United States, more than one-fifth of all children under age five whose mothers are employed are cared for by day care providers (Aguirre & Marshall, 1988). The provision of child care services has been a growth area in western economies for some years, with commercially provided facilities proving very profitable.

In some areas, industry has taken the lead in providing such resources. To attract and retain women workers, many companies provide various kinds of child care facilities. These may be on-site day care centers, vouchers for other facilities, or information and referral services (Conference Board, 1985). In some places, businesses too small to provide such services are forming consortia with similar firms to provide joint day care facilities. Others provide home services, such as visiting nurses, to employees ("Child Care," 1988).

The costs and gains of mothers working outside the home are complex and hard to quantify; even qualitative differences in satisfaction, children's educational progress, or the mental health of parent and/or child offer difficult methodological problems. The quality of outside care, however, can be and has been measured. In a somewhat dated report it was found that 11 percent of such children got poor care, and more than 50 percent received only custodial care (Keyserling, 1972). Consequently, doubts, ambivalence, and guilt undoubtedly exist and will grow as more women begin working. The need for social work services related to both families and the work world will increase as this phenomenon continues, although the use of social workers in child care centers is relatively small, such facilities usually being viewed as educational and consequently staffed primarily by teachers and their aides.

The same problem, to a lesser degree, arises with care of elderly people. With more women working outside the home, the need for care arrangements for the aged has continued to rise. This need is accentuated by the growing number of older people, and their lengthened life expectancy, as detailed in chapter 2.

The dilemmas of care for elderly people in the home, in the community, in an institution, or in some in-between arrangement will grow as more women enter the work force, because in most cases it is still the daughter who most often supports and cares for elderly relatives (Bond, 1984). Abrams (1980) said that, "Between mother and daughters in particular almost any call for help is legitimate and will if at all possible be satisfied."

Despite this dependence on daughters, there has been less of a focus on providing outside help for elderly people so that women may enter the work force than on providing such care for children. Probably a number of reasons exist for this, including the smaller number and proportion of elderly people as compared with children, or the assumption that elderly people are more capable of self-care. There may also be the widespread but unspoken assumption that care of the children is a desirable societal investment, whereas care of the elderly is simply an expense. Finally, there is the fact that while there exists societal pressure to make welfare mothers go to work, resulting in child care arrangements, there is no expectation that the aged— even aged welfare recipients—will take jobs.

Problems concerning child care might be relieved somewhat if the arrangements called "flexitime" and "flexiplace," mentioned in chapter 2, continue to grow as they have recently. Under flexitime arrangements, work schedules can vary (Best, 1981), and under flexiplace conditions, the work is done in or near the home. In 1988, 750,000 American men and 1.5 million women worked entirely at home (U.S. Department of Commerce, 1987). To date, this has been mostly confined to work that can be done on word processors, visual display terminals, or computers of various kinds. However, with the expected increase in rooftop satellite receivers ("Telecommuting," 1984) the amount of work done in the home may increase considerably, further lessening the need for outside-care arrangements.

The continued entry of formerly nonworking women into the labor force is a trend that shows no signs of diminishing. Even if there were to be a slackening in this trend, the high rate of the previous two decades will ensure that there will be a growth in problems arising from this phenomenon—problems primarily concerning intrafamily relationships and child and aged care. All of these are well within the province of social work activities.

WORK AND THE FAMILY

Also to be considered are the effects on the family that arise from working, or from the work itself. The problems that come up in the workplace may be the root of problems carried over into the home. (The attitudes and behaviors of workers, including their lack of satisfaction, is detailed in chapter 4.) It is unclear as to the extent to which work patterns affect nonwork behavior, however. On the one hand, the "spillover" theory holds that work patterns mold nonwork patterns, and that one tends to behave outside work as one does while on the job—that is, one seeks the same type of leisure-time pursuits, maintains the same pace, and reacts to events outside of work as one has been accustomed to doing at work. The "compensation" theory, on the other hand, holds that people react to their work during leisure time by seeking the kinds of situations and activities that are denied them on the job. Still another position holds that there is no connection between job and nonjob behavior. Little research has been done on the effect of work on families, although considerable attention has been paid to how family situations affect work patterns.

The effects of unhappiness at work and possible repercussions within the family are not confined to women, of course. However, the problem for women is made more complex by the fact that most women still receive lower salaries than men, despite legal prescriptions to the contrary and sincere efforts on the part of some companies and unions to arrive at equal pay for similar activities ("How Private Business Views," 1984). In addition, most women entering and currently in the work force hold part-time jobs. The growth of part-time employment is one of the strong trends in the world of work, and it is abetted by women who either choose or are assigned such work. Part-time work tends to be low paying and low status and affords little opportunity for advancement. Thus, family problems that might be created or exacerbated by women working are not generally compensated for by good salaries, interesting work, or meaningful career opportunities.

Lack of satisfaction at work, stress arising from work situations, fears concerning the future of the job, and all of the other problems that traditionally have been associated primarily with men at work will in the future also affect growing numbers of women as they join the work force, in addition to the problems arising from sexism.

UNEMPLOYMENT AND THE FAMILY

Despite the severity of problems that working causes families, the effect of unemployment on the family is probably much greater. The possibility of large groups of people undergoing long periods of unemployment will be discussed in more detail in chapter 4, but the effect of unemployment on individuals and families has been graphically illustrated both by statistics and anecdotes (Liebow, 1981). Not only is the loss of family income a problem, but changes also develop in roles, relationships, and ranks within the family, in self-images, and sometimes in behavior. The tensions and strains arising within families as a result of unemployment are quite likely to increase in both number and intensity as unemployment itself becomes more widespread.

The role of social welfare programs and of social work activity during periods of unemployment, or within groups of the unemployed, has not been spectacularly successful. At most, they are usually seen as holding actions until employment opportunities increase. In the future, however, social work and social welfare may be called on to help bring about necessary changes in values and structures and to help people not only endure their unemployment, but turn it into a positive experience. This may involve not only devising nonwork activities that are satisfying, time-structuring, and status-bestowing, but also counseling and advising with a new slant concerning unemployment.

MARRIAGE, DIVORCE, AND REMARRIAGE

Another prevailing change in family life can be anticipated with the growth of divorce and remarriage rates. The divorce rate has been growing steadily for the last several decades, having doubled between 1960 and 1980, and increasing by 111 percent between 1970 and 1988 (Visher & Visher, 1988). More than half of recent American marriages now end in divorce (United Nations, 1989), as do 60 percent of second marriages (Furstenberg & Spanier, 1984). Three-fourths of young divorced persons are likely to remarry (Glick, 1984). More specifically, 79 percent of divorced men and 75 percent of divorced women remarry, and it is estimated that by the year 2000, families with stepchildren will outnumber all other kinds of American families (Visher & Visher, 1979).

It is predicted that the divorce rate will rise even higher with the spread of "no-fault" divorce laws, with the decree granted on request (Glass, 1980). Even if the divorce rate declines somewhat in the future, it will undoubtedly remain much higher during the next 40 years than it was 40 years ago. In addition, the results of divorces already granted will persist in their effect on both divorced people and their children. One study indicates that divorce has more deleterious effects associated with it than does widowhood (Kitson, Babri, Roach, & Placidi, 1989). In both cases, however, there is likely to be an adverse financial result, at least for women. Forty percent of widows and 25 percent of divorced women fall into poverty for some time during the first five years of leaving marriage (Morgan, 1984). The United States does not have arrangements, such as some other countries have, in which the equivalent of the Social Security Administration insures women against nonpayment of alimony or child support payments. Consequently, rising or continuing high rates of divorce mean that American social workers are liable to deal with increasing cases of financial need.

Rising divorce rates are accompanied by rising remarriage rates, and in some cases the continuation of this trend can best be described as "serial marriages" or a "divorce chain," as the same person gets divorced and remarried a number of times. Remarriage rates increased 22 percent from 1970 to 1980 (Giles-Sims & Crosbie-Burnett, 1989). In 1984, 45.6 percent of all marriages were remarriages of one or both partners (U.S. Department of Commerce, 1987), and this figure rises even higher if unmarried cohabitation is taken into consideration (Glick, 1980). This last point is momentous, for divorced persons are more liable to cohabitate without marriage than are previously unmarried persons (Glick & Spanier, 1980). The number of unmarried cohabitating couples increased from half a million in 1970 to 1.6 million in 1980 and 2.3 million in 1986 (Glick, 1989). Further, it has been found that "divorced people choose other divorced people far more often than not" (Garfield, 1980). And remarriages are among comparatively young people—women average 27 years and men 29 (Garfield, 1980). The median interval between marriage and divorce in the United States is seven years, and the median period between divorce and remarriage is three years (Glick, 1980).

As Furstenberg and Spanier (1984) explained, divorce more often affects young married people, and widowhood more often affects older married people. In addition, each divorce introduces two additional persons to the "marriageable" group, whereas widowhood adds only one. Consequently, remarriage is more likely to involve divorced than widowed individuals.

Insofar as the effects of serial marriages, the divorce chain, or the marriage chain (Furstenberg & Spanier, 1984) are concerned, we have very little empirical—or even survey—knowledge. There is some demographic material available on such things as ages, length of marriage, time until divorce, and number of children, but as to the effects of even second marriages on the family members concerned—grandparents, parents, and children—the literature contains mostly broad generalities. There are almost no studies differentiating the effects on the basis of the ages involved, length of marriage, size and structure of previous and reconstituted families, and so forth.

Where third and subsequent marriages are concerned, the literature stands mute, with a paucity of information on even the number and demographics of such marriages.

Informal Marriages

Other changes in marriage (and nonmarriage) patterns can be anticipated. The practice of living together, without formal marriage, may increase considerably. The number of unmarried couples tripled during the 1970s (Glick, 1984), and tripled again by 1983 (*Jerusalem Post*, 1987). The tendency to live together without marriage has been strengthened in the past by the application of common law, such as "palimony" rulings, in which alimony is payable on the dissolution of such informal arrangements. It also has been given a boost by social welfare laws that pay individuals more than couples, thus placing a financial penalty on marriage. This phenomenon is especially noted among the elderly, whose joint income from old-age pensions would be less than their combined incomes from the same source. In some cases, obviating the secular law is less troubling for the individuals involved than violating religious laws, and there are cases of clergymen being asked to bless such currently unofficial unions (St. George, 1970).

There probably will be an increase in such marriages as women continue to enter the work force, freeing themselves of financial dependence on a mate, with the ties that this entails. The general move for sexual equality will also fuel this development, as will the general move toward a new sexual morality. This morality will include children born to parents who are single by choice, child adoption by single parents, and adoption by gay couples of both sexes.

Interfaith Marriages

There has also been a rising trend toward interfaith marriages, with or without conversion on the part of one partner. In addition to the strains inherent in many such unions, there are often problems regarding the religious affiliation and education of the children. In general, homogamous marriages have been found to be more satisfying (Heaton, 1984). However, it is highly probable that in the short run the number of interfaith marriages will continue to increase.

Counseling

With the continuing increase in rates of divorce and remarriage and the likelihood of more nontraditional marriages, the role of social

work in premarital counseling, marital counseling, and family counseling will have to be expanded. In the future, it must include more
counseling in the case of divorce, remarriage, and redivorce, and
more help of other sorts—financial, housing, and so forth—than now
exists. As Goldmeier (1980) pointed out, there is a continuum of
stressful situations—the period leading up to and including the divorce, the period of being single, and the reconstitution of a family
through remarriage.

Divorce not only strains the relationship between the couple involved; it may also involve their parents. Cicirelli (1984) found that,
"Up to 10 years later, many parents still regarded their child's divorce
as traumatic and upsetting to them, using such adjectives as sad,
disastrous, and so on." When parents regard the divorce as negative
or upsetting, the strain on their relationship with the divorced child
can result in a rebuff of efforts to return to previous relationships
(Cicirelli, 1984). The effect of the divorce on the couple involved may
be profound, and may accentuate ambivalence about remarriage. A
second divorce, to a greater degree, may trigger questions about
one's worth, behavior, attitudes, and much more. These problems
may be greatly exacerbated when coupled with problems of child/
parent, child/sibling, child/stepparent, and child/stepsibling relationships.

THE EVOLVING ROLES OF FAMILY MEMBERS

Children

The effect of divorce on individual children will vary owing to a large
number of factors. However, for most children it is a very upsetting
experience—the short-term trauma, in particular, is often quite considerable (Furstenberg & Spanier, 1984), particularly during the first
year following the divorce, and especially if it involves adolescent
children (Visher & Visher, 1988). If the divorce has been preceded by
a period of stress and tension between the parents, the stress, distress, anxiety, and problems of coping may be considerably increased. If there is a fight over custody of the children, and if the
children are drawn into this fight, overtly or covertly, the trauma may
be considerable and long continuing. Incidentally, the child or children in divorce cases and subsequent remarriages may not simply
be the passive victims: Schulman (1981) cited cases of children who
fill the gap left by the exodus of one parent and who try, by obnoxious
behavior, to drive out any replacement.

Children of divorced parents are likely to experience isolation, disruption, and suffering (LeCroy & Rose, 1986) and have been found
to be more oppositional, aggressive, lacking in self-control, distrac-

tible, and demanding of help and attention both at home and at school than children in nondivorced families with high rates of marital discord (Hetherington, Cox, & Cox, 1982). Parental divorce also has been found to affect children's own courtship patterns (Booth, Brinkerhoff, & White, 1984).

After the divorce (and sometimes before it), one parent—usually the father—moves out of the house, and contact with the children changes. Typically in such cases, the level of contact between the parent and child dwindles to an occasional visit, and many nonresident parents opt out altogether from an official custody role (Furstenberg & Spanier, 1984). In one study, nearly half of all children from maritally disrupted families had not seen one of their biological parents, usually the father, for five years (Furstenberg & Spanier, 1984).

The extent of child-centered problems is indicated by the fact that between 50 and 60 percent of all couples have children at the time of divorce (Wallerstein, 1983), and the number of children involved in divorce doubled between 1960 and 1980. Today, approximately one-third of all children encounter divorce before reaching 18 years of age, and this does not include children whose parents are separated but not divorced (Glick, 1979, 1984). When separations are included, the proportion of children who will experience such disruption is at least two in five (Bumpass, 1983).

Following a divorce, 90 percent of the children involved live with their mother. If the mother remarries when the children are still young, the possibility of the father gaining custody is strengthened, but not very much—only 4 percent of fathers have custody of all their children. There may, however, be joint custody, in which both parents are designated as custodians of one or more children, or split custody, with each parent being custodian of some of the children. This may result, of course, in brothers and sisters living in different households. There are also cases in which neither parent is deemed capable of custodianship, and foster homes, adoptions, and institutions are utilized.

When divorced parents remarry, the child in the family often acquires new relatives. It has been estimated that one-third of the children entering second families will have a half-sibling within four years, and about two-thirds, in total, will have either a stepsibling or half sibling; about one-sixth will have both (Bumpass, 1983). Although many children seem to have no great problem concerning the acquisition of new relatives, so to speak, one study found that children, especially adolescents, had a difficult time accepting and adjusting to the relationship with a stepparent (Kent, 1980). There are little data concerning the further repercussions on family structure, kinships, half siblings, stepsiblings, and so forth. However, Visher and Visher

(1979) noted that in the traditional nuclear family—four grandparents, two parents, and two children—there are 28 pairs and 247 possible relationships. If both parents remarry and bring four more children into the relationship structure, there are 253 pairs and more than 8 million possible relationships.

In 1981, the proportion of children living apart from their parents was 3.7 percent, and it was predicted that by 1990 this would rise to 4.1 percent. It was also predicted that the proportion living with both parents would drop almost 18 percent within the same period (Montemayor & Leigh, 1982). Of the children with parents absent (for any reason), the great bulk lived with relatives, and most of these with a grandparent (Kennedy & Keeney, 1988). In general, grandparents seek to maintain contact with the grandchildren of divorced parents, and there is reason to believe that such contact is growing (Cherlin & Furstenberg, 1988).

The growth in the number of divorces as such, and the manifold differences that may exist between the children of divorced parents—age, gender, position in the family (Toman, 1976), personality attributes, and relationships with parents—will require social workers to become very proficient in dealing with the feelings of both parents and children, as well as versed in the laws and regulations of custodianship, visitation rights, child-support payments, and other legal matters.

In view of the growth of child care problems with the increase in working women and in divorce and remarriage, it may become necessary for social workers to seek the appointment of ombudsmen for children, similar to those that exist in a number of other countries (Flekkoy, 1989; Rauche-Elnekare, 1989; Ronstrom, 1989). These officials are available to anyone who believes a child is being abused or neglected. It might also be advisable, as in the case of ombudsmen in institutions for the elderly, for social workers themselves to undertake this task, formally or informally.

It should be emphasized here that the family as such—whether from first or subsequent marriages—exhibits tenacity in western society, even in communal settings such as the Israeli kibbutz, and although its structure may change, the idea and role of the family is deep-rooted. Writing in 1972, George and Nena O'Neill spoke of "open marriage" as a new life-style for couples. Their intent was openness between marriage partners: sharing, honesty, and responsibility. Their title was misread and their book was misunderstood by a good many people who thought only in terms of sexually open marriages and who therefore announced that traditional families were finished. Five years later, Nena O'Neill (1977) felt impelled to write another book indicating that traditional marriage values persisted and probably would continue to do so.

Single Parents

With the continuation of high divorce rates and 40 to 50 percent of those divorced not remarrying, the number of single parents from this situation alone will grow. There are, in addition, widows and widowers, those who are separated from their spouses for a number of reasons, those who bear children outside of marriage, and, increasingly, unmarried individuals who adopt children.

In the United States in 1980, 18 percent of births were to single parents (Rose, 1989), and that percentage has risen since. Single parenthood is stressful (Faller & Ziefert, 1981). Single mothers in particular experience a decline in psychological well-being (McLanahan, 1985). When single parenthood arises from death or divorce, the parent and children sometimes return to the grandparents' home. Often, these arrangements are unworkable, with one or both of the grandparents knowingly or unwittingly usurping the parent's role and confusing the child (Weiss, 1975). Insofar as never-married parents are concerned, financial problems may be the most dominant, because almost no unmarried mother receives financial support from the father of the children (Weiss, 1979), although recent paternity suits may indicate this trend is changing.

The effect on children growing up in single-parent households must be considered. It is atypical today for a child to grow up in a two-parent household. About 60 percent of American children will live in a single-parent household at some point in their lives (Hamburg, 1987). The need for social work help is clear and growing in these instances (Schlesinger, 1989).

Stepfamilies

As parents remarry, the relationship of the child or children to the stepparent, and to the stepparent's children, can become a veritable maze. The problem is so new, relatively speaking, that terminology has not yet been formalized. Thus, writers speak of merged families (Kirby, 1981), reconstituted families (Kleinman, Rosenberg, & Whiteside, 1979), meta-families (Sager, Walker, Brown, Crohn, & Rodstein, 1981), linked families, binuclear families, new extended families (Giles-Sims & Crosbie-Burnett, 1989), blended families, recoupled families (Kent, 1980), and synergistic families (Visher & Visher, 1988). Yet, one-sixth of American children already live in remarried-couple households, and one child in four will grow up having more than two parents (Furstenberg & Spanier, 1984).

In 1987, 17.4 percent of American married families with children were stepfamilies, and before the youngest child becomes 18, 40 percent of families will be stepfamilies (Glick, 1989). As their biological parents remarry, children are called upon to relate to a stepparent, and in the case of additional marriages, to additional stepparents.

The child's relationship to these may take different forms of varying duration, calling for differential, and often confusing, responses from the child. Although adults tend to "trade" relatives with succeeding marriages, children add them. Children may easily have a half-dozen grandparents or more. How this complicates or enriches the child's life has not yet been explored (Furstenberg & Spanier, 1984).

In addition, current family law does not provide clear and comprehensive rules defining the responsibilities of parties in the stepparent/ stepchild relationship (Fine, 1989). This situation may be further complicated by the presence of grandparents on either or both sides, and the parents of the new mates, who then become the child's step-grandparents. With current lengthening of life expectancy, great-grandparents may also be involved in the situation. Saners and Trygstad (1989) found that the relationship with the stepgrandparent is weaker than that with the biological grandparent, but that, nevertheless, 48 percent of their grandchildren respondents indicated that they considered the former important, and 63 percent wanted more contact with the stepgrandparent.

Others speak of the problems involved in family functioning when the family consists of the entire remarried family, plus former spouses, grandparents, stepgrandparents, aunts, uncles, and cousins (Sager et al., 1981). Among the phases in reconstituting families after re-marriage, the child's necessity to form sibling alliances across family lines has been identified as a problem (Kleinman et al., 1979), as has the existence of a widely accepted stereotype—reinforced by fairy tales and folklore—of the wicked stepmother (Kompara, 1980; Visher & Visher, 1979).

With the prevalence of divorce and remarriage, the stepfamily has emerged in large enough numbers to be considered one of the several family types in contemporary society, but there has been comparatively little documentation and research in this area (Bergquist, 1984; Jacobson, 1980; Schlesinger, 1983; Walker et al., 1979). This leads to the fact that there are, as yet, few societal role prescriptions to regulate steprelationships with quasi kin—former spouses, their blood relations, and the people they remarry (Clingempeel, 1981). One example, resulting from greater longevity and rising divorce rates, is the "second chance" grandparent, whose divorced or widowed child comes back to the grandparents for a home. If the child works, the grandparents may find themselves carrying the major burden for rearing the grandchildren (Coulombe, 1985).

The increase in stepfamilies will not only pose questions of interpersonal family problems; there also will emerge the question of family responsibility in the areas of financing and caring, both from a moral and a legal point of view, as well as legal questions concerning adoption, inheritance, and much more (Macarov, 1978). The likelihood of increasing numbers of elderly parents needing help from their children, discussed in chapter 2, will be further complicated by divorces among adult children, especially among those of middle age, which will broaden their responsibilities to include those of several sets of parents. "The result is likely to be less help from adult children" (Cicirelli, 1984).

Grandparents and Great-grandparents

A further development to be expected is increasing remarriage by grandparents. With lengthened life expectancy and greater health in old age, the number of people living longer will grow, and among them will be larger numbers of people who have been divorced or widowed and remarried. Again, the question of family responsibility, moral and legal, comes to the fore. The grandfather, for example, whose inheritance was expected to go to his grandchildren but who remarries and later dies, leaving his estate, or a large part of it, to his new wife, may unwittingly and posthumously create a tangle of family disagreements. Conversely, the grandparent who has been supported by a child who now remarries and must share that support with her new husband's grandparents has also become an almost-familiar problem.

Then there is the previously mentioned fact that women in developed countries tend to live longer than men, with the gap growing with time (Lopez, 1984). Problems will thus arise not only from re-marriages, but from the search for marriage partners. The family contacts of widows generally increase, whereas those of widowers do not (Morgan, 1984). Thus, the lonely older man is more likely to need help searching for a marriage partner than the older woman. On the other hand, the preponderance of older women, as compared with men, means that men have more choice in the area of remarriage than do women. Carried to its logical conclusion, this means there will be fewer single older men than women, and that women will turn back to their families for the support and comfort they want, because they will have fewer chances of remarrying.

Longer lives also will result in changes in family configurations, as grandparents remain alive and healthy for many more years than was previously the case. Three-generation families living together will be augmented by increasing numbers of four-generation families, and even five generations under one roof will be found increasingly (Butler & Lewis, 1977). This will require of social workers that they reconceptualize normal family structure and functioning to include the grandparents as the focal people in family relationships (*Ageing International*, 1984). Social workers will also need to think of the dual role carried by parents regarding children and grandparents as continuing for a much longer period than at present. Further, even the grandparent sometimes may necessarily be viewed as a child, when the great-grandparents are still factors in the situation. The 70-year-old son or daughter of 90-year-old parents will become more common, and such children dying before their parents will present problems of financial and social support for remaining family members, as well as for social workers.

IMPLICATIONS OF FAMILY PLANNING

Family structure and dynamics also will be deeply affected by considerations less ethereal than values. The advances recently made—and soon to be made—in medicine and genetics will radically alter both the method and the impact of giving birth and child rearing, changing family structure and dynamics to an unprecedented degree. As recently as 10 years ago, the sex of an expected child was subject to guesswork, and the number of children to be expected included a good deal of error. Medical advances have now made it possible to know both the number and the sex of expected babies, and to detect at a very early period the presence of a number of diseases, conditions, and defects.

Simultaneously, new methods of avoiding pregnancy and of preventing the birth of unwanted babies, have been devised. Many are cheap, easy, and effective. These developments can solve some problems and obviate a good deal of unnecessary suffering; however, they raise questions of staggering implications and agonizing quality. The role of social workers working with clients involved in such situations has yet to be adequately discussed, defined, or clarified.

In addition, couples who once were condemned to be childless or to languish for years on a waiting list of prospective adoptive parents (often with a negative impact on marital relationships [Shapiro, 1982]) now have access to an array of new methods for producing babies, including hormone treatment, test tubes, surrogate parents, and others. There is little question that these new methods will proliferate and be improved. With such developments, however, there are also emotional, social, legal, and religious problems of great complexity, help with which may require a great deal of expertise from social workers—expertise that, as yet, many have not acquired.

Also to be considered are the effects on orphaned or unwanted children. With the opportunity for acquiring biological offspring increasing, the possibility of finding suitable adoptive families—especially for older, handicapped, or minority children of many kinds—may be curtailed, necessitating a return to institutional or group care homes.

From detecting the sex of the unborn child to determining what sex the child should be is probably only a matter of a relatively short time for medical science. The ability to determine in advance what sex a child should be has enormous implications for society, and even the short-term results cannot as yet be foreseen. For example, one possibility is that the desire for male children, widespread in certain parts of the world or among certain groups, will lead to relatively few girls being born. This could transform the status and role of women. They could be much sought after and greatly honored, either reaching positions of great power and responsibility, or being relegated to the status of pets. Lack of women could further change marriage and family structures. In any case, not only the societal but the individual implications of being able to choose a child's sex will undoubtedly become an area for social work thinking and practice.

ETHNICITY

Ethnicity has been a troublesome area as regards institutions for the elderly, for example, with older people clinging tenaciously to the rituals with which they have lived all their lives, to the point of wanting to be only with people of their own background or religion, and with regulations concerning governmental financing requiring an open-admittance policy.

Ethnically mixed married couples are more likely to get divorced and have a variety of other problems than couples of the same ethnicity. Their children indicate more personal problems and more relationship problems than children from ethnically homogeneous families (McGoldrick & Petro, 1984). Nevertheless, the number of interethnic marriages will undoubtedly increase in the future, as ethnicity becomes more an exotic than a practical aspect of personalities and society. Although it is true, as Hansen (1964) predicted, that in many cases the third generation of those who were immigrants feels secure enough to begin actively seeking for and trying to revive their ethnic roots, this is more in the area of song, dance, foods, costumes, and other aspects of folklore than in values or behavior patterns. And, as further noted by Hansen, unless this is institutionalized by the fourth generation, even this identification is gone. With the growth in the number of interethnic marriages, on the one hand, and the marriages being within succeeding generations, on the other, this area of social problems should recede.

SUMMARY

It is clear that current trends that probably will continue or intensify in the future will have profound impact on family structure and dynamics, calling for new stances and activities from social workers. These changes include those attendant upon more women continuing to enter the labor force, further rises in divorce and remarriage rates, lengthening life expectancy, growth and acceptance of interethnic marriages, new living arrangements in place of legal marriages, new methods of both guaranteeing and preventing births, and choosing the sex of the unborn baby.

Like all changes, each of these will cause strain, tension, problems, and perhaps misinformation. Each of these changes also will contain idiosyncratic problems. Social workers will need to be able to identify such societal changes to prepare themselves to handle them. They will also require knowledge and information concerning the shifts themselves and the laws and regulations that may apply. Their methods of intervention may have to change or be increased. Above all, they will need to be clear about their own values, those of the profession, and those of society to consciously and purposefully help families adjust to these changes as they occur.

REFERENCES

Abrams, P. (1980). Social change, social networks and neighborhood care. *Social Work Service, 22*, 12–23.

Ageing International. (1984). *11*, 5–6.

Aguirre, B. E., & Marshall, M. G. (1988). Training family day care providers using self-study written and video materials. *Child and Youth Care Quarterly, 47*, 115–130.

Andrisani, P. J. (1978). *Work attitudes and labor market experience*. New York: Praeger.

Bergquist, B. (1984). The remarried family: An annotated bibliography. *Family Process, 23*, 107–119.

Best, F. (1981). Changing sex roles and worklife flexibility. *Psychology of Women Quarterly, 6*, 55–71.

Bond, J. (1984). Abstracts: Sociology and social policy. *Ageing and Society, 4*, 205–213.

Booth, A., Brinkerhoff, D. B., & White, L. K. (1984). The impact of parental divorce on courtship. *Journal of Marriage and the Family, 46*, 85–94.

Bumpass, L. L. (1983). *Demographic aspects of children's second-family experience*. Working paper, Center for Demography and Ecology, University of Wisconsin, Madison.

Butler, R. N., & Lewis, M. I. (1977). *Aging and mental health*. St. Louis: Mosby.

Cherlin, A. J., & Furstenberg, F. F., Jr. (1988). *The new American grandparent*. New York: Basic Books.

Child care finds a champion in the corporation. (1988, August 4). *New York Times*, p. F14.

Cicirelli, V. G. (1984). Adult children's helping behavior to elderly parents. *Journal of Family Issues, 5*, 419–440.

Clingempeel, W. G. (1981). Quasi-kin relationships and marital quality in stepfather families. *Journal of Personality and Social Psychology, 41,* 890–901.

Conference Board, Inc. (1985). *The working woman: A progress report.* New York: Author.

Coulombe, G. (1985, September 8). "Second chance" parents. *Bridgeport Sunday Post,* p. B3.

Davis, K. (1984). Wives and work: The sex role revolution and its conse- quences. *Population and Development Review, 10,* 397–417.

Faller, K.C., & Ziefert, M. (1981). Causes of child abuse and neglect. In K. C. Faller (Ed.), *Social work with abused and neglected children.* New York: Free Press.

Fine, M. (1989). A social science perspective on stepfamily law: Suggestions for legal reform. *Family Relations, 38,* 55–58.

Flekkoy, M. G. (1989). Child advocacy in Norway: The ombudsman. *Child Welfare, 68,* 113–122.

Furstenberg, F. F., Jr., & Spanier, G. B. (1984). *Recycling the family: Re- marriage after divorce.* Beverly Hills, CA: Sage.

The Futurist. (1989). *23,* 6.

Garfield, R. (1980). The decision to remarry. *Journal of Divorce, 4,* 1–10.

George, V., & Wilding, P. (1984). *The impact of social policy.* London: Routledge & Kegan Paul.

Giles-Sims, J., & Crosbie-Burnett, M. (1989). Stepfamily research: Implica- tions for policy, clinical interventions, and further research. *Family Relations, 38,* 19–23.

Glass, B. L. (1980). No-fault divorce law: Impact on judge and client. *Journal of Family Issues, 1,* 455–478.

Glick, P. C. (1979). Children of divorced parents in demographic perspective. *Journal of Social Issues, 35,* 170–182.

Glick, P. C. (1980). Remarriage: Some recent changes and variations. *Journal of Family Issues, 1,* 455–478.

Glick, P. C. (1984). Marriage, divorce and living arrangements. *Journal of Family Issues, 5,* 7–26.

Glick, P. C. (1989). Remarried families, stepfamilies, and stepchildren: A brief demographic profile. *Family Relations, 38,* 24–27.

Glick, P. C., & Spanier, G. B. (1980). Married and unmarried cohabitation in the United States. *Journal of Marriage and the Family, 42,* 19–30.

Goldmeier, J. (1980). Intervention in the continuum from divorce to family reconstruction. *Social Casework, 61,* 39–47.

Hamburg, S. K. (Ed.). (1987). *Children in need: Investment strategies for the educationally disadvantaged.* Washington, DC: Committee for Eco- nomic Development.

Hansen, M. L. (1964). *The immigrant in American history.* New York: Harper & Row.

Heaton, T. B. (1984). Religious homogamy and marital satisfactions recon- sidered. *Journal of Marriage and the Family, 46,* 729–733.

Hetherington, E. M., Cox, M., & Cox, R. (1982). Effects of divorce on parents and children. In M. E. Lamb (Ed.), *Nontraditional families: Parenting and child development*. Hillsdale, NJ: Erlbaum.

How private business views comparable worth. (1984). *World of Work Report*, *9*, 7.

Howe, L. K. (1977). *Pink collar workers*. New York: Putnam.

Jacobson, D. S. (1980). Stepfamilies. *Children Today*, *9*, 2–6.

Jerusalem Post. (1987, August 2). p. 5.

Kennedy, J. F., & Keeney, V. T. (1988). The extended family revisited: Grand-parents rearing grandchildren. *Child Psychiatry and Human Development*, *19*, 26–35.

Kent, M. O. (1980). Remarriage: A family system perspective. *Social Casework*, *61*, 146–153.

Keyserling, H. D. (1972). *Windows on day care*. New York: National Council of Social Work.

Kirby, J. (1981). Relationship building in second marriage and merged families. *Journal for Specialists in Group Work*, *6*, 35–41.

Kitson, G. C., Babri, K. B., Roach, M. J., & Placidi, K. S. (1989). Adjustment to widowhood and divorce: A review. *Journal of Family Issues*, *10*, 5–32.

Kleinman, J., Rosenberg, E., & Whiteside, M. (1979). Common developmental tasks in forming reconstituted families. *Journal of Marital and Family Therapy*, *5*, 79–86.

Kompara, D. R. (1980). Difficulties in the socialization process of steppar-enting. *Family Relations*, *29*, 60–73.

Ladewig, B. H., & White, P. N. (1980). Dual-earner marriages: The family social environment and dyadic adjustment. *Journal of Family Issues*, *5*, 343–362.

LeCroy, C. W., & Rose, S. R. (1986). Helping children cope with stress. *Social Work in Education*, *9*, 5–15.

Liebow, E. (1981). The human costs of unemployment. In J. O'Toole, J. L. Scheiber, & L. C. Wood (Eds.), *Working: Changes and choices*. New York: Human Sciences Press.

Lingg, B. A. (1990). Women beneficiaries aged 62 or older, 1960–1988. *Social Security Bulletin*, *53*, 2–12.

Lopez, A. D. (1984). Sex differentials in mortality. *World Health Organization Chronicle*, *38*, 217–224.

Macarov, D. (1978). *The design of social welfare*. New York: Holt, Rinehart, & Winston.

McGoldrick, M., & Petro, N. G. (1984). Ethnic intermarriage: Implications for therapy. *Family Process*, *23*, 347–364.

McLanahan, S. S. (1985). Single mothers and psychological well-being: A test of the stress and vulnerability hypotheses. *Research in Community and Mental Health*, *5*, 253–266.

Montemayor, R., & Leigh, G. K. (1982). Parent-absent children: A demographic analysis of children and adolescents living apart from their parents. *Family Relations, 31,* 567–573.

Morgan, L. A. (1984). Changes in family interaction following widowhood. *Journal of Marriage and the Family, 46,* 323–334.

Morrison, P. A. (1990). Applied demography. *The Futurist, 24,* 9–15.

Moss, P., & Fonda, N. (1980). *Work and the family.* London: Temple Smith.

O'Neill, N., & O'Neill, G. (1972). *Open marriage: A new life style for couples.* New York: Evans.

O'Neill, N. (1977). *The marriage premise.* New York: Evans.

Pimlott, J. A. R. (1935). *Toynbee Hall.* London: Dent.

Raichle, D. R. (1980). The future of the family. In F. Feather (Ed.), *Through the 80s: Thinking globally, acting locally.* Bethesda, MD: World Future Society.

Rauche-Elnekare, H. (1989). Advocacy and ombudswork for children: Implications of the Israeli experience. *Child Welfare, 68,* 101–112.

Ronstrom, A. (1989). Sweden's children's ombudsman: A spokesperson for children. *Child Welfare, 68,* 123–128.

Rose, S. R. (1989). Teaching single parents to cope with stress through small group intervention. *Small Group Behavior, 20,* 259–269.

Sager, C. J., Walker, E., Brown, H. S., Crohn, H. M., & Rodstein, E. (1981). Improving functioning in the remarried family system. *Journal of Marital and Family Therapy, 7,* 3–13.

Saners, G. F., & Trygstad, D. W. (1989). Stepgrandparents and grandparents: The view from young adults. *Family Relations, 38,* 71–75.

Schlesinger, B. (1983). *Remarriage: A review and annotated bibliography.* Chicago: CPL Bibliographies.

Schlesinger, B. (1989). One-parent families under stress: Curriculum guidelines. *International Social Work, 32,* 129–138.

Schulman, G. L. (1981). Divorce, single-parenthood and stepfamilies: Structural implications of these transactions. *International Journal of Family Therapy, 3,* 86–112.

Shapiro, C. H. (1982). The impact of infertility on the marital relationship. *Social Casework, 63,* 387–393.

St. George, A. (1970). *The crazy ape.* New York: Philosophical Library.

Staines, G. L., & Pleck, J. H. (1983). *The impact of work schedules on the family.* Ann Arbor: Institute for Social Research, University of Michigan.

Telecommuting takes hold. (1984). *World of Work Report, 9,* 1–2.

Toman, W. (1976). *Family constellation.* New York: Springer.

United Nations. (1989). *Demographic yearbook 1987.* New York.

U.S. Department of Commerce, Bureau of the Census. (1987). *Statistical abstract of the United States 1988.* Washington, DC: Author.

Visher, E. B., & Visher, J. S. (1979). *Stepfamilies: A guide to working with stepparents and stepchildren.* New York: Brunner/Mazel.

Visher, E. B., & Visher, J. S. (1988). *Old loyalties, new ties: Therapeutic strategies with stepfamilies.* New York: Brunner/Mazel.

Walker, L., Brown, H., Crohn, H., Rodstein, E., Zeisel, E., & Sager, C. J.

(1979). An annotated bibliography of the remarried, the living together, and their children. *Family Process, 18,* 193–212.

Wallerstein, J. S. (1983). Children of divorce: Stress and developmental tasks. In N. Garmezy & M. Rutter (Eds.), *Stress, coping and development in children.* New York: McGraw-Hill.

Weiss, R. S. (1975). *Marital separation.* New York: Basic Books.

Weiss, R. S. (1979). *Going it alone.* New York: Basic Books.

Wellness Letter. (1989). 5, 1.

4

Responding to the Work World's Evolution

SOCIAL WORK AND EMPLOYMENT

Ever since the Elizabethan Poor Laws established the principle of "less eligibility," distinguishing between those who could work and those who could not, and instituted work tests and habitation in work houses as prerequisites for help (Macarov, 1978a), social workers have spent massive amounts of their time trying to help clients find work, motivating them to work, and preparing them to perform and hold their jobs, as well as tackle a host of problems arising from unemployment. Family service agencies in the United States report almost a quarter of their workload arising from problems associated with unemployment (Sunley & Sheek, 1986).

This is not surprising—such engagement with unemployment on the part of social workers stems from the attitudes and structures of society as a whole. It would be difficult to overstate the influence exerted by work on other aspects of life. The concept of work is one of the most widely spread and deeply embedded elements in individual psyches, the structure of societal institutions, and the value systems of industrial civilizations. It is the measuring rod for individuals, the goal of organizations, and the basis of society. Work is almost as encrusted with value orientations and transcendental meanings as is religion.

Work is seen as both necessary and desirable for the individual and for society. Political, social, and economic programs are all based on the assumption that people need and want to work and that society needs all the work that everyone capable of laboring can produce. On an individual basis, people are judged not only by the work they do, but also by the manner in which they perform it. People who do not or cannot work are viewed as somehow outside the mainstream of life. Work structures time, determines attitudes, shapes self- and others' images, and permeates every aspect of life, including education, family, religion, and even the prison system (Macarov, 1985a). Despite this emphasis on work by society as a whole, and the efforts of social workers to aid or induce their clients to comply with this insistence, relatively few social workers have been engaged in dealing with the problems that arise in and from the workplace, or from the world of work as such. In the future, however, social workers will have to be much more cognizant of the role of work in people's lives, the changing nature of work, the extent and effects of unemployment, and, in particular, the possibility of permanent unemployment for large numbers of people.

WELFARE AND INSURANCE

The welfare system has been shaped and constrained by developments in the world of work. For example, workers' disability programs—designed to relieve workers of the consequences of work accidents and thus encourage them to undertake work that might be dangerous or harmful—are almost invariably the first social insurance programs to be adopted in every country. Conversely, unemployment compensation programs, which are seen as enabling people to avoid work, are almost always the last to be adopted (Macarov, 1980). In addition, unemployment compensation programs are usually bound with more restrictions, pay less, and continue for shorter periods than most other compensation programs. The world of work shapes welfare programs in at least four areas: (1) coverage, (2) vestedness, (3) administrative regulations, and (4) the wage-stop.

Coverage

The great bulk of social insurance programs are intended only for workers. Throughout the world, 69 percent of children's and family allowance programs—designed to strengthen families and ensure the healthy development of children—are for workers' families and children only. Similarly, sickness and maternity programs are limited to workers in 94 percent of such programs, and old-age and survivors' insurance is only for workers in 89 percent of them. Obviously, workers' compensation and unemployment compensation require employment for coverage in every case (U.S. Department of Health and Human Services, 1986). Thus, nonworkers are excluded from most social insurance programs throughout the world.

Vestedness

It is not enough, however, that persons be covered by an insurance program to receive benefits. Eligibility for benefits almost always requires a prior period of employment. For example, the qualifying period of work for old-age programs varies throughout the world from five to 45 years, averaging around 15 years (U.S. Department of Health, Education, and Welfare, 1982). Persons who have not worked long enough, although technically covered, do not receive the programs' benefits and in many cases, such as in the United States, do not even receive back the amount of premiums they have paid in.

Administrative Regulations

Administrative regulations also play their part in linking welfare to work. Payment amounts are usually based on a percentage of salaries, and the length of time that payments are continued is determined by how long the recipient has worked previously. The waiting period required before actually receiving unemployment compensation is usually longer than for other programs and is often not compensated at all (Griffiths, 1974). Regulations may discriminate against non-workers in other ways: in Israel, for example, unemployed laborers must report to the labor exchange every day to be eligible for compensation.

The Wage-stop

The most powerful influence of the world of work on welfare programs is found in the wage-stop. This is the principle that no one should be able to receive from welfare as much, or even close to as much, income as they would receive if they were working. Obviously, the supposition is that if people had enough income they would choose not to work. This fear of a work disincentive is practically universal, and social welfare payments almost invariably are pegged at a point considerably lower than the prevailing, average, or minimum wage.

The desire to keep people at work underlies, shapes, and constrains all social welfare programs and is responsible for many of social work's activities (Macarov, 1980). Consequently, social workers' endeavors to fight unemployment are not based solely on ideological, moral, or value considerations, or on the effects of unemployment on clients' psychic, social, or immediate economic situations. These actions also arise from the realization that a nonworking client not only is prey to all the ills of present unemployment but will also suffer discrimination in the future, because of the links between work and welfare.

THE QUALITY OF THE WORK ENVIRONMENT

A Brief Overview

Recently, the area of occupational social work has been burgeoning as problems in the workplace have come more to the fore of public consciousness (Bargal & Shamir, 1981). Originally, most occupational social workers were concerned to a very large degree with alcoholism, drug abuse, absenteeism, and tardiness. They were employed either by unions or employers. The goal of the union-employed social workers was generally to help workers solve their problems so they would not lose their jobs, whereas the goal of employers was to increase productivity by solving or removing workers' problems.

More recently, the workplace has begun to be seen by social workers as a catchment area, with workers as clients with problems that do not necessarily have their roots in work and that might not even affect working behavior. In addition to seeking greater productivity, some employers have begun using social work services to try to move toward a better quality of working life for their workers, for its own sake.

Concern about workers' conditions has been expressed at least since the beginning of the Industrial Revolution, as Dickens's *Hard Times*, for example, illustrates. The deleterious effects of the working place—those "dark, satanic" places—were an important impetus both for formation of labor unions and populist political parties. These moves, however, were usually made by the workers themselves. It was not until the 1960s that social ferment in the form of student unrest, antiracist activities, and demands for sexual equality brought with them the activities subsumed under the title Quality of Working Life (QWL), in which employers—usually large corporations—took the initiative in trying to improve conditions in the workplace.

Being more obvious than social or emotional problems, health problems in the workplace garnered earlier and greater support than did social work. A parliamentary committee in England, for example, recently concluded that occupational health has improved to such an extent that occupational hygiene nurses are running out of work (House of Lords, 1982).

Attempts at Job Improvement

Insofar as nonhealth problems are concerned, the quality of working life is usually approached in one or both of two ways. The first is called job enlargement and consists of having people carry out more than one task on the assumption that repetitive work, or that which deals with only one segment of the operation, is the cause of dissatisfaction. This is, in effect, a horizontal enlargement of the job. The second method is called job enrichment and is intended to allow employees to participate in decisions on the assumption that lack of voice is the difficulty. In some cases this means joint decisions on the shop floor level, and in others it means representation on decision-making levels, up to and including the board of directors. This often is referred to as worker participation, or democratization of the workplace, and is essentially a vertical enlargement of responsibility.

Both of these aspects of QWL involve difficulties and problems (Macarov, 1982). In any case, the great majority of such experiments last a relatively short time (Simmons, 1984) and are generally a concomitant of prosperous, expanding businesses. When profits fall, or recessions set in, many of these experiments are abandoned in favor of old-fashioned division of tasks, centralization of authority, and tight supervision. The important fact, however, is that the very genesis and continuation of QWL activities are implicit acknowledgments that workers are not happy in their situations.

Although there are sometimes humanitarian or social-responsibility reasons for seeking a better quality of working life, most employers institute such programs on the assumption that satisfied workers are more productive. This assumption stems primarily from the Hawthorne studies of more than 60 years ago and the "human relations" school in industry to which they gave birth (Mayo, 1933). According to this school of thought, workers who felt management was concerned with their well-being, and who therefore were offered various satisfaction-inducing elements in their work, would develop loyalty to the company, which would evidence itself in hard work.

Despite early criticisms of the Hawthorne findings (Carey, 1967) and later analyses that found that satisfaction played little part in the results of that experiment (Franke & Kaul, 1978), belief in the connection between satisfaction and productivity continued and by 1976 had resulted in more than 3,000 published reports seeking confirmation of such a link (Locke, 1976). More recently, researchers and management experts have come to the conclusion that there is no generalizable, replicable, reliable continuing link between work satisfaction and work patterns (Aitkin & Hage, 1966; Anderson, 1964; Brayfield & Crockett, 1955; Lawler & Porter, 1971; Locke, 1976; Neider, 1980; Raskin, 1980; Smith, Kendall, & Hulin, 1969; Strauss, 1980; Tikhonov, 1977). Nevertheless, the assumption of such a connection continues to guide management policies.

Worker Satisfaction and Dissatisfaction

Social workers concerned with current and future problems in the workplace should understand that if they are employed by management, their success will probably be measured in terms of workers' increased productivity—a goal that workers may have trouble achieving from social work intervention alone. However, the question as to whether workers get satisfaction from their work, or suffer dissatisfaction, perhaps leading to other problems, is obviously an important one for social workers, because the ultimate goal of their activities is human happiness.

Work, and feelings aroused by work, can be major sources of stress. Indeed, stress has recently been legally recognized as a work disability under definitions of eligibility for workers' compensation programs. Stress may arise from unsuitable work, a pace not commensurate with the worker's ability, underuse of skills, relations with supervisors and peers, and a number of other sources, including the stress of being monitored at work by computers (Shostak, 1980). Occupational stress is said to play an important role in 75 percent of heart disease cases (Fraser, 1983), and job dissatisfaction is associated with many other psychological problems (Rizzo, Reynolds, & Gallagher, 1981).

The effects of work stress or other kinds of work problems often carry over into other aspects of the worker's life. Marital discord, family relations, neglect or abuse of children, and other ills often are related to the demands of work or feelings about the job. The example of the person who comes home from work and kicks the cat is a popular metaphor for the effects of work frustrations. In addition, both alcohol and drug abuse may result from continuing unhappiness at work and an inability to change the situation. In this connection, it should be noted that substance abuse—often seen by employers as negatively affecting job performance—may be the result of work patterns, not the cause.

Consequently, it is important that social workers understand the complexities of work satisfaction and dissatisfaction and the reporting of these. Work satisfaction or the lack thereof can arise from at least four different sources: (1) the need to work, (2) the job, (3) the workplace, and (4) the work itself.

THE NEED TO WORK

Under current conditions, there is little opportunity to provide for one's economic needs other than through the medium of work—employment or self-employment. Naturally, people react differently to this need. There are workaholics—people who not only love to work but do not seem to be able to get enough of it. They work long hours; take work home with them after hours, on weekends, and on vacations; and seem miserable when they are doing anything but working (Machlowitz, 1981). At the other extreme are the work-inhibited, who would do almost anything to avoid work. In between there are overworkers, underworkers, and—if they are not simply a statistical artifact—average workers. Both extreme cases are unusual. Most people go to work with varying amounts of enthusiasm or resistance because they must work, whether they like it or not.

Not much has been written or studied about the effects of having to work when one would rather not. Yet, there are, for example, many mothers of small children who are forced by economic circumstances—and sometimes so-called social welfare programs—to go to work when they would rather stay home with their children. There are also uncounted numbers of other working people who would prefer to study; or be creative through the arts; or engage in sports; or travel, garden, play chess, folk dance, read, watch television, or do myriad other things than work.

It seems people have never liked to work. Primitive people worked only hard enough to provide for their needs and had more than 100 free days a year (Buckingham, 1961). As late as the 18th century, laborers preferred leisure to increased income (Kuman, 1984), and in some modern cultures where small farms are in preponderance, nonworking days amount to 171 days a year (Ayalew, 1982).

The fact that people really do not like to work or want to work is evidenced by the admonitions, commands, fables, maxims, sermons, sayings, parables, and other forms of influence used since time immemorial to convince people to work. Obviously, people must be convinced to do only those things that they do not want to do. If there were a natural desire or innate need to work, such pressure would not be required. For example, no such pressure to engage in sexual activity is found anywhere—people do not need to be urged to do that which they desire to do. Because of this innate aversion to work, Russia, China, and Cuba (Bernardo, 1971) posit work as a patriotic duty, which recalls the days of mercantilism, when the wealth of the nation was considered more important than the welfare of the people (Macarov, 1977).

History is replete with evidence that people did not, and do not, work if they can get out of it. The institution of slavery, for example, clearly was based upon the desire to get someone else to do the work. Diocletian ordered sons to continue in their fathers' occupations, because they tended to seek easier work (Kranzberg & Gies, 1975). The ancient Athenians openly and publicly abhorred work: Socrates said work makes people bad friends and bad patriots (Kranzberg & Gies, 1975); Plato thought of work as of no great importance; and Aristotle saw work as corrupting citizens, making their pursuit of virtue more difficult (Anthony, 1978). In historic Judaism, work was not the primary source of pride or a major source of citizenship. Only male scholarship was valued (Cnaan, 1987). Indeed, even comparatively recently Sigmund Freud (1958), as a result of his many years of probing the human psyche, said there seems to exist "a natural human aversion to work."

Recognition of the human aversion to work is written into most social welfare programs, which do not allow people to receive from welfare as much as they could presumably receive from working. The assumption is that given sufficient money, people would almost automatically stop working—an assumption that is probably true and that certainly does not support the mythology that people have a psychological or physiological need to work or that they enjoy working.

It is therefore somewhat surprising to see social workers, who would ordinarily be sensitive to situations in which clients were forced by circumstances to do things repugnant to themselves, and who would try to help clients extricate themselves from the situation or to minimize the trauma to their psyches, view the desire not to work as perversity, deviance, or immorality, but rarely as a problem deserving help. Professionally and theoretically imbued with the principles of allowing clients freedom of choice and helping them to be happy with their choices, social workers nevertheless expend enormous amounts of time and energy trying to motivate people to work, consciously or unconsciously coercing them in the direction of work, seeking employment opportunities for them, training them in job seeking, and so on.

The number of social workers consciously and deliberately helping people who do not want to work to avoid working can probably be counted on one finger or less. There is very little chance that this situation will change, unless and until lack of necessity for human labor and legitimate methods of maintaining oneself through other means requires social workers to influence clients not to seek the few available jobs.

FACTORS OF WORKING

The Job

Insofar as satisfaction from the job, as distinct from working, is concerned, when people are asked what they want from their jobs, they essentially answer pay, permanence, and perquisites (Rubin, 1976).

Pay may be judged on many bases: whether it is enough for needs, for luxuries, or for desires; whether it is commensurate with the effort being expended, the importance of the work, or its dangers and discomforts; whether it compares with what others are being paid or with what one has or would like to earn; and whether it represents recognition for the work being done. Pay varies in its effect on different kinds of workers, for example, skilled and unskilled; the relatively well paid and the clearly underpaid; and those in affluent settings and those in other places. It often takes on symbolic meanings such as prestige or recognition that become more important than the amount as such (Macarov, 1980).

A second factor that people look for in their jobs is security—the potential of staying in the job or with the firm for long periods or, conversely, not being in danger of being summarily dismissed. Security also may include the opportunity to acquire skills or to be promoted and eventually reach a desired level of income. People may sacrifice some immediate or potential pay for security considerations. For example, toward the end of the Great Depression in the United States, many people applied for civil service jobs, with their relative permanence, rather than take the chance of being dismissed again from higher-paying jobs.

Finally, there are fringe benefits, which may range from good pension and health plans to reserved parking spaces or chauffeur-driven cars, from maternity leave to paid vacations. Fringe benefits may include the opportunity to buy stock in the company at preferred prices or to purchase its goods at a discount. Receiving or sharing in tips (monetary or investment) may be a fringe benefit in some jobs, whereas substantial bonuses might play the same role in others.

In any case, although workers may be more or less satisfied with their jobs, which means with their pay, with the prospects of permanence, and with their fringe benefits, there is little that social workers can do to make changes in these areas. These are aspects of company policy or practices that generally are not amenable to change by social workers. This is why Pahl (1984) said, "For many ordinary people, very little can be done at the workplace to improve their personal life chances."

The Workplace

Being satisfied with one's job is not the same thing as being satisfied or dissatisfied with the conditions under which one works. These may include the physical setup—light, dirt, noise, sanitary facilities, the food in the cafeteria, and so forth—as well as personal relationships with colleagues, supervisors, and subordinates. Because the work group is a classical example of enforced involuntary association with other people over long periods of time, it may be a source of great satisfaction, great dissatisfaction, and various feelings in-between.

In his seminal study of the workplace, Herzberg (1966) distinguished between sources of dissatisfaction, basically stemming from the conditions of work, which he termed "hygiene factors," and sources of satisfaction, which were based on the work itself. Studies of occupational social workers indicate that much of their time is engaged in trying to remove sources of dissatisfaction—the hygiene factors—that are amenable to minor changes, rather than the lack of satisfaction caused by having to work, the job, or the work itself, each of which is relatively impervious to changes on the part of social work activities.

The Work Itself

Workers may be satisfied or dissatisfied in various degrees with having to work, with the job, and with the workplace, whereas the work itself may have a different effect on them. Good work is said to be challenging and demanding, but not excessively so. It allows workers to see and to take pride in the product and it contributes to society. It is nonpolluting, nondiscriminatory, and so forth.

These presumed desirable aspects of work often are subsumed under Maslow's (1954) rubric: self-actualization. Unfortunately for such formulations, there is empirical research indicating that work seen as self-actualizing has no effect upon work patterns or workers' satisfaction (Macarov, 1976). In fact, it is doubtful if more than a small part of the work done in any modern society can be self-actualizing in this manner (Macarov, 1981). As Fein (1976) said, it is possible that attempts to make work as we know it self-actualizing would be disastrous:

> It is because *workers choose not to find fulfillment in their work* that they are able to function as healthy human beings. . . . Workers would indeed become mentally ill if they took the behaviourists' proposals to heart. . . . By rejecting involvement in work which cannot be fulfilling, workers save their sanity.

Taken together, it is obvious that workers may be more or less satisfied with various aspects of their careers. They may be very happy with some, and very miserable with others. The net balance of their satisfaction, however, depends upon how important they see some factors as compared with others, and the extent to which they view their work as important in the totality of their lives. With this in mind, it is advisable to look at people's satisfaction with their work, as indicated by what they say and do about it.

RESPONSES TO WORKING

Workers' Attitudes

In most surveys that simply ask people if they are satisfied with or at work, the response is overwhelmingly positive. However, overreporting the positive is a well-known feature of survey research (Gutek, 1980; Haavio-Mannila, 1971). Take, for example, the question of marital happiness: 86 percent of couples questioned say they are happy in their marriage, but the divorce rate exceeds 50 percent. Similarly,

Argyris (1959) found that although 92 percent of his sample claimed to be satisfied in their jobs, and 67 percent said management was "wonderful," 67 percent said they experienced no intrinsic satisfaction from their jobs.

There may be many reasons for facile positive survey responses. Strauss (1980) likened many such questions to "How are you?" for which the socially acceptable and expected response is "Fine." Any more meaningful answer requires baring oneself to a stranger, perhaps being exposed as deviant in one's response, being asked for explanations one is reluctant to give or even to explore. Schrank's (1978) experience was that questions about work satisfaction were too devastating and were therefore to be cut off at the source. It is only when research becomes more probing and asks for the source of satisfaction or for the amount to be graded that responses become more meaningful.

Despite such overreporting of the positive, 40 percent of workers reported that time drags at work; 36 percent felt their skills were underused; and 55 percent said they had inadequate leisure time (Walfish, 1979). Ruch (1937) found long ago that a third of workers in the United States were dissatisfied. As recently as 1973 to 1978, job satisfaction was reported to be declining by "large percentages." No occupational group reported gains, or even stability, insofar as satisfaction was concerned, and losses ranged from 11 percent to 43 percent (Walfish, 1979). During that period, job satisfaction among all employee groups was at "its lowest level ever" (Opinion Research Corporation, 1977). As a result of such feelings, a solid majority of workers say they would forgo future pay raises for more time away from work. Twenty-five percent of workers would give up 10 percent or more of their income for more time off (Olmsted, 1985).

It should be noted in this connection that the lower the level of the job in terms of prestige, salary, responsibility, and interest, the more dissatisfaction there seems to be. People with ego-satisfying, power-wielding, decision-making jobs tend to enjoy their work and to work hard and resist retirement. The irony in this situation is that these are the people who tend to determine employment policies and write laws and regulations concerning work and welfare. They project onto other workers their own attitudes and are surprised when told, and reluctant to believe, that all workers do not feel the same way about their jobs.

There have been a number of studies that have gone beyond survey research and that have interviewed people in depth, spending more time creating a friendly relationship, probing answers with further questions, and asking for opinions (Baim, 1981; Garson, 1975; Howe, 1977; Kanter & Stein, 1979; Lasson, 1971; Rubin, 1976; Terkel, 1972, 1980). In very few of these reports does there appear any active personal satisfaction arising from work. Most speak of boredom, frustration, and unhappiness.

Some of our knowledge about life at work comes from researchers who took jobs of various kinds with the intention of documenting what went on around them. Other sources are former workers who have written of their experiences. These observations coincide with the results arrived at by others, ranging from dissatisfaction and unhappiness to more severe problems (Fein, 1976; Roy, 1976; Schrank, 1978).

More revealing than what people say about their work is what they do about it. They fight for shorter work hours and early retirement and certainly do little for which they are not paid—hardly symptoms of happiness at or enjoyment of work.

Thus, although there is a prevailing mythology concerning how much people enjoy working, or enjoy their work, and an even more prevalent ideology as to how much people should enjoy working, it is clearly understood by everyone that nobody will work without pay. As Ernest Bevin (circa 1944) said when he was general secretary of Britain's Transport and General Workers' Union (but before he was prime minister and changed his opinion): "Few of us desire work for its own sake."

As noted previously, all of the limitations on welfare payments—for example, that they must not approach the wage level—are based upon the fear that if people are given sufficient money, they will stop working. Indeed, the fact that people (with the possible exception of workaholics and some creative artists) work primarily for the income involved is so well accepted that it requires little further discussion. Skeptics need only envision a situation in which no one is paid for working and project how many people would do so.

Because most people need to work in order to live, they accept that need as they do many other things that are necessary, even if annoying or unpleasant, such as brushing their teeth, walking the dog, washing the dishes, or dusting the furniture. However, workers use many devices to make the work time pass faster. Some fantasize; others create challenges for themselves, like the tuna packer who tried to see how high she could pile the fish before they fell over, or the ping-pong paddle packer who worked with his eyes closed to show he could do it (Garson, 1975). Some engage in games and rituals (Roy, 1976).

As workers become more aware of the reality of daily work, their previous illusions wear off and their expectations diminish. Something sets in that Lasson (1971) called "the surrender process," resulting in "fatalistic contentment" (Robinson, 1969). Indeed, the higher work satisfaction reported by some older workers can be seen as a result of the surrender process. Having lowered their expectations, through experience, as to what they can expect from work, older workers are more easily satisfied and report themselves as such (Bourne, 1982; D'Arcy, Syrotuck, & Siddique, 1984; Macarov & Yanay, 1982; Price, 1971).

To summarize, although most people assert that they enjoy and get satisfaction from their work, both deeper probing and their behavior indicate that for most people there is little positive, active happiness at work; indeed, for many there is reluctance, boredom, problems, and unhappiness. Not only is this entire area proper for social work intervention—currently underemphasized in theory, education, and practice—but it is one that, as noted in some of the studies quoted above, seems to be growing.

Reducing Work Time

One of the striking historical phenomena of our times is the reduction of work time, which continues without respite. In the 19th century, the average worker put in 4,000 hours a year; the modern worker puts in less than half that amount. The average workweek in the United States shrank from 68 hours in 1860 to 53 hours in 1900 (McCarthy & McGaughey, 1989) and to 35 hours in 1987 (International Labour Office, 1988). From 1870 to 1970, the spare time of the American worker increased from 360 hours a year to 1,700 hours (Patruchev, 1977).

The amount of leisure time available to people in the United States today is only 2.75 hours less than work time, even when second jobs are included, and this gap is rapidly narrowing. Leisure time will outweigh work time very shortly (Bell, 1978). In 1975, the average American had four more hours of leisure a day than his or her grandparents had (Kaplan, 1975), and as the workweek has contracted and life expectancy has been extended, the same average American has added 22 years of leisure to life (Cunningham, 1964). According to poll results, if workers had their way, average work hours would drop from the present 2,000 to about 1,500 (Kendrick, 1979). As Jallade (1982) noted, "A reduction of working time is considered by everyone to be a step forward both socially and economically."

Early Retirement

In addition to demanding shorter work hours, the number of people opting for early retirement grows every year (as discussed in chapter 2). In 1989, more than 68 percent of all OASI beneficiaries were receiving reduced payments because of early retirement—an increase from 45 percent in 1970 (*Social Security Bulletin*, 1990). In short, they had elected to give up three years of full pay and 20 percent of their lifetime Social Security benefits to retire at age 62 instead of 65. Further, Parnes (1983) tracked the same workers for almost 25 years, asking among other things when they hoped to retire. In 1966, 27 percent of the 45-to-49 age group intended to retire early; in 1971, when the same workers were in the 50-to-54 age group, 38 percent announced their intention to retire early; in 1976, at 55 to 59, the proportion exceeded 60 percent. In fact, in 1984, 33 percent of males between 55 and 64 left work (*U.S. News & World Report*, 1985).

This is not just an American phenomenon. Average retirement ages in Austria, West Germany (preunification), Spain, and the United States range from 58.1 to 63.9 years, although normal pensionable age in each of these countries is 65 (*Ageing International*, 1988). Early retirement in the United States is accelerating, and 61 is now the median retirement age (Loftus, n.d.).

THE EFFECTS OF TECHNOLOGY

As technical devices take over jobs formerly done by human beings, a number of counteracting effects can be expected (see chapter 5). For example, technology usually enters to do the dirty, disagreeable, dangerous jobs (Glenn & Feldberg, 1979; Kraft, 1979; Zimbalist, 1979), thus relieving people of such tasks. On the other hand, it removes the interesting aspects of much work, thereby contributing to worker boredom and alienation (Richardson & Henning, 1984). On balance, it seems that technology polarizes work between a few highly paid, interesting, power-wielding, ego-satisfying jobs and many low-paid, dull, rote jobs. The majority of new jobs being created today are low skilled and low paid (*World of Work Report*, 1985), and technology seems to be one of the factors leading to the "deskilling" of workers (Immerwahr, 1982; Sparks, 1984).

Another technological factor has to do with the use of computers for many kinds of information technology. It is possible to monitor workers' time on the job, speed, accuracy, and other factors continually and with much more precision through the use of computers. For many workers, this amounts not only to a work speed-up, but also to feelings of being constantly watched, with the attendant stress this creates. There are also situations in which the computer takes the place of certain workers, thus contributing to the breakdown of informal social networks that made the work bearable, if not enjoyable.

With the continuing growth in use of technology, most workers will probably find their work as banal as in the past, if not more so. There also may be additional problems brought about through the use of technology itself. The consequent growth of unhappiness with work will require more and more attention from social workers.

"CONTINGENT" WORKERS

Another current trend that seems destined to continue is the growth in the number of so-called contingent workers—part-time and temporary employees. There are about 25 million part-time workers in the United States, and approximately 40 percent of them are involuntary, that is, they are doing part-time work only because they cannot find full-time work (*Monthly Labor Review*, 1988). The proportion of part-time jobs is growing. About 20 percent of all new jobs are part-time, and most of them are paid close to the minimum wage (*New York Times*, 1988a). The seriousness of this trend is not always understood. Klein and O'Higgins (1985) indicated that our present social security system is based on the assumption that paid work is a full-time activity and part-time work an occasional aberration. This situation is no longer true. Indeed, the current announced trend of large-scale organizations and corporations is to be "lean and mean"—that is, to maintain a skeleton staff of permanent workers while hiring others as needed, on a part-time and/or temporary basis (Hall, 1984; Kumpke, 1986; Lewis, 1986). Having learned the costs of unemployment insurance, health insurance, pension plans, and other fringe benefits, these companies will tend to avoid fixed costs by using as few full-time and/or permanent employees as possible.

This trend is equally true in service industries. From sales personnel to nurses, and short-order cooks to computer programmers, service providers will be leased, rented, put on short-term contracts, used occasionally, used temporarily, and then released. Social workers as employees are also affected by this trend. A study of social welfare agencies in Australia found that employers of social workers prefer part-time workers for a variety of reasons, even though it involves discontinuity regarding client treatment (Puckett & Frederico, 1988).

Temporary workers typically are paid less than full-time workers, receive fewer benefits, and can be laid off at a moment's notice. The use of temporary workers is not only advantageous for employers, it is also profitable for the organizations that offer temporary employees. In 1987, Britain's largest nursing employment agency reported profits of more than £2 million (approximately $4 million) (Park, 1987), whereas the number of Britons working for substandard wages increased from 8 million in 1979 to 9.4 million in 1988 (Raines, 1988). Of the 10 million jobs created in the United States in the last six years, 1 million to 3 million are temporary, and "likely to disappear quickly if a recession hits" (Uchitelle, 1988a). Further, "the proliferation of full-time temporary jobs helps explain why the civilian unemployment rate [has fallen]" (Uchitelle, 1988a).

Although the Labor Department does not keep records concerning temporary employees as such, temporary-employee firms are known to have employed more than 1 million workers, and a "significant portion" of the 8.3 million self-employed workers fall into this category (Uchitelle, 1988b). For such workers, temporary work means reduction in or loss of benefits, including Social Security, pensions, unemployment insurance, vacations, paid time off, child care facilities, and union protection. In fact, the number of people covered by unemployment insurance declined by about 25 percent from 1980 to 1988 (Uchitelle, 1988a). The growth in poorly paid part-time and temporary work may be one of the reasons why, between 1979 and 1986, for every $9.50 in income added to the top fifth of the American economic strata the bottom fifth lost a dollar (Levy, 1988). Added to the current problems involved in working sporadically or only part-time are future problems in regard to payment from entitlement programs based on, or proportionate to, work records.

WORKING WOMEN

The unemployment of women (and children) once was seen as a positive societal factor—as evidence of the wealth of a country that could afford to protect women from the need to work. Increasingly, however, work opportunities for women are seen both as evidence of sexual equality and as indicators of family financial need. Women, including married women and those with children, are entering the labor force in ever-increasing numbers. This phenomenon has many implications. For example, the growth of part-time work is both cause and result of this movement. Many women whose basic motivation for working is to increase the family income only want or are only free for part-time work. Conversely, the availability of women on a part-time basis makes it easier for employees to enlarge their part-time labor force at the expense of full-time workers.

Furthermore, the entrance of women into the work force raises obvious questions and problems in terms of child care and care of the dependent elderly, as depicted in previous chapters. In some cases this situation results in more sharing of caregiving on the part of both spouses. In others, the result is need for additional social welfare and social work services to assume more of the caregiving. These solutions are not always easily or amicably arrived at, and strains and tensions arising from them may necessitate family or marital counseling.

Women in the workplace have also raised public consciousness concerning sexual harassment on the job and sexual equality in general. Although legal safeguards against sexism and sexual harassment in the workplace exist, many women workers need help in handling such situations, and helping them get the assistance needed must become part of social workers' repertoires. Further, women have not yet arrived at a situation of equal pay for equal work, nor are they represented in the upper levels of corporations and organizations in proportion to their numbers in the work force. For the most part, working women tend to hold part-time jobs that offer little innate satisfaction or career potential. The amount of dissatisfaction that such jobs create is only partially offset by salaries, which tend to be low.

In summary, we can look for more problems to arise from changes in the world of work, including growing discontent with work or—at the least—lack of satisfaction, as most jobs become more routine, become less secure, and offer fewer fringe benefits, and as they encompass more women, specifically mothers of small children.

THE GROWTH OF THE SERVICE SECTOR

One of the most prominent changes taking place in the world of work today is the shift from an industrial to a service economy. In 1929, only 40 percent of the jobs in the United States were in the service sector (Gersuny & Rosengren, 1973); in 1950, 51 percent were (Gartner & Reissman, 1974); in 1967, this had risen to 55 percent; and by 1980, more than 80 percent of all jobs were in the service sector (Thurow, 1981). Of all new jobs created between 1973 and 1980, more than 70 percent were in the services, and in the 1970s, 50 percent of total job growth came from the white-collar and service sectors (Leon, 1981). Today, the services account for more than two-thirds of the total value of production, more than three-quarters of all jobs, and more than 90 percent of new jobs (*New York Times*, 1989). Martin Rein (1985) said 35 percent of all women workers hold service jobs, and 28 percent of all women workers in the United States work in what he termed the social welfare industry. According to this source, 48 percent of the increase in female employment in the United States between 1968 and 1983 was due to the social welfare industry. Further, two-thirds of the self-employed workers in the United States produce services (Newland, 1982), and there are predictions that by the end of the century, service employment will constitute 90 to 97 percent of all employment (Best, 1973; Stellman, 1982).

Despite the importance of this trend, it has not been given the attention it deserves either in research or literature concerning the world of work. For example, there is no generally accepted definition of service employment. In Great Britain in 1978, half of the people who were said to have service jobs performed functions that were in direct support of production activities (Gershuny, 1978), and about one-third of the people who worked in goods-producing activities had service jobs (Newland, 1982). Although there have been many attempts to categorize service jobs (Morris & Murphy, 1950; Robinson, 1969; Roe, 1956; Super, 1957), there still are many conceptual problems in grappling with this question (Cooperman, 1989; Mark, 1982; Shelp, 1981). Consequently, one useful way of looking at service employment is as a continuum, extending from people who manufacture, transform, or handle material items on one end, to those in the human services dealing with the physiological, educational, emotional, or social problems of individuals on the other.

As the shift toward the service end of this continuum continues, a number of unanswered questions become pertinent (Macarov, 1986). For example, does it require a certain type of personality, or specific personality traits, to become a human-services worker? Some people claim human-services workers must have special talents and abilities (Pines & Kafry, 1978), or specific qualities such as being responsible or caring (Albeda, 1983), or that they must need to be loved (Levinson, Price, Munden, Mandl, & Solley, 1962). Katz (1963) put special emphasis on empathic ability—an ability that may not exist (Macarov, 1970, 1978b). Then there are those who argue that women are naturally more suited than men for certain roles (Flick, 1983; McGill, 1985), or, conversely, that women are inherently unsuited for certain positions and roles (Goldberg, 1989). Some argue that unemployed unskilled male workers are unsuitable recruits for the service sector (Pearson, 1982), and there are said to be 1.5 million workers who are already displaced because their skills are obsolete because of the shift from manufacturing to high-tech and service industries (*American Association of Retired Persons Bulletin*, 1987). Finally, some say only people who express the importance of self-development (Zetterburg & Frankel, 1983), or who can resist role strain (Shamir, 1980), or who have initiative (Moos, 1983), can operate successfully in the human-services sector.

Screening for specific personality attributes or attitudes is sometimes an important element in accepting candidates for professional human-services training. Some schools of social work, for example, require written autobiographies, tests, interviews, and second interviews, whereas other schools accept all technically qualified applicants. Unfortunately, despite some elaborate, lengthy, and expensive experiments in related fields (Office of Strategic Services, 1947), there is little empirical evidence that either method results in better practitioners or students.

A related question has to do with whether professional training can overcome or inculcate specific traits. Bargal (1981) indicated that social work students' values are accentuated, rather than changed, during their education. On the other hand, in an empirical study of students' work satisfaction and their relationships with clients, differing amounts of work satisfaction did not seem to affect the quality of these relationships (Macarov, 1987). Possibly the students had learned to control the effects of their own feelings when dealing with clients, which would seem to indicate that professional training can overcome individual attitudes.

Concerning the service sector, there is also the question as to whether the sources of job satisfaction and dissatisfaction are the same in the service sector as in the industrial sector. Despite the shift to the service sector by 1950, almost all of the research on workers' attitudes, patterns, satisfaction, and so forth has been done in industrial settings. For example, if one examines the 400 sets of tests of workers' responses published in two compendia (Cook, Hepworth, Toby, & Warr, 1981; Stewart, Hetherington, & Smith, 1984), 399 of them were done in industry. Similarly, of the 3,000 studies of workers located by Locke in 1976 (see the section "Attempts at Job Improvement" in this chapter), almost all of them were done in industry.

Consequently, little is known about human-services workers' sources of satisfaction or dissatisfaction. One empirical study found that the primary sources of social workers' satisfaction were rooted in relationships with clients and their families, contact with multidisciplinary staff, and having the resources to do a good job (Meller & Macarov, 1985). In a study of satisfaction in an Israeli kibbutz, educational staff indicated satisfaction arising from their relationships with students, but dissatisfaction from their relationships with parents (Macarov, 1982). Such sources of satisfaction and dissatisfaction do not arise in industrial research.

As more workers move into service jobs and deal with people rather than with things, training and retraining courses will need to deal more with attitudes, relationships, and professional behavior than with technical skills, dexterity, and precision. Changing from industrial to service jobs will not be easy for many of the people engaged in pursuits closer to the industrial end of the continuum outlined previously, and they may need help in making the transition.

Service jobs do not necessarily offer more satisfaction than industrial or semiservice jobs. One-third of the nurses in the United States, for example, usually are not working, and one-third work only part-time (*The Nurses' Almanac*, 1978; U.S. Department of Health, Education, and Welfare, 1981). The same figures hold good for nurses in Israel (Handles, Apel, & Sagin, 1982). Because employer turnover is a constant problem in both teaching and social work, work in the service sector, including the personal social services, may create as many individual problems as does work in industry. With the continuing move toward a service society, these problems likely will increase.

This raises the question of whether service organizations will be as willing, or as unwilling, to employ social workers to help their staffs as industry has been. The fact that productivity has been found to be much more difficult to define and measure in the services than in industry will militate against employment of social workers if greater productivity is the goal. On the other hand, employers in the services might be much more sensitive and receptive to helping workers as such.

MAKING WORK MORE FLEXIBLE

Flexitime/Flexiplace

One rather recent development that may ease the work situation, at least insofar as time is concerned, is the previously mentioned flexitime arrangement. Under flexitime, workers may put in their assigned hours at various times. Sometimes there are specified time segments that workers may choose to work at different times; sometimes there is a core period when the worker must be at work, with discretionary time in addition, to be worked at the individual's convenience. Alternatively, the worker may be free to work the assigned daily, weekly, monthly, or even annual hours completely at his or her own convenience. All of these arrangements require a good deal of prior thought and preparation, especially in industrial settings. However, the success of even the most extreme of these possibilities is exemplified by a furniture factory in an Israeli kibbutz, where members are committed to a certain number of hours per month, but can work nonstop for days, or during mornings only, or only during the middle of the night, all completely within the choice of the worker.

Such arrangements offer solutions for workers who are also caring for children or elderly people at home, because they allow them to schedule their work so they can be available when needed at home. Flexitime also sometimes makes job-sharing (to be discussed below) easier, by dovetailing work and nonwork sequences with another person.

In 1988, 12.3 percent of all American workers were on flexible schedules (U.S. Department of Commerce, 1987). However, despite the logic of flexitime and the independence of choice that it offers as well as its problem-solving possibilities, this form of working has not grown to the extent previously predicted. The difficulty of arranging the work that needs doing in such a way that the time and/or the sequence is not important may be one of the reasons for this. Lack of demand by workers may be another. Best (1989) said experiments with time schedules, as well as other novelties, tend to be abandoned when the economic situation worsens, which may have happened in this case. Finally, there is simply the innate conservatism of most organizations and a reluctance to experiment with new methods unless there are overwhelming reasons to do so. With the continued entrance of women into the labor force, however, and the growth of sharing in all tasks on the part of married couples, this might yet become the preferred and accepted way of working.

Related to, and sometimes connected with, flexitime is the work form known as flexiplace. This is a system that enables employees to choose where they want to work—in the normal workplace, at home, or somewhere else. The proliferation of work that can be done on computers or through other information technology makes it possible for much work that formerly could be done only in the office or workplace to be done elsewhere.

The use of flexiplace brings with it certain dangers, however, among them the fear of sweatshop operations, where work is paid on a piecework basis, leading to the possibility of long work hours and exploitation of other family members. There are also questions of disability liability for work being performed outside the controlled area of the workplace, weakening of labor unions, and availability of fringe benefits.

In any case, experience has indicated that people choosing not to work in the traditional workplace prefer work centers (group work places near, but not in, the home) that make it possible to avoid constant contact with the people at home—child, spouse, parent, invalid—but allow workers the possibility of returning home as quickly and as often as necessary.

Job Sharing

The burgeoning area of job sharing also deserves mention. In this instance, two people hold the same job, getting one salary but dividing the hours of work. In some cases, this arrangement makes it possible for married couples to share both the work and the housekeeping duties. In others, it offers partial retirement or part-time work to two people who desire it. Unfortunately, it is sometimes forced upon people involuntarily to avoid firing one of them and thus increasing the unemployment rate. However, when job sharing is undertaken, it can be combined with flexitime and flexiplace if either of those options is available.

Social workers should know and understand all of these alternative work arrangements, with their advantages and disadvantages, as they move in the future into the area of helping people with their work problems.

UNEMPLOYMENT: PAST AND PRESENT

Social workers have been concerned with the problem of unemployment from the earliest days of the profession. Today, the unemployed, and those with problems stemming from that condition, make up a large part of many social workers' caseloads, particularly in certain areas such as inner cities, or in respect to certain client groups, such as youth or minorities. Consequently, it is not surprising that both social welfare programs and much social work activity center around the area of work. Nevertheless, what should be considered work, unemployment, or full employment is not always clear.

Definitions

Some dictionaries use as many as 12 pages for definitions and examples of work. There are also researchers who seek to distinguish between "work" and "labor," or paid and unpaid work, or market and nonmarket work, and so on. For this discussion, however, suffice it to designate work as that activity in which people engage in order to acquire the goods and services they want. It is possible to take exception to that definition, or to enlarge upon it, but pragmatically, that is what most people mean when they speak of work, including the employed, the self-employed, and the unemployed. It should be noted that this definition specifically excludes activities undertaken for psychological, emotional, or social reasons, although these elements also may be present in work.

Employment is a bit more difficult to define, because it can include not only people who are working full-time, but those who are working less than they would like. This has been termed underemployment. One could also argue that people working at less than their capacity are, at least, part-time unemployed. This is known as subemployment. Then there are those who hold jobs for which they are unfit or jobs that do not use their abilities or training. This is malemployment. For most purposes, however, the official definition used by the U.S. government is sufficient: anyone who has worked for more than one hour in the previous week is employed.

Unemployment, too, has an official definition: anyone who is not working and looking for work. In the United States, the official count of unemployed people is taken from a survey of 60,000 families, in which people are asked whether they are now working and whether they are looking for work. (If they have worked more than one hour per week, they are defined as employed.)

Full employment is the most difficult term to define and the most arguable one. Lord Beveridge (1930) defined unemployment as "more men looking for work than there are jobs available." Conversely, full employment might be defined as more jobs available than there are people looking for work. However, this would ignore the fact that some of these jobs are so undesirable that no one is willing to accept them, or that they include part-time jobs or require skills that job-seekers do not have. On the other hand, one might define full employment as does the Long Island Coalition for Full Employment (Kogut & Aron, 1980): "The right of all persons able, willing and seeking work for full opportunity for useful paid employment at fair rates of compensation." Because this definition holds that the employment should be "useful," which itself requires definition, and should pay fair rates, which is no less debatable, the extent to which this is a useful definition for policy purposes is questionable. Generally, full employment is defined as an unemployment rate that is considered natural, or acceptable, or impossible to reduce, and thus varies from commentator to commentator. Thus, Sherraden (1988) posited 3 percent unemployment as full employment in the United States; Sweden claimed only 1.9 percent unemployment in 1989 (Ministry of Labour, 1989) and did not call that full employment; and 20 percent unemployment was said to constitute full employment in Newfoundland in 1989 (Canadian Council on Social Development, 1989).

A Brief History

The problem of maintaining maximum employment has occupied governments since antiquity. Mendelssohn (1977) maintained that the construction of the later pyramids was a makework project; Herod began a road around the Temple Mount in Jerusalem when the Second Temple was finished to give work to the newly unemployed workers; Vespasian forbade the use of rivers for moving construction materials, in order to give more jobs to people (Garraty, 1978). Since then, governments have engaged in a large variety of job-creation schemes, few of which have produced long-term success (Taggart, 1977).

Finding jobs for people is becoming increasingly difficult, especially full-time, decent-paying jobs. Despite temporary fluctuations, the unemployment rate throughout the West has been rising inexorably. After every recession or period of economic difficulty, the "floor" of unemployment rises. In 1930, Beveridge saw 2 percent unemployment among unskilled workers as the irreducible minimum, but by 1973, the American Council of Economic Advisors was speaking of 3.5 percent unemployment as the "natural" (unavoidable) rate (Reich, 1983). In 1979, the Humphrey-Hawkins Act called 4 percent unemployment "full employment" (*World of Work Report*, 1979). In 1983, the Council of Economic Advisors spoke of 6 to 7 percent unemployment as the natural rate (Reich, 1983). At this writing, the unemployment rate in the United States hovers between 5 and 6 percent and seems to cause little concern except among the unemployed themselves. In Europe, the rate varies from country to country, between 1 percent and 21 percent, with a median of about 8 percent (United Nations, 1988).

The rise in unemployment has occurred despite continual reduction in hours of work. For example, in 1900, the average workweek in the

United States was 53 hours; in 1979 it was 35.5 hours (*World of Work Report*, 1980); and in 1987 it was 34.8 hours (International Labour Office, 1988). During January 1991 alone, the average work week in the United States was reduced by 30 minutes (*New York Times*, 1991). Over the past half-century, the average hours worked per year has been reduced by close to 0.5 percent a year (Kendrick, 1979). In addition to this reduction in working hours, there is the increase in the amount of time wasted on the job, noted below, as well as an increase in maintenance of unneeded jobs.

Statistics

With the official definition of "unemployed" used by the U.S. government (one who has not worked during the past week and is looking for work), the unemployment rate in the United States at the time of this writing is between 6 and 7 percent (*New York Times*, 1991). However, as many commentators are quick to point out, the official rate is not the real rate. Every government attempts to minimize the extent of unemployment. In the United States, for example, unemployment figures omit "discouraged workers"—those who have ceased looking for work because it is obvious there are no jobs for them—and part-time workers, many of whom work more than one hour a week but are seeking full-time work. Unemployment figures do not include transient workers, seasonal workers, agricultural farm laborers, school leavers, and illegal immigrants. In 1983, the official figures listed 1.5 million discouraged workers, but some estimates ran as high as 15 million (Schwartz & Neikirk, 1983). In 1985, 5 million discouraged workers and 6 million involuntary part-time workers were left out of the unemployment figures (*International Herald Tribune*, 1986; *New York Times*, 1986). In Israel, differences in definition and in methods of counting have been shown to result in unemployment figures ranging from 19,000 to 115,000 (Sicron, 1986). Similarly, a recent redefinition of unemployment in the Netherlands succeeded in reducing the official figure from 683,000 to 443,000 (Verduyn, 1989).

In addition, there are the nominally unemployed, who are taking various kinds of training and retraining courses and who are considered students or trainees getting stipends, rather than unemployed people. This device, among others, is used extensively in Sweden, which accounts in large part for that country's 1.9 percent official unemployment rate (Yankelovich, Zettenberg, Strumpel, & Shanks, 1983). In Sweden, only 84,000 persons are listed as unemployed, but there are another 34,000 in training courses. These are mainly unemployed people required to undergo retraining and thus are considered students rather than unemployed, which they are. Another 41,500 Swedish citizens are "working," but their salaries are paid at least in part by the government; another 17,600 have been given "temporary public employment" (makework), and 21,000 are in "youth teams," made up of unemployed youngsters, but listed separately. Taking into consideration the various devices used to conceal the unemployed, the actual unemployment rate in Sweden is 5.5 percent rather than 1.9 percent (Ministry of Labour, 1989).

Then there are those who have not worked but would like to if they could find suitable jobs and make the necessary arrangements; included in this group are an unknown number of housewives. Due to these methods of undercounting, it is estimated that actual U.S. unemployment figures range from 50 to 300 percent more than the officially quoted rate (Field, 1977; Kogut & Aron, 1980; Levinson, 1980; Macarov, 1984; Schwartz & Neikirk, 1983; Yankelovich et al., 1983).

Further, one must take into account the hidden unemployment present in those jobs that are maintained just to give employment but that serve no useful purpose. For example, there are 5,000 military installations in the United States, none of which has been closed since 1977. Not only are many of these not needed for military purposes, but shutting them down would probably improve the environment. But the fact that shutting down bases means employees will lose their jobs usually ends any discussion (*New York Times*, 1988b).

In addition, there are numerous examples of people being guaranteed jobs that are not needed in order to allow for the entrance of technology that is desired. This was the case when container ships were introduced and longshoremen were guaranteed their salaries whether they worked or not. Steel workers are paid for a 30-hour week even if they work less, or not at all. Employers have given long-term or lifetime contracts to unneeded workers as compensation for introducing technology (Gorz, 1982; *World of Work Report*, 1984; Zimbalist, 1979). In Great Britain, some crew members on cross-channel ferries work fewer than 80 days a year for a full year's pay (Petty, 1987). In Japan there are "window gazers"— people on the payroll who have nothing to do but look out the windows (Jones, 1982).

Finally, there is that aspect of hidden unemployment that consists of time wasted on the job. Walbank (1980) estimated that the average worker uses 44 percent of his or her potential at work; 78 percent of Gyllenhammer, Harman, and Yankelovich's (1981) respondents said they could work harder; all of Macarov's (1972) kibbutz respondents said the same thing. Wasting time is not an indication of laziness on the part of the worker, but rather stems from the maintenance of more workers than necessary—to support them, on the one hand, and reduce the unemployment figure, on the other. In any case, the amount of time wasted on the job is growing; between 1965 and 1975, it increased by more than 10 percent (Kendrick, 1979; Yankelovich & Immerwahr, 1983).

Social Effects

Although the effects of unemployment have been outlined extensively (Barrington, 1976; Briar, Fiedler, Sheen, & Kamp, 1980; Marsden, 1982; Maurer, 1978; Travers, 1985), nowhere has any positive effect been noticed. Unemployment, under current circumstances, leads to negative changes in self-image and in relations with others, mental and physical illness, economic distress, changed family roles, and changed behavior. A 1-percent increase in unemployment has been found to be associated with more than 30,000 deaths, more than 20,000 of them from heart attacks (Pelletier, 1983).

There seems to be, however, a certain tipping point, or critical mass, in unemployment. Up to a certain point, joblessness is seen as the fault of the unemployed person—he or she is not really trying, or is unwilling to do certain kinds of work, or prefers to live on unemployment compensation. This has been termed "blaming the victim" (Ryan, 1974). But when the number of unemployed people reaches large proportions, as it did during the Great Depression and during some recessions since then, it begins to be seen as a societal or governmental problem—that jobs are not being provided by those who should provide them. This seems to have its effect on the psyche of the unemployed person. A study done in Edinburgh found that after the number of people unemployed reached a certain point, the incidences of parasuicidal behavior decreased (Platt, 1987). One possibility is that seeing the extent of unemployment, the unemployed stopped blaming themselves, or stopped seeing others as blaming them.

In any case, it is small wonder that so many social workers find themselves dealing with the unemployed, or the problems arising from unemployment.

The Role of Social Workers

The question of what social workers do about unemployment and the unemployed can only partially be answered by reviewing the professional literature. Only a small portion of what is done is recorded, an even smaller part of that is prepared for publication, and many articles submitted for publication do not appear. On the other hand, that which is published probably represents a reasonable sample of what is being done.

A survey of 15 English-language social work journals published from 1977 through 1988 indicates at least a beginning recognition that a situation of permanent unemployment is emerging and includes some proposed theories as to how it should be viewed (Macarov, 1988b). However, very little practical knowledge exists to indicate the best way of handling the situation while dealing with clients. The articles appearing in the English journals dealt with four areas: (1) descriptions of the unemployed and the effect of unemployment upon them; (2) job-seeking behavior and motivation; (3) principles, policies, and programs; and (4) theories for practice and practice experience.

Descriptions of the Unemployed and Effects of Joblessness. Differences between the employed and the unemployed are outlined by a number of authors. For example, several authors stress the need to differentiate between categories of the unemployed, such as different age groups (Briar et al., 1980; Figueria-McDonough, 1978) and women as differentiated from men (Koller, Wade, & Godsden, 1980; Rosenman, 1979). Other authors note that the longer one is unemployed, the less chance one has of getting a job (Garfinkle, 1977) and that discouraged workers often are more needy than the unemployed (Madonia, 1983). Braithwhite and Biles (1979) noted that unemployed people have a strikingly higher rate of criminal victimization than employed people and also are more likely to be subject to victimization by the police.

Other writers look at the problem of unemployment and the toll that it takes on those afflicted (Barrington, 1976; Briar et al., 1980; Travers, 1985). Fopp (1983) found that families of the unemployed are bearing increasing responsibility for young unemployed people, and Sunley and Sheek (1986) found that sooner, rather than later, the support networks of the unemployed begin to weaken and even family members withdraw support. Hanlon (1981) looked at the factors that influence the amount of assistance the unemployed receive from relatives and friends and found that help tended to be "spot, crisis-induced," with age an important factor in determining whether help would be given and in what amount.

From this group of articles, it seems social workers are concerned and informed about unemployment and its effects on different categories of people. The need to individualize unemployed clients and groups of clients to provide appropriate services, emphasized in these articles, will be as necessary with the long-term and permanently unemployed in the future as it is now.

Job-Seeking Behavior and Motivation. Another set of writers studied the attributes, motivations, and behaviors of the unemployed. Studies of differences between employed and unemployed welfare recipients (Glass, 1982) and between the employed and unemployed generally (Tiggeman & Winefield, 1980) found few differences, although family stability (Chambri, 1976), past experiences in job-seeking (AuClaire, 1979a), economic factors (Chrissinger, 1980), and higher wages (Nichols, 1979) all have some effect on job-seeking and its success. Mildred Rein (1982) found that pay, permanence, and perks are as important to welfare clients seeking jobs as they are to others. AuClaire (1979b) commented that the factors making for self-support among welfare clients are beyond the control of individual recipients.

The conclusion one is led to by these studies is that neither individual motivation nor attachment to the work ethic has little (if any) influence on the job-seeking behavior of the unemployed, and even less on successful job-finding. Thus, efforts by social workers to "motivate" clients to work are irrelevant and will be increasingly so as jobs, especially good jobs, become more difficult to find.

Principles, Policies, and Programs.   The major thrust of these articles deals with the principles underlying current staffing and employment policies (Briar, 1983) and calls for a reassessment of current thinking and changes in assumptions (Ensley, 1980; Macarov, 1985b). Work and its meaning are seen to be constantly changing phenomena (Borrero, 1980b) requiring dynamic policies (Coleman, 1985) that change with the situation. For example, the current thinking that more industrialization will solve welfare problems is not seen as valid, because the model required "is a social image of community and family life that . . . does not exist" (Burghardt & Fabricant, 1981). In short, these writers believe that the assumptions underlying employment and unemployment policies are faulty and therefore lead to ineffective programs.

Insofar as enunciated policies themselves are concerned, they are subject to a number of criticisms—that they are nonexistent (Kogut & Aron, 1980), insufficient (Briar, 1983), inconsistent (Borrero, 1981), and directionless (Sherraden & Adamek, 1984). Proposed policies include more state-employed people (Stanback, 1980), more welfare spending at the expense of military spending (Lowenthal, 1976/1977), an income-subsidy program for hard-core unemployed black youth (Moss, 1982), public-sector job creation (Tomer, 1985; Toomey, 1980), more social insurance income (Danzinger & Plotnick, 1978), shorter working hours (Weeks, 1980), and a national youth service (Sherraden & Adamek, 1984). Lurie (1978) opposed plans for making welfare recipients work ("workfare"), on the basis that the costs of such a program would exceed both the savings in government expenditure and the increase in recipients' earnings. In short, none of the writers is happy with current policies, but they do not agree as to what should be done to reduce or relieve unemployment.

A few articles analyze specific programs for helping the unemployed. Koller, Godsden, and Wade (1980) examined Australia's Community Youth Support Scheme (CYSS), which was intended to provide employment-centered activities, including training in completing job applications, interviewing skills, basic work-related skills, community service, and hobby and interest-expanding activities. These activities were of doubtful value in procuring jobs but seemed to provide social contact and emotional support. Peel (1981) detailed one volunteer's efforts to find work for youngsters by loaning them tools, teaching them skills, and so forth, and Borthwick and Diamond (1980) reported on a 16-week program for 15 youngsters, eight of whom found jobs.

On a more conceptual level, Hasenfeld (1975) studied two employment placement services and found that their activities were more directed toward meeting the needs of low-wage industries than helping the unemployed as such. Soothill (1976) described the effort involved in finding employment for white-collar offenders and the quandary of whether it is more appropriate to help large numbers of relatively easy-to-help people or to try to assist those who prove much more difficult as placement propositions.

Examination of the articles in this section indicates that although efforts to help the unemployed find work continue, the track record of such efforts, and that of job-creation schemes, is not encouraging. Indeed, the problems with such schemes have been described as "almost inherently intractable" (Tyrell & Shanks, 1982), and there are calls in the literature that such courses begin to stress personal development and general life skills rather than work preparation or work-related skills (Salmon, 1983).

Practice Theories and Practice Experience.   Another group of published articles deals with theories for use in practice with the unemployed. Unemployment is compared with bereavement, loss, or separation, and recognition of the validity of the suffering is proposed, as well as concern for psychological changes, social results, alcoholism, violence, effects on children, and possible suicide caused by unemployment (Borrero, 1980a; Krystal, Moran-Sackett, Thompson, & Cantoni, 1983). Unemployment is also seen as a period of learned helplessness (Barber, 1982), loss of control, and alienation (Keefe, 1984). Neikrug (1982) spoke of the effects of meaninglessness, although from a somewhat different perspective.

It is interesting to note that although each of these theories is rather generally based on crisis intervention, each also may be useful in dealing with long-term or permanent situations; that is, grief from bereavement can be overcome, but the loss itself remains. Insofar as unemployment is concerned, these theories deal with the crisis of unemployment from the same long-term point of view, being concerned with the effect on the individual and the family, rather than being based on the "get 'em back to work" school of thought.

Turning to actual practice, rather than theories, Briar (1980) emphasized use of both "people-changing" and "situation-changing" strategies in working with the unemployed. Figueira-McDonough (1978) emphasized concrete help with everyday needs as the most important buffer to psychological strain among the unemployed. Halladay (1980) called for social workers to reorient themselves and their responses toward unemployment and proposed some practical steps to take. A few writers make the important point that although unemployment has many adverse effects and creates new needs, it can also be a period of growth and change (Krystal et al., 1983; Sunley & Sheek, 1986).

In some places, an additional and different tactic is being pursued—that is, organizing the unemployed into a network, which in some respects acts like a labor union. The network in Europe has now existed for almost 10 years and has annual national and European conferences (Bothmer, 1989). There is also a union of the unemployed in Australia (Windshuttle, 1981), and a national network of unions of the unemployed has emerged in the United States (Briar, 1988).

On a more empirical basis, family-service agencies in the United States report that 23 percent of their cases have had problems engendered by unemployment. In 43 percent of these cases, the agencies felt they had rendered "some help"; another 43 percent reported "minimal help"; 15 percent reported that they had been unable to help. In 30 percent of the cases affected by unemployment, the clients were helped to secure work or training (although whether the work derived from the training is not indicated) (Sunley & Sheek, 1986).

The relative paucity of articles concerning social work activities with unemployed people other than trying to help them find work reflects the general societal dictum that working is better than not working. An official British report, for example, concluded that, "The Commission does not regard with favour suggestions that people should now be educated or trained for unemployment" (Manpower Service Commission, 1978); and a response to the author's article urging social workers to help people use periods of unemployment constructively (Macarov, 1988b) argued against legitimizing unemployment (Cattell-Gordon, 1988).

Taken as a totality, these articles indicate the needs of the unemployed should not be neglected, although there is increasing awareness that unemployment now must be viewed differently, and even can be seen as a positive opportunity once daily needs are met. It is revealing, however, that articles describing hands-on, front-line practice with the unemployed constitute by far the least numerous of any category. However, there are sources that prescribe direct social work practice approaches with the unemployed (Briar, 1988), although the extent to which these prescriptions are actually carried out is unclear. In short, other than trying to get work for the unemployed, social workers—at least as revealed in their literature—do seem to have ideas about how the unemployed should be helped, and these ideas will be increasingly necessary in the years to come.

In summary, as the results of the literature search detailed above indicate, there is a good deal of unhappiness among social workers concerning current approaches to unemployment. Despite documented evidence concerning the adverse effects of being out of work, government policies are not reflective of reality; current programs are ineffective; and social work practice is, at best, ameliorative rather than curative.

Viewing unemployment as a temporary phenomenon through which the client should be supported until he or she finds a job is becoming increasingly obsolete, as levels of unemployment in the United States indicate that six out of every 100 workers cannot find jobs. Adding hidden unemployment to that figure raises it to 10 to 20 out of every 100, and applying it to specific groups, such as young, black, inner-city populations, results in figures ranging from 20 to 60 percent unemployed. The need to view unemployment from a new perspective is becoming increasingly clear and important, particularly in view of the possibility, if not the probability, that the need for human labor is constantly diminishing and that despite many rear-guard actions, unemployment will, in the long run, continue to rise (Macarov, 1984).

In this connection, it should be noted that although the "baby boomers" (the result of high birthrates immediately after World War II) will pass out of the labor force toward the end of this century, creating less of a labor surplus than now exists, by 2010, the "baby boom echo" again will result in an enlarged pool of job seekers (Vu, 1985). In addition, an unknown proportion of previously nonworking women will be entering the labor force in the interim.

THE FUTURE OF UNEMPLOYMENT

Popular Theories

There is good reason to believe that the problem of unemployment will become more urgent with the passage of time. Although there is some disagreement, a large and growing body of opinion maintains that technological changes will reduce the need for human labor in the future. For example, microelectronic devices are much simpler to manufacture than their predecessors, require much less labor to operate, and have longer life expectancies (Norman, 1980). The productivity of the individual worker rises constantly: In 1850, people used 13 percent of their total energy at work; today, they use less than 1 percent (Ministry of Health, 1988). Between 1950 and 1978, the average output per hour of persons in private business in the United States almost doubled (*Monthly Labor Review*, 1979), and the output per hour of all workers doubled from 1947 to 1972 (Moss, 1979). Using 1977 as the base of 100, output per worker in the United States was 67.6 in 1960, but 107.9 in 1986 (U.S. Department of Commerce, 1987). Put another way, in 1950, every employed civilian worker in the United States produced $5,000 of the gross national product. In 1975, this had risen to $16,000. It is predicted that by the year 2000, this will be $85,000. If current increases continue, by the year 2100, every worker will produce $5 million worth of the gross national product (Calloway, 1976). On a national basis, productivity rises on average 2.5 percent a year (United Nations, 1988). Consequently, just as the use of technology reduced the number of people engaged in agriculture from more than 90 percent at one time to less than 3 percent today, it has reduced human labor in industry until industrial jobs now account for less than 20 percent of those being performed, and, as noted previously, there are estimates that this will be reduced to between 3 and 5 percent by the end of this century.

In the services, too, technology is making great inroads into human employment, as will be detailed in the next chapter. The greatest changes in this area are in the information/communication services, including such areas as banking, printing, and communications. However, increased productivity due to the introduction of technology has been recorded in areas as diverse as laundries (Carnes, 1978), retail food sales (Carey & Otto, 1977), and automobile dealers (Duke, 1977), among many others. Technology has also made a dramatic impact on some areas of human services, with medicine being the most obvious example—from CAT-scanners to blood pressure measurements with finger caps, to laser beam surgery, as a few examples. In both teaching and nursing, technology has led to greater efficiency, if not always to greater effectiveness.

As the next chapter indicates, the use of technology in social work has been concentrated mainly in the information and retrieval area (Levinson & Hayne, 1984)—with considerable gains in efficiency and effectiveness—but there are also examples of its use in decision making (Shapira, 1990), predicting behavior (Klein, Greist, & van Cura, 1975), and therapy (Weizenbaum, 1976). The growing use of computers in the social services is evidenced by an increasing number of centers concentrating on this area and by the appearance of publications on the subject, such as the *Computer Use in Social Services Network Newsletter*.

The use of technology over the long term has resulted in constantly rising unemployment, despite constant reductions in work hours. At the same time, efforts to mask or mitigate these realities have resulted in more time wasted at work, as well as the creation and maintenance of jobs that are no longer necessary. Because there is no reason to believe technology has run its course and there will be no further changes in this area, it is highly probable that the amount of human labor necessary in the future will continue to diminish and that there will be a growth in both overt and covert unemployment.

Although there is no complete consensus on this score, there is, nevertheless a large and growing school of thought that predicts this kind of future. Economist Wassily Leontief (Leontief & Duchin, 1984), a Nobel prize recipient, took into consideration new occupations and new services in his prediction that all of the goods and services produced in another 20 years will require 10 percent less human labor than at present. Others use different time frames and parameters but agree with the basic premise (Freedman, 1983; Gerard, 1978; Griffiths, 1977; Jenkins & Sherman, 1979; Jones, 1982; Macarov, 1988a, 1988c). A report by the International Labour Office concluded, "Although there is evidence to support diverse views on the new technology's impact on work, levels of employment are likely to decline in the long term, either in numbers fully employed or through part-time employment or shorter working hours" (Kaplinsky, 1987).

The continuing existence of unemployment has given rise to a generally accepted categorization that includes "frictional," "structural," and "cyclical" unemployment, each of which is time limited, requiring only short-term or temporary help. With the inexorable growth of unemployment, however, especially among certain groups at risk, like inner-city black youths, and the prospect that despite plans, programs, boondoggling, and statistical juggling, unemployment will continue to grow as technology replaces humans, an additional category of unemployment has emerged as a growing challenge to social workers: permanent unemployment.

The growth of technology will continue to cause more unemployment. More people will be unemployed, and for longer periods of time. This prediction has become so widely accepted that a terminology has evolved to describe it. We are said to be heading toward a process of "hysteresis," under which two types of workers develop in the labor market. There are "attached" workers, who remain employed without a break or are rehired after a brief period, and "unattached" workers, who are "permanently unemployed, with little skill, no knowledge of the market, no work habits, and no contacts in workplaces" (Temkin, 1989).

Counterarguments

There are three counterarguments often used to question this view of the future: technology-produced jobs, infrastructure rebuilding, and human-services staffing.

Technology-Produced Jobs. The first counterargument is that the creation of the technology itself, or the creation of new industries made possible by technology, will provide more jobs than technology eliminates. This is possible, but the track record so far does not offer much comfort. Technology seems to create jobs in the short run but to eliminate even more jobs in the long run. Take, for example, predictions about the need for cardpunch operators in the early days of computers. These jobs were predicted to more than make up for the jobs lost by shorthand stenographers, typists, and file clerks. With the subsequent rapid introduction of computer tapes and diskettes, however, computer cards have gone the way of the abacus, and so have the many jobs that they were to offer. Even computer programmers have short half-lives, because new technology makes their knowledge obsolete.

The continued growth of unemployment casts doubt on the long-term employment potential of technology. For every job created by the computer industry, two will be eliminated (Norman, 1980; Rada, 1980). Once a high-technology unit finds its market, automation quickly follows and employment usually falls (Russel, 1986). In short, high technology promises to generate relatively few jobs (Reich, 1983).

Rebuilding of the Infrastructure. The second rebuttal to the job-reduction theory holds that by using unemployed people to rebuild the infrastructure of cities, roads, bridges, and so forth will be preserved and unemployment eliminated. Putting aside the number of unemployed people who are incapable of engaging in physical construction, the number of people needed for such work is usually grossly overestimated. For example, insulating all the homes in Great Britain would give employment to just 30,000 people for 10 years. To rebuild all the necessary railroads, roads, and sewers in Great Britain would give employment to only 62,000 workers (House of Lords, 1981). Together these projects would hardly create a ripple in British unemployment figures, which hover around 3 million.

Using a similar but broader example, it has been estimated that to build homes for every family in the Third World would give employment to 8 million people (Sethuraman, 1985). However, in India alone, "tens of millions of people are registered as looking for jobs" (*New York Times*, 1988c).

Staffing the Human Services. Finally, there is the hope that unemployed people can be induced or coerced to reinforce the undermanned social services. This argument does not consider that most unemployed people are male manual workers and that the great bulk of the caring jobs currently are being done by part-time married women (Bosanquet, 1985). It also ignores the questions of whether service jobs require certain personal characteristics that many unemployed people may not possess (Macarov, 1986) and of whether unemployed people can be retrained (or would agree) to perform service jobs, not to mention the costs of such a massive effort (*New York Times*, 1988d).

The basic question still remains as to how many additional workers are required to bring the services up to optimal conditions. Here, too, although the folklore envisions massive personnel needs in the social services, the few scattered empirical studies that exist cast doubt on that vision. In the United States in 1988, for example, there were 1.6 million nurses working, and it was estimated that an additional 300,000, at most, would satisfy the need for more (*New York Times*, 1988e). Similarly, to reduce American classroom sizes from the average of 24 students today to a maximum of 15 (and it is not at all agreed on that this would improve education) would require only 1 million new teachers (*New York Times*, 1988d). Also, the National Association of Social Workers estimated that there would be need for 700,000 geriatric social workers. Yet, taken together, these optimal conditions would provide only 2 million jobs in the United States at a time when official unemployment exceeds 6.5 million, to which should be added 9 million involuntary part-time workers (*Monthly Labor Review*, 1988).

Further, it would be naive to believe that all of the 2 million added jobs would be filled by the presently unemployed. Many of them would be filled by new entrants into the labor force, primarily previously nonworking part-time women workers (Olsson, 1987). Consequently, many researchers agree that the number of new jobs involved would not make a great impact on the overall level of unemployment (Bosanquet, 1985).

Finally, it should be recognized that technology is invading the services just as it did industry, as is described in chapter 5. In short, even if governments could afford the tremendous costs of training for the services for everyone who becomes unemployed, the unemployment rate will continue to rise as technology replaces human beings.

Helping the Permanently Unemployed

Increasingly, social workers will have to deal with people ready, willing, and able to work but for whom there simply are no jobs. At best, such people will live their working lives with part-time or temporary jobs, alternating with long periods of no work; at worst, they will never be able to find employment. For many of them, unemployment will be the norm and working will be a sporadic and uncertain activity (Schwartz & Neikirk, 1983). They will never achieve the ideal of permanent, full-time, decent-paying jobs under acceptable conditions.

Many of those working will be underemployed, doing part-time work for part-time salaries while both wanting and needing full-time work with its augmented income. And many of those working full-time will do so in jobs that pay so little that they become part of that most neglected portion of the population (insofar as social welfare programs are concerned)—the working poor.

Consequently, the traditional activities of social workers trying to help unemployed clients—motivating, training, helping clients find jobs or seeking jobs for them, and being supportive during periods of unemployment—will not only be useless, but irrelevant. Indeed, the unreal expectations and the consequent frustrations engendered by these activities will be counterproductive and therefore discouraged. Social workers will need to view unemployment, especially long-term and permanent unemployment, from a new perspective. Practitioners will have to learn to help clients live fulfilling lives despite their lack of jobs, to engage in satisfying activities, to not feel stigmatized, and to maintain positive self-images.

These tasks may be made somewhat more manageable because the diminishing role of human labor in society eventually will require radical changes in value systems. Work will be replaced as the major criterion of human worth by other activities and attributes. Simultaneously, structural changes will be required to distribute the resources of an automated economic system on a basis other than jobs held or work done. As Sherer (1987) said, "An answer must be found to bridge the gap between society's decreased need for manpower and the need that people have for work," especially when that need is economic. Despite the seeming difficulty of achieving these changes, some scenarios indicate that they may be attained more easily than first seems possible.

Social welfare systems will, of course, be part of these changes, as Bridge and Campling (1978) summarized:

> If the forecasts of . . . long-term technical displacement of labour are fulfilled and work plays a completely different part in our lives, the expectations of social work would also change radically. The British Association of Social Workers has said that the focus of social work will shift as society adjusts itself to cultural and technological changes which alter the pattern of living.

If the need for human labor were to be practically eliminated, the fear of a work disincentive from welfare payments would cease to guide welfare policies. Income-maintenance payments would be made on a basis other than work performed, perhaps through expansion of universal programs, or through the performance of other kinds of activities (Macarov, 1985a), or purely on the basis of need. In Smith's (1960) terms, one will be entitled to whatever welfare is necessary simply by virtue of being alive, as in the Israeli kibbutz. At a 1989 conference on work and nonwork held in Holland by the European Region of the International Council on Social Welfare, one of the resolutions adopted was to attempt to acquire payment for what has been termed "informal work"—housekeeping, taking care of children and elderly people, and so forth. In any case, it is clear that work cannot continue to be the sole pillar on which life is based. This represents a "very major development in society, involving alternative bases of status and self respect, alternative sources of friendship and fulfillment" (Prior, 1980).

However, during the interim period, the major activities engaging social welfare and social work will entail dealing with (1) the intensification of problems already associated with work; (2) difficulties arising from the shift to service jobs; and (3) a growing number of long-term and permanently unemployed clients. As Walker (1985) stated, "The effort to live with unemployment and redistribute jobs may be more extensive and radical than anything required for a return to full employment."

Dealing with the unemployed in a manner that removes the stigma of unemployment, that helps them apply their enforced leisure to satisfying ends, and that enables clients to find meaning in a life in which work plays little part is the emerging challenge to social work. Meeting that challenge will require social workers to undergo a wrenching reorientation concerning the meaning of work and life— a reorientation that will necessitate use of all the instruments of socialization currently used to prepare social workers for their profession.

REFERENCES

Ageing International. (1988). *15*, 42–43.

Aitkin, M., & Hage, J. (1966). Organizational alienation: A comparative analysis. *American Sociological Review, 31*, 497–507.

Albeda, W. (1983). *Social progress for world solidarity: Reflections on full employment.* Geneva: World Social Prospects Study Association.

American Association of Retired Persons. (1987). *AARP Bulletin, 28*, 13–14.

Anderson, N. (1964). *Dimensions of work: The sociology of a work culture.* New York: McKay.

Anthony, P. D. (1978). *The ideology of work.* London: Tavistock.

Argyris, C. (1959). The individual and the organization: An empirical test. *Administrative Science Quarterly, 4*, 145–167.

AuClaire, P. A. (1979a). Employment search decisions among AFDC recipients. *Social Work Research and Abstracts, 15*, 18–26.

AuClaire, P. A. (1979b). The mix of work and welfare among long-term AFDC recipients. *Social Service Review, 53*, 586–605.

Ayalew, S. (1982). Ethiopia: Time-budgeting for development. *World Health Forum, 3*, 129–131.

Baim, J. I. (1981). *Work alienation and its impact on political life: Case study of District Council 37 workers.* Unpublished doctoral dissertation, City University of New York, New York.

Barber, J. G. (1982). Unemployment and helplessness. *Australian Social Work, 35*, 3–10.

Bargal, D. (1981). Social values and social work: A developmental model. *Journal of Sociology and Social Welfare, 8,* 45–61.

Bargal, D., & Shamir, B. (1981). Personnel directors' and welfare officers' views of occupational welfare's role. *Social Work Papers, 19,* 56–64.

Barrington, J. (1976). Young and unemployed. *Australian Journal of Social Issues, 11,* 291–294.

Bell, D. (1978, Spring). The future that never was. *Public Interest,* p. 42.

Bernardo, R. M. (1971). *The theory of moral incentives in Cuba.* University: University of Alabama Press.

Best, F. (1973). *The future of work.* Englewood Cliffs, NJ: Prentice Hall.

Best, F. (1989). *Flexible life scheduling: Does the idea have a future?* Paper presented at 14th International Congress on Gerontology, Acapulco.

Beveridge, W. H. (1930). *Unemployment: A problem of industry.* London: Allen & Unwin.

Bevin, E. (ca. 1944). *My plan for 2,000,000 workless.* London: Victoria House Press.

Borrero, I. M. (1980a). Psychological and emotional impact of unemployment. *Journal of Sociology and Social Welfare, 7,* 916–934.

Borrero, I. M. (1980b). Toward a meaning of work. *Journal of Sociology and Social Welfare, 7,* 880–894.

Borrero, I. M. (1981). The price of unemployment and inflation and who pays. *Journal of Sociology and Social Welfare, 8,* 122–131.

Borthwick, J., & Diamond, C. T. P. (1980). Back on your feet and into the world: An interpretation of an educational program for unemployed youth (EPUY). *Australian Journal of Social Issues, 15,* 225–268.

Bosanquet, N. (1985). Welfare needs, welfare jobs and efficiency. In R. Klein & M. O'Higgins (Eds.), *The future of welfare.* Oxford: Basil Blackwell.

Bothmer, J. (1989). *First European network of unemployed people.* Utrecht, Netherlands: Samenwerkingsverband/Mensen Zonder Betaald Werk.

Bourne, B. (1982). Effects of ageing on work satisfaction, performance and motivation. *Ageing and Work, 5,* 37–47.

Braithwhite, J., & Biles, D. (1979). On being unemployed and being a victim of crime. *Australian Journal of Social Issues, 14,* 192–195.

Brayfield, A., & Crockett, W. (1955). Employee attitudes and employee performance. *Psychological Bulletin, 52,* 396–424.

Briar, K. H. (1980). Helping the unemployed client. *Journal of Sociology and Social Welfare, 7,* 895–906.

Briar, K. H. (1983). Unemployment: Toward a social work agenda. *Social Work, 28,* 211–215.

Briar, K. H. (1988). *Social work and the unemployed.* Silver Spring, MD: National Association of Social Workers.

Briar, K. H., Fiedler, D., Sheen, C., & Kamp, P. (1980). The impact of unemployment on young, middle age, and aged workers. *Journal of Sociology and Social Welfare, 7,* 907–915.

Bridge, B., & Campling, J. (1978). *Employment problems: The social work involvement*. Birmingham, England: British Association of Social Workers.

Buckingham, W. (1961). *Automation*. New York: Mentor.

Burghardt, S., & Fabricant, M. (1981). Reindustrialization and the future of social welfare. *Journal of Sociology and Social Welfare, 8*, 674–697.

Calloway, M. D. (1976). Men, machines and social security. *Black Aging, 1*, 20–22.

Canadian Council on Social Development. (1989). *The future of work: Consultation report*. Ottawa, Canada: Author.

Carey, A. (1967). The Hawthorne studies: A radical criticism. *American Sociological Review, 32*, 403–416.

Carey, J. L., & Otto, P. F. (1977). Output per unit of labor input in the retail food store industry. *Monthly Labor Review, 100*, 42–47.

Carnes, R. B. (1978). Laundry and cleaning services pressed to post productivity gains. *Monthly Labor Review, 101*, 38–42.

Cattell-Gordon, D. (1988). Don't socialize unemployment. *Social Work, 33*, 384.

Chambri, S. M. (1976). Welfare, work and family structure. *Social Work, 21*, 103–108.

Chrissinger, M. S. (1980). Factors affecting the employment of welfare mothers. *Social Work, 25*, 52–56.

Cnaan, R. A. (1987). The evolution of Israel's welfare state. In R. R. Friedmann, N. Gilbert, & M. Sherer (Eds.), *Modern welfare states: A comparative view of trends and prospects*. New York: New York University Press.

Coleman, M. (1985). Unemployment and the future of social policy. *Australian Journal of Social Issues, 20*, 3–11.

Cook, J. D., Hepworth, S. J., Toby, D., & Warr, P. B. (1981). *The experience of work*. New York: Academic.

Cooperman, D. (1989). Structural accounts of services. *International Journal of Sociology and Social Policy, 9*, 5–17.

Cunningham, R. L. (1964). *The philosophy of work*. New York: National Association of Manufacturers.

Danzinger, S., & Plotnick, R. (1978). Can welfare reform eliminate poverty? *Social Service Review, 53*, 244–260.

D'Arcy, C., Syrotuck, J., & Siddique, C. M. (1984). Perceived job attributes, job satisfaction and psychological distress: A comparison of men and women. *Human Relations, 37*, 603–611.

Duke, J. (1977). New car dealers experience a long-term gain in productivity. *Monthly Labor Review, 100*, 29–33.

Ensley, R. (1980). Full employment: An outmoded objective in a technological age. *Australian Journal of Social Issues, 15*, 277–282.

Fein, M. (1976). Motivation to work. In R. Dubin (Ed.), *Handbook of work, organization, and society*. Chicago: Rand McNally.

Field, F. (1977). Making sense of the unemployment figures. In F. Field (Ed.), *The conscript army*. London: Routledge & Kegan Paul.

Figueira-McDonough, J. (1978). Mental health among unemployed Detroiters. *Social Service Review, 52,* 382–399.

Flick, R. (1983). The new feminism and the world of work. *The Public Interest, 71,* 33–44.

Fopp, R. (1983). Unemployment, youth homelessness, and the allocation of family responsibility. *Australian Journal of Social Issues, 18,* 304–315.

Franke, R. H., & Kaul, J. D. (1978). The Hawthorne experiments: First statistical interpretation. *American Sociological Review, 43,* 623–643.

Fraser, T. M. (1983). *Human stress, work and job satisfactions*. Geneva: International Labour Office.

Freedman, D. H. (1983). Seeking a broader approach to employment and worklife in industrialised market-economy countries. *Labour and Society, 8,* 107–122.

Freud, S. (1958). *Civilization and its discontents*. New York: Paperback.

Garfinkle, S. H. (1977). The outcome of a spell of unemployment. *Monthly Labor Review, 100,* 54–57.

Garraty, J. A. (1978). *Unemployment in history: Economic thought and public policy*. New York: Harper & Row.

Garson, B. (1975). *All the livelong day: The meaning and demeaning of routine work*. Harmondsworth, England: Penguin.

Gartner, A., & Reissman, F. (1974). *The service society and the consumer vanguard*. New York: Harper & Row.

Gerard, D. (1978). Democracy—a fiction? *Social Service Quarterly, 52,* 24–27.

Gershuny, J. (1978). *After industrial society? The emerging self-service economy*. London: Macmillan.

Gersuny, C., & Rosengren, W. R. (1973). *The service society*. Cambridge, MA: Schenkman.

Glass, B. L. (1982). Comparing employed and unemployed welfare recipients: A discriminant analysis. *Journal of Sociology and Social Welfare, 9,* 19–36.

Glenn, E. L., & Feldberg, F. L. (1979). Proletarianizing clerical work: Technology and organizational control in the office. In A. Zimbalist (Ed.), *Case studies on the labor process*. New York: Monthly Labor Review Press.

Goldberg, S. (1989). The theory of patriarchy. *International Journal of Sociology and Social Policy, 9,* 15–62.

Gorz, A. (1982). *Farewell to the working class: An essay in post-industrial socialism*. Boston: South End Press.

Griffiths, D. (1974). *The waiting poor: An argument for abolition of the waiting period on unemployment and sickness benefits*. Fitzroy, Victoria, Australia: Brotherhood of Saint Laurence.

Griffiths, D. (1977). *Whither work*. Bundoora, Victoria, Australia: Preston Institute of Technology Press.

Gutek, B. (1980). The relative importance of intrapsychic determinants of job satisfaction. In K. D. Duncan, M. M. Gruneberg, & D. Wallis (Eds.), *Changes in working life*. Chichester, England: John Wiley & Sons.

Gyllenhammer, P., Harman, S., & Yankelovich, D. (1981). *Jobs in the 1980s and 1990s: Executive summary*. New York: Public Agenda Foundation.

Haavio-Mannila, I. (1971). Satisfaction with family, work, leisure and life among men and women. *Human Relations, 24*, 585–601.

Hall, K. (1984). How shall we ever get them back to work? *International Journal of Manpower, 5*, 24–32.

Halladay, A. (1980). Social work's response to unemployment: A time for decision. *Australian Social Work, 33*, 3–12.

Handles, Y., Apel, L., & Sagin, M. (1982). *Satisfactions of nurses at work*. Tel Aviv: General Federation of Labour. (Hebrew)

Hanlon, M. D. (1981). Determinants of primary group assistance during unemployment. *Journal of Sociology and Social Welfare, 8*, 623–639.

Hasenfeld, Y. (1975). The role of employment placement services in maintaining poverty. *Social Service Review, 49*, 569–587.

Herzberg, F. (1966). *Work and the nature of man*. Cleveland: World.

House of Lords Select Committee on Science and Technology. (1982). *Subcommittee II: Occupational health*. London: Her Majesty's Stationery Office.

House of Lords Select Committee on Unemployment. (1981). *Report of the House of Lords Select Committee on Unemployment*. London: Her Majesty's Stationery Office.

Howe, L. K. (1977). *Pink collar workers*. New York: Putnam.

Immerwahr, F. (1982). The future of the work ethic. In D. Macarov (Ed.), *People, work and human services in the future*. Garden City, NY: Adelphi University, School of Social Work.

International Herald Tribune. (1986, May 3–4).

International Labour Office. (1988). *Yearbook of labour statistics*. Geneva: Author.

Jallade, J. P. (1982). Central issues in part-time work. In L. Bekeman (Ed.), *The organization of working time*. Maastricht, Holland: European Centre for Work and Society.

Jenkins, C., & Sherman, B. (1979). *The collapse of work*. London: Methuen.

Jones, B. (1982). *Sleepers, wake! Technology and the future of work*. London: Oxford University Press.

Kanter, R. M., & Stein, B. A. (Eds.). (1979). *Life in organizations: Workplaces as people experience them*. New York: Basic Books.

Kaplan, M. (1975). *Leisure: Theory and policy*. New York: John Wiley & Sons.

Kaplinsky, R. (1987). *Micro-electronics and employment revisited: A review*. Geneva: International Labour Office.

Katz, R. C. (1963). *Empathy: Its nature and uses.* New York: Free Press.

Keefe, T. (1984). Alienation and social work practice. *Social Casework, 65,* 145–153.

Kendrick, J. W. (1979). Productivity trends and the recent slowdown. In W. E. Fellner (Ed.), *Contemporary economic problems.* Washington, DC: American Enterprise Institute.

Klein, M. J., Greist, J. H., & van Cura, L. J. (1975). Computer psychiatry. *Archives of General Psychiatry, 32,* 837–843.

Klein, R., & O'Higgins, M. (1985). *The future of welfare.* Oxford: Basil Blackwell.

Kogut, A., & Aron, S. (1980). Toward a full employment policy: An overview. *Journal of Sociology and Social Welfare, 7,* 85–99.

Koller, K., Godsden, S., & Wade, R. (1980). Youth unemployment: Observations of the community youth support scheme. *Australian Journal of Social Issues, 15,* 148–155.

Koller, K., Wade, R., & Godsden, S. (1980). Youth employment: The special case of young women. *Australian Journal of Social Issues, 15,* 43–48.

Kraft, P. (1979). The industrialization of computer programming: From programming to 'software revolution.' In A. Zimbalist (Ed.), *Case studies on the labor process.* New York: Monthly Labor Review Press.

Kranzberg, M., & Gies, J. (1975). *By the sweat of thy brow.* New York: Putnam.

Krystal, E., Moran-Sackett, M., Thompson, S. V., & Cantoni, L. (1983). Serving the unemployed. *Social Casework, 64,* 67–76.

Kuman, K. (1984). Unemployment as a problem in the development of industrial societies: The English experience. *Sociological Review, 32,* 184–233.

Kumpke, T. (1986). *Works organization in the post-industrial company.* Paper delivered at the conference on New Technologies and the Future of Work. Maastricht, Holland: European Centre for Work and Society.

Lasson, K. (1971). *The workers.* New York: Grossman.

Lawler, E. E. III, & Porter, L. W. (1971). The effects of performance on job satisfaction. In G. A. Yukl & K. Wexley (Eds.), *Readings in organizational and industrial psychology.* New York: Oxford University Press.

Leon, C. B. (1981). Employed but not at work: A review of unpaid absences. *Monthly Labor Review, 104,* 18–22.

Leontief, W., & Duchin, F. (1984). *The impacts of automation on employment, 1963–2000.* New York: New York University, Institute for Economic Analysis.

Levinson, A. (1980). *The full employment alternative.* New York: Coward, McCann & Geoghehan.

Levinson, H., Price, C. R., Munden, K. J., Mandl, H. J., & Solley, C. M. (1962). *Men, management and mental health.* Cambridge, MA: Harvard University Press.

Levinson, R. W., & Hayne, K. S. (1984). *Accessing human services: International perspectives.* Beverly Hills, CA: Sage.

Levy, F. (1988, May 1). Income distribution. *New York Times.*

Lewis, A. (1986). *Vocational training: Education as an investment.* Paper delivered at experts' meeting on new technologies and the future of work. Maastricht, Holland: European Centre for Work and Society.

Locke, E. A. (1976). The nature and causes of job satisfaction. In M. D. Dunnette (Ed.), *Handbook of industrial and organizational psychology.* Chicago: Rand McNally.

Loftus, D. F. (n.d.). *Early retirement policies and practices in the United States: Implications for midlife workers.* Washington, DC: American Association of Retired Persons, Worker Equity Department.

Lowenthal, M. D. (1976/1977). Government spending and welfare employment. *Journal of Sociology and Social Welfare, 4,* 1203–1233.

Lurie, I. (1978). Work requirements in income-conditioned transfer programs. *Social Service Review, 52,* 551–566.

Macarov, D. (1970). The concept of empathy and the educational process. *Applied Social Studies, 2,* 107–113.

Macarov, D. (1972). A test of the two-factor theory of work motivation in an Israeli kibbutz. *Personnel Psychology, 25,* 121–124.

Macarov, D. (1976). Reciprocity between self-actualization and hard work. *International Journal of Social Economics, 3,* 39–44.

Macarov, D. (1977). Social welfare as a by-product: The effect of neo-mercantilism. *Journal of Sociology and Social Welfare, 4,* 1135–1144.

Macarov, D. (1978a). *The design of social welfare.* New York: Holt, Rinehart, & Winston.

Macarov, D. (1978b). Empathy: The charismatic chimera. *Journal of Education for Social Work, 14,* 86–92.

Macarov, D. (1980). *Work and welfare: The unholy alliance.* Beverly Hills, CA: Sage.

Macarov, D. (1981). Humanizing the workplace as squaring the circle. *International Journal of Manpower, 2,* 6–14.

Macarov, D. (1982). *Worker productivity: Myth and reality.* Beverly Hills, CA: Sage.

Macarov, D. (1984). The concept of employment in social welfare programs: The need for change in concept and practice. *Journal of Sociology and Social Welfare, 11,* 1–24.

Macarov, D. (1985a). The prospect of work in the western context. In H. F. Didsbury, Jr. (Ed.), *The global economy: Today, tomorrow and the transition.* Bethesda, MD: World Future Society.

Macarov, D. (1985b). Planning for a probability: The almost-workless world. *International Labour Review, 123,* 629–642; also appears as Un monde quasiment sans travail: Comment s'y preparer, *Futuribles, 104,* 15–36; also appears as La planificacion para un mundo casi exento de trabajo, *GRUPCAIXA Magazine, 11,* 62–68.

Macarov, D. (1986). *The service society: Knowledge, ignorance, hopes and fears.* Paper delivered at the Fourth World Congress, International Society for Social Economics, Toronto.

Macarov, D. (1987). Changing values of work and leisure. *European Journal of Education, 22*, 233–246.

Macarov, D. (1988a). The world of work revisited. In J. S. Eaton (Ed.), *Colleges of choice: The enabling impact of the community college.* New York: ACE/Macmillan.

Macarov, D. (1988b). Reevaluation of unemployment. *Social Work, 33,* 23–28.

Macarov, D. (1988c). Quitting time: The end of work. *International Journal of Sociology and Social Policy, 8,* 1–181.

Macarov, D., & Yanay, U. (1982). Use of the task force in the human services: A documented experience. *Administration in Social Work, 6,* 29–35.

Machlowitz, M. M. (1981). *Workaholics: Living with them, working with them.* New York: Mentor.

Madonia, J. F. (1983). The trauma of unemployment and its consequences. *Social Casework, 64,* 482–496.

Manpower Service Commission. (1978). Manpower service commission review and plan. London: Author.

Mark, J. A. (1982). Measuring productivity in service industries. *Monthly Labor Review, 105,* 3–8.

Marsden, D. (1982). *Workless.* London: Croom Helm.

Maslow, A. H. (1954). *Motivation and personality.* New York: Harper & Row.

Maurer, H. (1978). *Not working: An oral history of the unemployed.* New York: Holt, Rinehart, & Winston.

Mayo, E. (1933). *The human problems of an industrial civilization.* New York: Viking.

McCarthy, E., & McGaughey, W. (1989). *Nonfinancial economics: The case for shorter hours of work.* New York: Praeger.

McGill, M. E. (1985). *Keeping it all inside: Male intimacy.* New York: Holt, Rinehart, & Winston.

Meller, Y., & Macarov, D. (1985). Studying satisfactions in human service organizations: An exploration. *International Journal of Sociology and Social Policy, 5,* 1–15.

Mendelssohn, K. (1977). *The riddle of the pyramids.* London: Sphere.

Ministry of Health. (1988). *How to avoid heart disease.* Jerusalem: Author.

Ministry of Labour. (1989). *The labour market and labour market policy in Sweden.* Stockholm: Author.

Monthly Labor Review. (1979). *102,* 107.

Monthly Labor Review. (1988). *111,* 71–73.

Moos, M. (1983). The training myth: A critique of the government's response to youth unemployment and its impact on further education. In D. Gleeson (Ed.), *Youth training and the search for work.* London: Routledge & Kegan Paul.

Morris, R., & Murphy, R. (1950). The situs dimension in occupational literature. *American Sociological Review, 23,* 231–239.

Moss, J. A. (1982). Unemployment among Black youth: A policy dilemma. *Social Work, 27,* 47–52.

Moss, M. (1979). Welfare dimensions of productivity measurement. In *Measurement and interpretation of productivity*. Washington, DC: National Academy of Sciences.

Neider, L. L. (1980). An experimental field investigation utilizing an expectancy theory view of participation. *Organizational Behavior and Human Performance, 26*, 425–448.

Neikrug, S. M. (1982). Meaning in work: Toward a clinical approach to work dissatisfaction. *Journal of Sociology and Social Welfare, 9*, 134–139.

Newland, K. (1982). *Productivity: The new economic context*. Washington, DC: Worldwatch Institute.

New York Times. (1986, July 22).

New York Times. (1988a, March 31). p. A18.

New York Times. (1988b, April 29). p. A38.

New York Times. (1988c, May 29). p. A22.

New York Times. (1988d, April 6). p. A23.

New York Times. (1988e, April 18). p. A37.

New York Times. (1989, October 26). p. A12.

New York Times. (1991, February 3). p. 8IE.

Nichols, A. C. (1979). Why welfare mothers work: Implications for employment and training services. *Social Service Review, 53*, 378–391.

Norman, C. (1980). *Microelectronics at work: Productivity and jobs in the world economy*. Washington, DC: Worldwatch Institute.

The Nurses' Almanac. (1978). Germantown, MD: Aspen.

Office of Strategic Services. (1947). *Assessment of men*. Washington, DC: Author.

Olmsted, B. (1985). 'V-time' pleases employees, helps employers cut costs. *World of Work Report, 10*, 3.

Olsson, S. (1987). Towards a transformation of the Swedish welfare state. In R. R. Friedmann, N. Gilbert, & M. Sherer (Eds.), *Modern welfare states: A comparative view of trends and prospects*. New York: New York University Press.

Opinion Research Corporation. (1977). *National executive briefing on changing work values in America*. New York: Author.

Pahl, R. E. (1984). *Divisions of labour*. Oxford: Basil Blackwell.

Park, M. (1987, November 15). *London Times*, p. 71.

Parnes, H. S. (Ed.). (1983). *Policy issues in work and retirement*. Kalamazoo, MI: Upjohn.

Patruchev, V. A. (1977). The problem of organizing spare time of society in conditions of the scientific and technological revolution. In M. R. Haug & J. Dofny (Eds.), *Work and technology*. Beverly Hills, CA: Sage.

Pearson, R. (1982). Personnel planning: The importance of the labour market. In G. Mensch & R. J. Niehaus (Eds.), *Work, organization and technological change*. New York: Plenum.

Peel, M. (1981). Clive's kids: An employment scheme for unemployable youth. *Australian Journal of Social Issues, 16*, 315–322.

Pelletier, K. R. (1983, September 8). The hidden hazards of the modern office. *New York Times*.

Petty, J. (1987, December 5). *Daily Telegraph* (London), p. 4.

Pines, A., & Kafry, D. (1978). Occupational tedium in the social services. *Social Work, 23*, 499–507.

Platt, S. (1987). *Unemployment and parasuicide*. Paper delivered at annual meeting, British Association for the Advancement of Science, Belfast.

Price, C. R. (1971). *New directions in the world of work*. Kalamazoo, MI: Upjohn.

Prior, J. (1980). Quoted by R. Grover in *Work and the community*. London: Bedford Square Press.

Puckett, T. C., & Frederico, M. (1988). Part-time workers in welfare: Who wins, who loses, and why? *Australian Journal of Social Issues, 23*, 50–62.

Rada, J. (1980). *The impact of micro-electronics*. Geneva: International Labour Office.

Raines, H. (1988, April 19). Britain's bitter debate: Will welfare state perish? *New York Times*, p. A6.

Raskin, A. H. (1980). Toward a more participative work force. In C. S. Sheppard & D. C. Carroll (Eds.), *Working in the twenty-first century*. New York: John Wiley & Sons.

Reich, R. B. (1983). An industrial policy for the right. *The Public Interest, 7*, 3–17.

Rein, Martin. (1985). Women, employment and social welfare. In R. Klein & M. O'Higgins (Eds.), *The future of welfare*. Oxford: Basil Blackwell.

Rein, Mildred. (1982). Work in welfare: Past failures and future strategies. *Social Service Review, 56*, 438–447.

Richardson, J., & Henning, R. (1984). Policy responses to unemployment: Symbolic or placebo responses? In J. Richardson & R. Henning (Eds.), *Unemployment: Policy responses of western democracies*. London: Sage.

Rizzo, C., Reynolds, I., & Gallagher, H. (1981). Job satisfaction: A study of Sydney adults. *Australian Journal of Social Issues, 16*, 138–148.

Robinson, J. P. (1969). Occupational norms and differences in job satisfaction: A summary of survey research evidence. In J. P. Robinson, R. Athanasiou, & K. B. Head (Eds.), *Measures of occupational attitudes and occupational characteristics*. Ann Arbor: University of Michigan.

Roe, A. (1956). *The psychology of occupations*. New York: John Wiley & Sons.

Rosenman, Z. S. (1979). Unemployment of women: A social policy issue. *Social Work, 24*, 20–25.

Roy, D. F. (1976). Banana time: Job satisfaction and informal interaction. In R. M. Kanter & B. A. Stein (Eds.), *Life in organizations: Workplaces as people experience them*. New York: Basic Books.

Rubin, L. B. (1976). *Worlds of pain: Life in the working class family*. New York: Basic Books.

Ruch, F. L. (1937). *Psychology and life*. New York: Scott, Foresman.

Russel, R. A. (1986). *Winning the future*. New York: Carroll & Graf.

Ryan, W. (1974). Blaming the victim: Ideology serves the establishment. In P. Roby (Ed.), *The poverty establishment.* Englewood Cliffs, NJ: Prentice Hall.

Salmon, H. (1983). *Unemployment: Government schemes and alternatives.* London: Association of Community Workers.

Schrank, R. (1978). *Ten thousand working days.* Cambridge, MA: MIT Press.

Schwartz, G. G., & Neikirk, W. (1983). *The work revolution.* New York: Rawson.

Sethuraman, S. V. (1985). Basic needs and the informal sector: The case of low-income housing in developing countries. *Habitat International, 9,* 299–316.

Shamir, B. (1980). Between service and servility: Role conflict in subordinate service roles. *Human Relations, 33,* 741–756.

Shapira, M. (1990). Computerized decision technology improves decision practice in social service: Decision support system in youth probation service. *International Journal of Sociology and Social Policy, 10*(6/7/8), 138–164.

Shelp, R. K. (1981). *Beyond industrialization: Ascendency of the global service society.* New York: Praeger.

Sherer, M. (1987). Welfare states: An overview of trends and prospects. In R. R. Friedmann, N. Gilbert, & M. Sherer (Eds.), *Modern welfare states: A comparative view of trends and prospects.* New York: New York University Press.

Sherraden, M. (1988). *Full employment is both feasible and desirable.* Paper delivered at the North American Conference on Employment and Unemployment, Adelphi University, Garden City, NY.

Sherraden, M., & Adamek, M. E. (1984). Explosive imagery and misguided policy. *Social Service Review, 58,* 539–555.

Shostak, A. B. (1980). *Blue-collar stress.* Reading, MA.: Addison-Wesley.

Sicron, M. (1986). *How many unemployed are there in Israel?* Paper delivered at annual meeting of Israel Industrial Relations Research Association, Bar-Ilan University, Ramat Gan, Israel.

Simmons, J. (1984). When quality circles fail. *World of Work Report, 9,* 5.

Smith, A. D. (1960). *The right to life.* Chapel Hill: University of North Carolina Press.

Smith, P. C., Kendall, L. M., & Hulin, C. L. (1969). *The measurement of satisfactions in work and retirement: A strategy for the study of attitudes.* Chicago: Rand McNally.

Social Security Bulletin. (1990). 53(3), 60.

Soothill, K. B. (1976). The effort involved in finding employment for white-collar offenders. *British Journal of Social Work, 6,* 449–463.

Sparks, L. (1984). Retail employment in the current recession. *International Journal of Manpower, 5,* 3–10.

Stanback, H. J. (1980). The political economy of unemployment. *Journal of Sociology and Social Welfare, 7,* 870–879.

Stellman, J. (1982). *Human and public health aspects of telecommunications.* Paper delivered at Fourth General Assembly, World Future Society, Washington, DC.

Stewart, B., Hetherington, G., & Smith, M. (1984). *British Telecom survey item bank*. Bradford, England: MCB Universities Press.

Strauss, G. (1980). Book review. *American Journal of Sociology, 85,* 1467–1469.

Sunley, R., & Sheek, G. W. (1986). *Serving the unemployed and their families*. Milwaukee: Family Service Association.

Super, D. (1957). *The psychology of careers*. New York: Harper.

Taggart, R. (Ed.). (1977). *Job creation: What works?* Salt Lake City: Olympus.

Temkin, A. (1989, May 12). Unemployment is making a comeback. *Jerusalem Post*, p. 15.

Terkel, S. (1972). *Working*. New York: Random House.

Terkel, S. (1980). *American dreams: Lost and found*. New York: Ballantine.

Thurow, L. C. (1981). *The zero-sum society: Distribution and the possibilities for economic change*. Harmondsworth, England: Penguin.

Tiggeman, M., & Winefield, A. H. (1980). Some psychological effects of unemployment on school leavers. *Australian Journal of Social Issues, 15,* 269–276.

Tikhonov, A. (1977). The content and organization of work as specific factors in the process of formulation of attitudes to work (Quoted in V. A. Yadov & A. A. Kissel, Job satisfaction: Analysis of empirical data and attempt at their theoretical interpretation). In M. R. Haug & J. Dofny (Eds.), *Work and technology*. Beverly Hills, CA: Sage.

Tomer, P. (1985). Public sector and private sector employment programs as competing solutions to unemployment. *Australian Journal of Social Issues, 20,* 56–71.

Toomey, G. B. (1980). Work ethic and work incentives: Values and income maintenance reform. *Journal of Sociology and Social Welfare, 7,* 148–160.

Travers, P. (1985). Unemployment and the downward trail. *Australian Journal of Social Issues, 20,* 12–22.

Tyrell, R., & Shanks, M. (1982). Long-term unemployment: Why it is a problem and what we can do about it. In *Work and society*. Brighton, England: Institute for Manpower Studies.

Uchitelle, L. (1988a, March 16). Reliance on temporary jobs hints at economic fragility. *New York Times*, p. 1.

Uchitelle, L. (1988b, May 1). Pensions and other benefits erode. *New York Times*, p. F25.

United Nations. (1988). *Statistical yearbook 1985/86*. New York: Author.

U.S. Department of Commerce. (1987). *Statistical abstract of the United States 1988*. Washington, DC: Author.

U.S. Department of Health and Human Services. (1986). *Social Security programs throughout the world—1986*. Washington, DC: Author.

U.S. Department of Health, Education, and Welfare (1981). *Sourcebook of nursing personnel*. Washington, DC: Author.

U.S. Department of Health, Education, and Welfare. (1982). *Social Security programs throughout the world—1982*. Washington, DC: Author.

Verduyn, J. (1989). *Work and non-work: Summary of exposé for participants in the 15th European symposium of the International Council on Social Welfare*. IJmuiden, Holland: Hoogovens Groep.

Vu, M. T. (1985). *World population projections 1985*. Baltimore: Johns Hopkins University Press.

Walbank, M. (1980). Effort in motivated work behaviour. In K. D. Duncan, M. M. Gruneberg, & D. Wallis (Eds.), *Changes in working life*. Chichester, England: John Wiley & Sons.

Walfish, B. (1979). Job satisfaction declines in major aspects of work, says Michigan study. *World of Work Report, 4*, 9.

Walker, A. (1985). Policies for sharing the job shortage: Reducing or redistributing work? In R. Klein & M. O'Higgins (Eds.), *The future of welfare*. Oxford: Basil Blackwell.

Weeks, W. (1980). Shorter working hours give working parents an alternative to traditional patterns of employment. *Canadian Journal of Social Work Education, 6*, 25–41.

Weizenbaum, J. (1976). *Computer power and human reason: From judgment to calculation*. San Francisco: Freeman.

Windshuttle, K. (1981). *Unemployment: A social political analysis of the economic crisis in Australia*. Harmondsworth, England: Penguin.

World of Work Report. (1979). 4, 29.

World of Work Report. (1980). 5, 52.

World of Work Report. (1984). 9, 8.

World of Work Report. (1985) 10, 8.

Yankelovich, D., & Immerwahr, J. (1983). *Putting the work ethic to work*. New York: Public Agenda Foundation.

Yankelovich, D., Zettenberg, H., Strumpel B., & Shanks, M. (1983). *Work and human values: An international report on jobs in the 1980s and 1990s*. New York: Aspen Institute.

Zetterburg, H., & Frankel, G. (1983). The changing work ethic in Sweden (Quoted by R. M. Greve & A. Gladstone). In D. Gaudart, R. M. Greve, & A. Gladstone (Eds.), *Changing perceptions of work in industrialized countries: The effect on and implications for industrial relations*. Geneva: International Institute for Labour Studies.

Zimbalist, A. (Ed.). (1979). *Case studies on the labor process*. New York: Monthly Labor Review Press.

5

Technology's Ongoing Development

Early in the 19th century, a bill was proposed to the British Parliament that the patent office be closed, because everything conceivable had already been invented. There is no more reason now than there was then to believe technology has run its course. The reasons for the continued growth of technology are deeply rooted in individual and societal needs and desires, and there is very little chance of technological change coming to a halt or even slowing down. Consequently, the implications of future technology for social work require examination.

Changes in technology cause great shifts in societal situations and, therefore, the matters with which social work deals. One might cite as an example the effect of improved safety measures and devices in industry, which reduce the number of accident victims needing help, and, conversely, the growth in the number of fatalities and injuries from traffic accidents as vehicles have become faster and more numerous. Similarly, smallpox with all its attendant problems has been eliminated through easily administered vaccinations, but the number of AIDS victims has increased through similar blood bank and blood transfusion techniques.

THE HISTORY OF TECHNOLOGY

Technology is coeval with human existence. The first person who picked up a stick to reach a piece of hanging fruit was making use of technology. When animal power augmented human power, and

129

when mechanical and electrical power took the place of most animal power, these were technological changes. In fact, from before the invention of the wheel to whatever was invented this morning, the march of technology has been continuous and inexorable. As with many other overarching concepts, however, there are difficulties in arriving at a universally applicable, generally accepted definition of technology, because it arises in different contexts and is used for different purposes. For example, one dictionary published just 25 years ago defines technology as "the sum of ways in which a social group provide themselves with the material objects of their civilization" (*Random House Dictionary*, 1966)—a definition that does not distinguish between human effort and mechanical devices. For heuristic reasons, therefore, technology is defined here as changes in methods, machines, materials, and energy that result in quantitative and qualitative changes in the production of material goods and services.

There are at least four major reasons for the invention and application of technology: (1) simplifying work, (2) increasing production, (3) reducing costs, and (4) overcoming obstacles.

Simplifying Work

The first impulse toward technology was probably a desire to make work easier. There is a good deal of evidence that earlier humans did not see production as a goal in itself. Other than satisfying their own immediate needs, there was no sense in producing a surplus. In the absence of roads, storerooms, markets, and a money economy, surplus goods would just rot, so any improvement in methods was based almost entirely upon a desire to lighten the burden of work. In the third century, Diocletian required sons to follow their fathers' occupations, since they were wont to look for easier work (Kranzberg & Gies, 1975). Even as late as the 18th century, laborers did not desire income beyond a certain level, preferring leisure to increased income (Kuman, 1984). Hence, Adam Smith, the economist, anticipating modern technology, found in his investigation of a pin factory that "A great part of the machines . . . were originally the invention of common workmen who . . . naturally turned their thoughts to finding out easier and readier methods of performing [their jobs]" (Mazlish, 1961). Indeed, part of the rationale for so-called "worker participation" or "joint decision making" in industry today is the assumption that the person doing the actual job will find the easiest way to get the work done (Cummings & Molloy, 1977).

History supports the search for easier work as one basis for technological change. For example, the beginnings of automation, or cybernation, came about because of the desire of a 12-year-old boy to avoid onerous work. In 1713 in Britain, Thomas Newcomen invented a steam engine to draw water from mine pits. But since the pressure in the engine could rise to dangerous heights, Newcomen hired 12-year-old Humphrey Potter to open a valve when the pressure reached a certain point and to close it when the pressure dropped. Soon growing bored with this task, young Potter rigged up an ingenious device that caused the valve to open by itself as the pressure rose and to close when it dropped—in short, one of the first self-regulating machines (Wilson, 1960).

Technology has succeeded in relieving human beings of much of the physically difficult work that required large inputs of human energy. One hundred years ago, people used about 13 percent of their total energy in work, whereas today they use less than 1 percent (Ministry of Health, 1988). Even on the job, it is estimated that people use less than half of their potential ability (Walbank, 1980). Certainly, few people today work as long or as hard as their grandparents did. In this respect, technology has eased the human condition.

Increasing Production

With the onset of the Industrial Revolution, however, when most people began working for others, the ease of workers was no longer a salient factor, because the emphasis was on production. Technology then began to be used mainly to produce more goods and services without hiring more people. The productivity of the individual worker began to rise as he or she activated mechanical devices. This rise was not caused by people working harder, or even better. As former AFL-CIO president Lane Kirkland (1982) said, "If efficiency depended on human labor, we would have reached the peak of efficiency in the building of the pyramids."

The success of technology in increasing production and productivity is evidenced by the fact that throughout the West today almost nothing is in short supply because of lack of productive capacity. In fact, production is held down to the level of expected sales; when more demand is anticipated, production is easily increased. Take another example: 200 years ago, one farmer produced enough food for three people; today, primarily because of the use of technology, that ratio is 1 to 57 (U.S. Department of Agriculture, 1976). On the average, and over the long term, productivity in the West increases at about 2.5 percent per year, which amounts to more than 30 percent in 10 years (United Nations, 1988). The reason for increased productivity is clearly technology; people simply do not work 30 percent harder than they did 10 years ago.

Reducing Costs

The third impetus for technological change is the desire to reduce costs, which, of course, is expected to result in increased profits. An industry that manufactures 1 million units per year, whether automobiles, refrigerators, or computers, makes an additional $1 million in profit each time it manages to cut construction costs $1 a unit. Because social and political pressures do not allow employers to continue reducing salaries indefinitely, or even to hold them constant, the solution lies in using new methods, machines, or materials to cut costs. Despite their initial costs, machines can produce goods more inexpensively than humans can, especially in countries with the relatively high standards of living that result from relatively high salaries.

Machines can operate 24 hours a day, every day of the year; never strike, dawdle, come late, or leave early; never get tired, bored, or vengeful; can be speeded up without resistance; perform with the same accuracy at the end of a run as at the beginning; have prodigious memories; and perform extremely intricate operations. Such "workers" are highly desired in many areas of industry and services, especially when they prove less expensive than human workers. In a profit-motivated economy, a machine that costs less to employ than humans eventually comes into use.

Overcoming Obstacles

Finally, technology does tasks and solves problems that human beings alone cannot handle. Space flight was impossible until the invention of computers to do the necessary calculations, and the creation of metals capable of withstanding heats and pressures hitherto irresistible was delayed until the machinery necessary to make them was available. Similarly, many surgical procedures today were unthinkable until the invention of certain technology. The promises of superconductivity and room-temperature fusion energy, to name but two, are completely dependent upon solving the technological problems involved.

All of these historical reasons—the desire to simplify work, to produce more, to cut costs, and to solve the hitherto insoluble—exist today. Therefore, it is inevitable that technology will continue to be developed and used.

THE IMPACT OF TECHNOLOGY ON SOCIETY

Technology is amoral. It is neither good nor bad. It is completely dependent upon human users for its application, and humans make judgments concerning its results. These results are profound and widespread. However, perhaps due to the relative novelty of some areas of technology, such as information technology, the implications of societal changes resulting from these inventions have hardly begun to be investigated on either a theoretical or an empirical basis (Nelson, 1989). Indeed, there is said to be "an empirical vacuum of startling proportions on the social consequences of technology" (Fischer, 1985).

However, some effects of technology that have implications for social work can be documented. The format used here is that adopted by the Working Group on the Impact of Technology at the 15th European Symposium on Social Welfare, which met in Holland in 1989. Recognizing the primacy of work in much of human activity and in societies, that group concentrated on the impact of technology on the economic and social aspects of work. Further recognizing that not only does work influence nonwork activities, but that technology also has a decided impact on the nonwork areas of life, the latter was also examined in terms of its economic and social implications.

Effects on the Economy

Improved Products and Services. One of the most visible results of technology is the production of more and better products and services. The continuing growth in productivity and in production is due primarily to changes in methods, machines, materials, and energy, not changes in human behavior or work patterns. For example, efforts to increase productivity by making changes in methods of supervision or by changing the makeup of the work group or the methods by which the work group is organized may lead to differences in productivity of 7 to 15 percent, but changes in methods of working themselves can lead to increases ranging from 20 to 200 percent (Sutermeister, 1976). When productivity increases, human effort accounts for only 10 to 25 percent of the increase; technology, however, accounts for 75 to 90 percent (Walbank, 1980).

Further, a study of the effect of technology on the American economy found that technology alone accounted for 54.5 percent of the growth in the national economy per employed person, with capital investment, education, research and development, and changes in energy sources all playing a part in the remainder. Since World War II, the contribution of technology to economic growth has been four times greater than that of business investment, 2.8 times greater than investment in education, and 3.8 times higher than improvements from more efficient use of resources. Without technology, the growth rate of the postwar economy would have been cut in half (Wilson, 1980).

Direct production is not the only beneficiary of technology. Management is one of the greatest beneficiaries of information technology. Current professional literature regarding management is so devoted to new uses of communication technology for improvement that one wonders how management possibly functioned previously. Computer-aided decision making, computer-generated decisions, record keeping, information retrieval, inventory control, monitoring, and dissemination of information, to name a few, have all been improved and speeded up. For example, the facsimile machine—the fastest growing of all recent inventions—has enormously speeded up communications, especially pictorial information, handwritten memos, signed contracts, charts, pictures, annotated memos, and so forth.

In the services, too, decision making can be improved, and the decisions can be more objective, more standardized or individualized, better recorded, and more quickly disseminated and carried out. Coordination between and collaboration with other agencies may be quicker and fuller, and evaluation of results may be achieved in more depth and with greater objectivity. Information technology contains two unique features. One is the unprecedented rate of improvement, which is about a 10-fold increase in capacity every five years, and the second is its great impact on the service sector (Organization for Economic and Cultural Development, 1981).

In addition, the computer fulfills many of Weber's (1952) prescriptions for beneficial bureaucracy, without the pathologies that creep in when bureaucracy is left to humans. The computer keeps records; provides continuity; makes decisions objectively, uninfluenced by power, prestige, or outside influence; and treats clients alike. The computer is immune to the inherent malaise of every bureaucracy: that the reward for making proper decisions is not commensurate with the punishment for making wrong decisions. In such a no-win situation, the human bureaucrat has a tendency to avoid making decisions by putting them off; inventing difficulties; or passing them on to a colleague, a superior, or a subordinate. The computer has no such inhibitions (Remus, 1986). Consequently, the computer has been found to be superior to human beings in certain decision-making situations.

Cheaper Products and Services.   Not only has technology increased productivity, it has also reduced costs. A set of office transactions that cost $1.25 in 1956 can now be done for a small fraction of a cent, for example (*World of Work Report*, 1985b). To produce a single page of text might take a hand compositor 22 hours, a machine compositor 5.5 hours, a teletypesetting unit 1.3 hours, and an electronically controlled photocomposing machine only 15 seconds (Jones, 1982). Such instances could be repeated almost indefinitely.

Not all of the savings made possible by technology are passed on to the consumer. Much goes back into capital investment, profits, taxes, and so forth. In the final analysis, however, it is because of technology that the populations of the most industrialized countries enjoy a standard of living undreamed of in nonindustrialized countries. And technology has the possibility of making technologically advanced countries more competitive in world markets.

Increased Employment Opportunities for Marginal Groups.
The introduction of technology into the workplace has increased employment opportunities for formerly restricted groups, such as those
suffering from various kinds of disabilities and those subject to environmental restraints, such as mothers of small children. It has also
paved the way for employment of semi-literate people. In some cases
this is true of repetitive work, inspection and monitoring tasks, and
areas of narrow responsibility. However, it has also opened up supervisory, management, and executive possibilities that such groups
were formerly barred from, through use of computer-aided decision
making, computer-aided designs, simplified communication methods, and so on.

As technology grows, the economy becomes less dependent on
demographic indicators such as prime-age workers, disadvantaged
groups (such as new immigrants—legal and illegal), previous birth
rates, married versus unmarried workers (especially women), and
other indicators. Technology also offers workers the opportunity for
more job mobility, because technological skills often are exportable
from one area to another.

Not all of the implications of technology for the world of work are
positive, of course. For example, the dependence of industry and
services on technology, rather than on human workers, tends to make
workers less necessary and therefore depresses their pay levels. This
is particularly true as technology makes part-time and temporary work
more feasible. And, as pointed out in chapter 4, rising levels of long-
term and permanent unemployment are largely attributable to the
growth of technology.

In addition, technology generally requires relatively large initial in-
vestments, which militate against the type of small enterprises that
some commentators advocate as solutions to unemployment. In this
vein, it is also true that technology often requires more technology.
New improvements, new capabilities, and new possibilities require
that technology be replaced, or at least updated, relatively frequently.

Effects on the Job

Making Work Easier.   Technology often begins with those jobs
that are difficult, dangerous, dirty, or demeaning—in short, the jobs
humans tend to avoid. One area in which this can be seen is in the
reduction of pure physical energy required in many jobs. The auto-
matic concrete-mixing truck, with its long hose to deliver mixed concrete wherever needed, replaces the wheelbarrow full of hand-mixed
cement sent to the top of a building on an elevator, which in turn
replaces the buckets on ropes and tackle pulled by humans, which
replaces the person laboriously climbing a ladder with a small load

of concrete. In many places, even the concrete mixer is being phased out by prefabricated units.

Garbage collectors may no longer lift garbage containers up to dump them into trucks. In many cities today, garbage trucks automatically connect to waste containers, pick them up, empty them, and return them, while the driver and helper hardly soil their white uniforms. These instances can be repeated indefinitely, for one of the contributions of technology to the human condition has been to remove the premium once placed upon physical strength, with its concomitant feature—human tiredness or exhaustion from work.

In addition to removing the emphasis on strength, technology has relieved human workers of difficult tasks (Glenn & Feldberg, 1979; Kraft, 1979; Zimbalist, 1979). In automobile factories, for example, the first use of robots is usually to weld and paint hard-to-get-at corners and parts that cause difficulty for human workers. Nor is use of technology confined to physical difficulty. Complicated statistical computations, problematic equations, perpetual inventory control, simulations, multivariate comparisons, and other complicated mental jobs that caused headaches for generations of white-collar workers now are done easily by computers.

Making Work Safer.   Further, work safety records indicate that jobs today are much safer than they were in the past. Built-in "fail safe" devices, better engineering and construction, activities that are mechanically or electronically confined to safe limits, and other such devices all have contributed to a reduction in occupational accidents. In addition, jobs that are dangerous for humans, whether they involve mixing chemicals or detonating suspicious objects, handling asphalt, or exploring the seabed, now are routinely done by machines.

However, stress at work has been found to play an important part in 75 percent of heart disease (Fraser, 1983), and whether use of technology leads to more or less work stress is not yet clear. Some think the need to keep up with machines, including computers, is more stressful than being supervised by humans, because computers can keep a better record of speed, errors, and so forth, than human managers can (Shostak, 1980).

Making Work More Dignified.   Finally, demeaning jobs, such as sifting garbage, can be done by robots equipped with vision, smell, and feeling facilities. Libraries, stores, and airports use mechanical devices instead of security guards to detect smuggled items. In this way, not only are the guards relieved of jobs that require them to be forever suspicious of others, but also the clients or customers are no longer subjected to the indignity of package, luggage, and body searches.

In short, technology is doing away with jobs that rob people of their dignity, that are dangerous, that are difficult to accomplish, and that require brute strength. Technology thus has the capacity to make work more humane.

Deskilling. Conversely, there is the danger that work will become deskilled. The introduction of automation in its various forms may reduce workers' tasks to pushing buttons and watching dials, with subsequent changes in their attitudes, gratifications, and self-images.

Some fear has been expressed that although more education may be required for upper-level jobs in an automated society, most workers will need only minimal skills to be able to perform their jobs. This may lead to a depression in educational levels, because there are many sections of society that see education's primary task as preparing people for the world of work—although not everyone agrees with this approach (Anthony, 1978; Berg, 1971; Bowles & Gintis, 1976; Caplow, 1954; Ginzberg, 1976; Herzberg, 1966; O'Toole, 1977; *Work in America, 1973*).

Baran (1985) proposed that previously deskilled people are simply being eliminated from the labor force and that the deskilling taking place is among professional workers. Using the insurance industry as an example, he found that people previously using their judgment and skills now find that their jobs are dead-end, boring, stressful, and deeply unsatisfying.

Dehumanization. There is also a fear that work will become dehumanized as workers and clients relate to machines rather than people. One aspect of this prediction has to do with workers' relationships among themselves in the workplace—that instead of talking to one another, sharing in the completion of tasks, and playing out social roles, workers will instead relate with machines. This results in a loss of social contacts and sociability and in frustration of gregarious needs on the job. Indeed, so strong is the need for relationships that workers in technologically centered jobs have been known to give names to their machines and to talk to and about the machine as though it were a person. However, there is also the opinion that use of new technology increases free time on the job, with subsequent opportunities for socializing with other workers. A number of studies indicate that time wasted at work is growing (Cherrington, 1980; Gyllenhammer, Harmon, & Yankelovich, 1981; Kendrick, 1979; Olson, 1983; Yankelovich & Immerwahr, 1983), and technology may be one reason for this.

Another aspect of this attitude is that in the services, the human touch or relationship between one person and another, such as between client and worker, will be lost as decisions are made by machines and as interactive computer programs lead clients to interact with machines rather than people. There is little evidence to support this notion, although at least one study found that the human inter-action is different, but not less (Aydin, 1989).

Another fear accompanying technological advancement is that workers' social circles outside the workplace will contract as they have less personal contact with fellow workers on the job. However, re-search dating back over 30 years indicates that most personal rela-tionships do not arise in the workplace and those that do are not carried over to the nonwork environment (Goldthorpe, Lockwood, Becchofer, & Platt, 1968; Kornhauser, 1965). Nevertheless, the pres-ence of fellow workers may make the work itself—or, at least, the workplace—more bearable (Garson, 1975; Kanter & Stein, 1979).

Polarization. As machines begin to do "the dirty, dead-end jobs of society" (Gans, 1967), they replace and make unemployed the most unskilled, inexperienced, poorly paid workers—those with the least chance of finding alternative employment. If these workers do find work—perhaps in operating the very machines that replaced them—it tends to be boring, repetitive work, even though mechanized (Rich-ardson & Henning, 1984). Thus, there is a good chance the labor force will become polarized between a minority with challenging, in-teresting, ego-satisfying work in power-wielding and influential po-sitions and a majority with banal, monotonous jobs.

Povertization. The growth of technology may lead to an increase in underpaid and underemployed workers, particularly if the feasibility of part-time work results in its spread from those who are simply augmenting the family income to wage earners themselves.

Because a symbiotic relationship exists between part-time, under-paid work and the entry of women into the labor force, the result increasingly is that the low-paid workers are women, leading to a description of "the feminization of poverty" (Goldberg, 1988). For both sexes, the danger of rising levels of poverty is very real, both from technologically induced part-time work and from unemploy-ment, as outlined in chapter 4.

Unemployment. Machines replace people. Consequently, the growth of technology has been closely correlated with a reduction in the use of human labor. Not only have hours and lifetimes of work been reduced, as noted previously, but jobs have been eliminated. During the past 50 years, despite short-term fluctuations, unemploy-ment figures have continued to rise even as the hours of work have continued to drop (Macarov, 1988b). In short, despite a masking effect caused by the growth in the number of part-time workers, who are not included in the unemployment figures, the latter numbers continue to grow. Further, as many researchers have pointed out, the official figures must be increased by 50 to 300 percent to account for the definitional and statistical manipulations used to try to minimize the official rates (Field, 1977; Kogut & Aron, 1980; Levitan & Johnson, 1983).

Part-Time and Temporary Work. During the last several years, the labor market has been marked by an increase in part-time and temporary work. As noted in chapter 4, this has become the mode of choice for many large industries, which have discovered that in the case of recession, too many permanent full-time employees are costly to the firm, whether retained or made redundant. They have therefore announced their policies as becoming "lean and mean"—keeping a skeletal full-time staff and hiring temporary workers that can be laid off, as occasions demand (Hall, 1984; Kumpke, 1986; Lewis, 1986). Because part-time and temporary workers are less well protected in terms of social benefits, are not unionized, and earn lower salaries, this often represents savings as well as flexibility for the firm.

For this reason, as well as others, part-time work has become a growth industry in many countries, with a large portion of new jobs consisting of part-time workers and another large portion of temporary workers. Such "contingent workers" make up 28 percent of the American work force (*World of Work Report*, 1985a). About 20 percent of all new jobs are part-time and up to 30 percent of new full-time jobs are temporary (*New York Times*, 1988). Here, too, technology has played a part. It is possible for part-time and temporary workers to pick up where their co-workers on previous shifts left off by punching some buttons. Upon leaving for the day, they can report what they did during their shift. Many of the jobs available require only minimum skill in using the technology (for example, a checkout person at the supermarket simply needs to run the items over the decoder and makes change when necessary, and a bartender simply has to punch in the name of a requested cocktail to have the finished product delivered to his or her hand).

This situation offers flexibility to the worker as well as to the firm. One can work as little or as much as one likes. However, because part-time work pays part-time salaries (Olmsted, 1985), the growth of part-time work invariably means a cut in workers' incomes (Morehouse & Dembo, 1988).

More Options for Women. Women have been entering the labor force in most western countries in increasing numbers. In virtually every industrialized country, the proportion of women in paid employment has risen dramatically, especially during the past quarter century (Macarov, 1988a). There are several reasons for this, but technology has made the trend more practical. With the removal of physical strength as a condition for some jobs, the availability of part-time work during convenient hours, and the possibility of temporary work from time to time, the difficulty associated with women performing multiple roles—as workers, spouses, parents, and children caring for parents and grandparents—has eased somewhat. Indeed, although there are many women seeking careers and self-fulfillment in work, the great majority report themselves as working to augment the family income (Moss & Fonda, 1980), for which part-time and temporary work may not only be sufficient, but desirable.

Both flexitime, in which full-time work can be performed in hours of choice, and flexiplace, in which the work can be performed in or near the home, are heavily dependent upon the kind of technological infrastructure that allows work to be performed in this way, and that infrastructure is growing.

Health Factors. Although technology tends to replace humans in dangerous situations, the effects of technology itself on health must also be considered. Perhaps the most widely debated of these is the effect of computer monitors on the health of the operators, particularly pregnant women. A great deal has been written and claimed on both sides of this argument, and a definitive answer has not yet been given. If, however, unequivocal evidence of negative effects were to be produced, it is almost certain that new technology would be devised to circumvent the danger; the use of computers is too deeply ingrained in society to abandon them. Other concerns related to computer use involve eye and back problems, both of which, some claim, can be offset by proper attention to ergonomics. All in all, however, it would seem that the positive effects of machines undertaking dangerous jobs once done by humans outweighs the possible negative effects of technology on workers' health.

Education and Training

The use of audiovisual aids in formal educational efforts has a long history, but the use of self-taught courses of various kinds has grown by leaps and bounds with the advent of appropriate computer and video programs. In addition, courses in the use of computers, and the use of computers in courses, have begun to offer many advantages. In particular, many computer-based programs devised to attract and hold youths have been found successful, at least in engaging them in computer activities.

Programs such as those on video that teach signing to both hearing and hearing-disabled people or cassette courses in foreign languages and similar devices are examples of using technology to deepen formal and informal education. There is also the extension of formal education, such as the use of remote classes taught by an instructor in a distant city via television and connected by direct link for interactive questions and discussion.

Conversely, technology may widen the gap between computer-literate people and those with no knowledge of or experience with communication technology. The balance of power sometimes changes in the classroom as students to whom computers always have been part of life outstrip their teachers, to whom computers may remain new and unfamiliar ground. Students may confer with each other, move beyond the teacher's competence, and effectively bar the teacher from participating in what they are doing.

Impact on the Homebound and Handicapped

One of the most gratifying uses of new technology is in helping the elderly, homebound, and disabled people become more independent and more secure. For example, technological improvements such as power-assisted seat belts in cars, advanced security systems in the home, and other forms of physical care can greatly aid daily life for older adults (Czaja & Barr, 1989). Many similar examples can be cited, including electronically operated wheelchairs, "kneeling" buses, and chairs that rock to ease rising. Communication technology also makes possible wider social contacts for the homebound through participation in computer networks, telephone group discussions, and electronic bulletin boards, as evidenced by the existence of the *Computer Use in Social Services Network*, and offers everyone new leisure opportunities through computer games; traditional games such as chess, backgammon, and bridge, for which human partners are no longer necessary; and discussion about these games, as a form of social contact.

Summary

Technology will continue to make work less physically demanding, less dangerous, less difficult, and less demeaning. It also will continue to reduce the number of jobs available, resulting in growing numbers of permanently unemployed people. The jobs that remain will be polarized between a few "good" jobs and many "bad" ones, but in both cases, the amount of free time on the job probably will continue to increase. Due to technology, the number of part-time and temporary jobs will increase, which will make it easier for increasing numbers of women to enter the labor force. The amount of leisure time available will grow owing to both a reduction in work times and increased longevity, and technology will help make this a satisfying part of life.

It is possible, of course, that not all of these predictions will come to pass, but if even a few do, the need for social work to reconceptualize and retrain will constitute a most important task.

THE BEGINNINGS OF COMPUTERIZATION IN SOCIAL WORK

In addition to technology's impact on society and, therein, its indirect influence on social work, its direct impact on the profession must be considered. Technology, particularly communication technology, may change the nature of social work in several areas. These areas are ones in which computerization has begun to play a significant role. They include research, agency management, case management, policy/planning, direct service, and education and training.

Research

Computers were generally first used in research, and social work researchers were usually the first to take advantage of their speed and abilities. The ability to do multivariate analysis, as well as depict spatial relationships, has increased the capabilities of researchers enormously. Increasingly, professional journals are requiring that articles indicate the use of methodology sophisticated enough to indicate even small nuances in the findings. In addition, computerized searches of literature allow researchers to build on the work of others. Literature searches are available from a number of commercial companies, from library networks, and from programs offered in computer-oriented journals. All of these factors have changed the whole nature of social science research.

Agency Management

The next step in the adoption of technology in the human services is usually administrative/supervisory: record keeping, filing and retrieving information (Levinson & Haynes, 1984), bookkeeping and other office management tasks, keeping track of changes in laws and regulations, and the like. At present, this is probably the most developed area of computer use in social work, and many articles as well as papers delivered at meetings describe information and retrieval systems or databases concerning clients. An examination of the contents of one publication devoted to the subject indicates that more than half the programs described are devoted to management (*Computer Use in Social Services Network Newsletter, 1988/1989*).

Case Management

Management, in another sense, is also a burgeoning area for the use of computers. This has to do with case management—that is, keeping track of clients and their situations (Rosenholm, 1990). Perhaps the most visible of such programs involves keeping track of children in care; but, in general, case management includes information about client demographics and clinical data, enrollment in programs, use of external services, referrals, special incidents and events, goal selection, and progress monitoring (Epstein, 1989). Also, clients in many categories are being helped by multifarious agencies (health, education, financial, family, psychological, and others), and the use of computers makes a holistic view of the client's situation possible.

The use of computers in case management is somewhat less widespread than in research or agency management (Blennerhassett, 1988). One reason for this is that the former involves the needs of service givers, whereas the latter are related to the needs of clients (Geiss & Viswanathan, 1986), which presumably are less compelling. In other words, service organizations use computers because they offer greater control over operations and decision making and thus maximize efficiency, not because they are more effective in dealing with clients.

Policy and Planning

Policy and planning use computers in working with statistics, trends, demographics, and other quantitative data. Increasingly, however, computer-aided decision making is taking place, with projections and simulations indicating the probable end result of policy changes.

Direct Service to Clients

Programs that are directly applicable to clients have grown. The entire 1988/1989 issue of *Computer Use in Social Services Network Newsletter*, in fact, was devoted to the availability of such direct-service programs as the following:

- cognitive rehabilitation of the injured and handicapped
- self-administered psychiatric diagnostic interviews
- self-administered programs dealing with assertiveness, self-esteem, and stress
- one finger/stick programs (for those with very limited movement ability or control)
- hospital/social work discharge planning
- clinical assessment for mental health
- child abuse intake prioritization

There are also many descriptions of computer use in aiding clients. Computer technology has produced work aids for the physically disabled (Howey, 1988), improved the prognosis for stroke victims (Thompson & Coleman, 1988), helped in the everyday life of older adults (Czaja & Barr, 1989), assisted people with Alzheimer's disease (Arber, 1987), created games for disadvantaged youth (Sherer, 1990), predicted behavior (Klein, Greist, & van Cura, 1975), and offered decisions in many different situations (Wilson, 1988).

In addition to computer programs operated by social workers, there are a growing number of interactive programs in which clients themselves operate the technology and relate to the program. Some of these entail games (Resnick, 1988), whereas others are more directly therapeutic (Weizenbaum, 1976) or help clients make decisions (Starkshell & Rivlin, 1987). Such programs will become more user-friendly and, thus, more widely used, with advances in current leading-edge technologies such as voice-activated programs, holograms, three-dimensional graphics, language recognition, and artificial intelligence applied to social problems.

Education and Training

One of the areas in which technology is least used in social work is in social work education. Beyond a course or two intended for use in administration or research, computers are hardly acknowledged. Cases where technology is used primarily in the interests of education itself are few and far between. An examination of issues of *The Journal of Social Work Education* from 1985 to 1989 indicates only eight articles on the use of computers. Similarly, a University of Minnesota study conducted while videodisks for teaching social work were being prepared found no other school of social work preparing or using such disks (Maypole, 1983).

THE FUTURE OF COMPUTERIZATION IN SOCIAL WORK

Despite the unevenness of computer use in various aspects of social work and social welfare, movement toward such usage has begun, and the infrastructure for it now is being put into place. Computer programs are being devised for many different situations. Because the experience of using information technology is by and large a positive one, this in itself will call for continued growth.

Publications and Conferences

Interest and activity in use of computers in social work are indicated by the existence of publications devoted to this area (*Computer Use in Social Services Network Newsletter; New Technology in the Human Services; The Journal of Computers in Human Services;* and the *Bitnet* newsletter). A number of national and international meetings have been devoted to the same topic, for example, the conference held at Aspen Institute in 1984; the Human Service Information Technology Application international conference held in Birmingham, England, in 1987; and the European Experts' Consultation on the Use of Computers in the Social Services, held in Jerusalem in 1989.

Extent of Computer Use

A recent study in the United States found that 48 percent of private nonprofit agencies currently use microcomputers primarily for office use, but increasingly for clients (Finn, 1988/1989). The same article estimated that within the next few years, at least two-thirds of the agencies will be using microcomputers. Altogether, it is estimated that somewhere between 25 and 68 percent of all human-service agencies in the United States are now using computers.

Benefits of Computer Use

Time Saving. Insofar as technology saves time in social work without sacrificing other attributes, it inevitably will find its way into agencies and services, as time saved is money saved. It has been found that one of the positive results of using technology in the services is a savings in time devoted to peripheral or administrative tasks, which often permit a reduction in staff and the attendant cost savings (Epstein, 1988). This also makes more time available for contact with clients (Geiss & Viswanathan, 1986). This achievement should be of great help to social workers, who list a lack of resources, including time, as one of their major sources of professional dissatisfaction (Meller & Macarov, 1986).

In social work education, too, the savings in time will prove important. Teacher time needed at the college level for computer-based instruction is 36 percent less than for conventional courses (Kulick, Kulick, & Cohen, 1980).

The failure of educational institutions, including schools of social work, to exploit computer-based courses has led to the entry of commercial firms into this area. There already are an enormous number of teaching programs available from such companies. In fact, there exists a danger that schools of social work and social welfare will fall behind in learning to use and develop information technology applications (Visser & Monasso, 1988).

Nor is it enough simply to teach the use of computers in isolated courses. Educators must learn to teach *via* technology, not just about technology (Kirst, 1983). Failure to integrate technical issues with educational policy and experience can result in outdated concepts that do not correspond with real-life situations (Pogrow, 1983).

Job Effectiveness. The role computers play in increasing the effectiveness of social work practice has not yet been documented through sufficient generalizable empirical studies, probably because effectiveness must be measured differently in various areas. Effectiveness in child care may be different from effectiveness in prison programs, or in dealing with the elderly, for example. Consequently, one can only examine the evaluations of specific programs as they appear. For example, computers can predict suicide attempts more accurately than can experienced clinicians (Schoech & Arangio, 1979), and there has been documented more than 70 percent agreement between computers and juvenile probation officers concerning recommendations to judicial authorities (Shapira, 1990). Other such success stories appear in the social work literature.

There even appears evidence that clients are more comfortable asking for information from computers than from social workers, perhaps because computers are not seen as stigmatizing (Epstein, 1988/1989). In addition, Epstein found that clients felt they received (and they did receive) more accurate information this way. However, because failures do not often appear in print, it is still not possible to make general statements about the effectiveness of computer programs in direct practice.

Problems in Computer Use

Resistance to Change. One of the factors deterring wider use of computers in the human services is the normal fear of and resistance to new methods inherent in all attempts at change. To those in the age range or social group where computer familiarity—even through use of video games—was not part of their developmental repertoire, electronic mechanisms may still contain an element of strangeness and thus fear. This fear may be compounded by factors as simple as inability to type; memory problems that inhibit retention of instructions; dyslexia, which leads to spellings that even computerized dictionaries cannot unravel; and rejection of even the simplest mechanical tasks. The major part of this element of resistance, however, is ignorance of new methods and fear that such ignorance will become evident to others or will continue.

Where purely clerical tasks are concerned, there are volumes of literature about methods of introducing computer technology, particularly in offices, as well as continuing efforts by software manufacturers to make the systems as user friendly as possible. For computer usage by professional staff, however, the resistance may arise from a more complex congeries of reasons. Nevertheless, as Shapira (1990) has demonstrated with youth probation officers, it is possible to start with the premise that professionals really do want to do the best possible job and to involve them in examining the help computers can give so they begin to demand such help and improve on it.

The entry into social work by young graduates for whom computers have always been a part of their lives and their learning, coupled with increasing use of and teaching about computers in schools of social work, will cause whatever resistance remains to melt away. Currently, the resistance of social work students to new technology is less than that of psychology students (Monnickendam & Morris, 1989). There-fore, instead of resisting such technology, social workers will even-tually demand it for the help it offers workers and clients.

Shifting Power Relations. Knowledge is power, and those who understand, or even have access to, computers may begin to play a more powerful role than they have previously. As youngsters gain familiarity with computers, they may confer more often with each other, may discover possibilities their instructors are unaware of, and may sometimes freeze the teacher out of their conversations and activities, thus shifting the balance of power in the classroom from the teacher to the students. In the human services, too, practitioners with computer skills can become an elite (real or imagined). If more experience with computers results in greater ability and familiarity on the part of the clerical staff or the practice staff, the control of the supervisory or executive staff may be reduced. It has already been found, in other settings, that the computer "experts" among the staff may tend to hoard their information, to clothe it in esoteric language, and to indicate to others that the process is too complex for them to understand. Thus, power is accumulated through possession of real or pretended knowledge.

In the same vein, as interactive programs designed for social work practice continue to increase, clients may become less dependent on, and thus less under the control of, practitioners. Although many may see this as desirable, the new situation may require different attitudes and activities from practitioners and be reflected in their training needs. Further, the strains inherent in adjusting to the new situation will require flexibility from practitioners, programmers, and planners.

Just as clerical staff or computer experts in commercial settings sometimes conceal time-wasting or personally pleasurable activities from their supervisors, so human-services practitioners might be able to behave or perform in a manner that escapes the knowledge of their less-computer-literate superiors.

Mechanical Monitoring. Conversely, resistance to computeriza-tion may arise from workers' fears of being monitored easily and efficiently. Clerical workers have been found to resent the fact that the computer can determine their typing speed, number of mistakes, and total productivity quickly and correctly, thus not only evaluating their skill, but also reducing the amount of unproductive work time that workers sometimes feel is necessary to make the work bearable. Similarly, computerized human services can record social workers' activities in a different manner than hitherto, keeping them constantly under surveillance, as it were. This factor may have great impact in those services in which malpractice suits and complaints have become commonplace.

Changes in Recording and in Practice. The use of computers for recording information in human-service settings may involve standardized language, keywords, prescribed formats, or inclusion of only certain kinds of information. This can lead to changes in which information regarded as important by some is omitted from the record. For example, the inclusion of tentative diagnoses, preliminary treatment plans, half-formed hypotheses, and value judgments—in short, that which has been described as the "metaphysical musings" of the practitioner (*Experts' Consultation on Client Access to Personal Social Service Records*, 1987)—may be omitted in favor of empirically verified facts, or worker/client-agreed entries, leading to loss of important insights.

Further, prescribed requirements for recording may alter practice methods. As Etzioni (1964) pointed out, emphasis on counting leads to doing countable things, and thus records tailored to the needs of the computer may lead to doing only those things in practice that will fit the record. This fear has also been expressed in terms of practice being analyzed piecemeal rather than holistically (Gripton, Licker, & De Groot, 1988).

This same argument has arisen around the growing requirement for client access to records—the knowledge that the client will see the record may affect what is recorded. To keep the record honest, practice may be trimmed to fit. This may become an increasing problem with the advent of magnetic cards (similar to credit cards) that contain all of the information concerning a client and that might remain in the client's possession, to be used whenever he or she feels the need for help.

Client Resistance. The knowledge that the contents of an interview or the details of an activity will be computerized and kept in a mechanical memory may increase client resistance to cooperation, especially if the setting is a statutory one, such as probation, parole, child placement, and the like. For some people, the handwritten or typed record kept in a file folder is psychologically less threatening than the presumably omniscient, immortal, and amoral computer memory bank. This consideration is even more important with reference to the interactive programs, which despite their built-in user-friendliness may overawe, confuse, or repel some clients, who may prefer contact with a human professional.

Finally, there are cases in which interacting with a computer may be less threatening than interacting with a human professional—for example, in determining the most appropriate birth control methods

(Starkshell and Rivlin, 1987) or in seeking information about sexual proclivities and abilities, venereal disease, and so forth.

Inappropriateness. There is also the danger that arises from indiscriminate and uninformed uses of computer technology. There is a natural tendency, especially on the part of newcomers to the field, to become fascinated by the possibilities of computer technology and to try to use it "because it is there," or to see how far it can be pushed. Just as most human services require that the client be individualized, so the use of new technology requires that it first be demonstrated to be not only appropriate for the existing situation, but better than existing systems. The old adage still holds: "If it ain't broke, don't fix it."

Dehumanization. One of the most frequently voiced concerns about the use of computers in social work is about the dehumanization of the client—that a relationship with a computer deprives the client of important elements involved in a relationship with a social worker.

Undoubtedly many occasions arise when the need for personal contact is an important part of the client's problem, or, conversely, where personal contact is an important part of the treatment process. Quantitatively, however, this need is limited to those problem areas where emotional support and at least semitherapeutic measures are necessary. When social workers are acquiring resources, making placement judgments, finding (and fighting for) openings in institutional settings, giving information, helping with forms, or engaging in other activities in which the emotional element is not primary, the dehumanization fear may be greatly exaggerated.

Further, the current role of personal contact with a professional may be highly overestimated. Not many hospital patients have a chance to talk at any length with a social worker, or even a nurse, let alone a doctor; nor does the doctor or nurse in the public health service have time for more than a few cursory words. Children in care may not be seen by a professional for weeks, or even months, at a time, and the probation officer may see his or her client only at the scheduled intervals required by law. In many cases, the loss of personal contact is minimal and can be more than compensated for by the efficiency and effectiveness the use of computers introduces.

On a more empirical basis regarding the need for human contact, there are now radio-therapy programs in the United States with 20 million or more listeners, and surveys show that more than half of those who call in feel they were helped (Schommen, 1984). Because there are also successful therapeutic computer programs, it is possible that the computer can personify the clinician. The relationship may be largely or completely in the mind of the client, with little difference whether the "significant other" is a telephone voice, a computer screen, or a person.

Some clients seem to prefer giving personal information to the computer, and there is some indication that the information they give is more accurate than the information reported directly to a social worker. This is akin to the "white coat syndrome," in which the appearance of a doctor increases blood pressure, whereas blood pressure taken by a machine tends to be lower.

Finally, insofar as dehumanization is concerned, one cynical observer put it thus: "I know some people in the human services whose sense of humor is even below the built-in humor of some programmed dialogues. And the same applies to 'originality' and 'creativity'" (Grundiger, 1988/1989).

Confidentiality. One of the first and most often mentioned fears concerning the use of computers in social work has to do with loss of confidentiality. This includes fears of a central data bank concerning individuals, which raises images of "Big Brother," as well as concern that information such as income tax reports, employment records, police records, welfare payments, school achievements, and family problems will be shared among agencies to the detriment of the individual. There is also fear that unauthorized persons will gain access to personal information, with results ranging from gossip to lawsuits. This fear is exemplified by a recent court ruling that appointments with a psychiatric professional are to be considered privileged information (Horty, 1981).

Concern for confidentiality seems to arise from three roots: (1) that clients who are not convinced of confidentiality will withhold information, which will render help less efficient (Dulchin & Segal, 1982; Levy, 1976); (2) that confidentiality is a basic human right, regardless of its efficiency (Butz, 1985); and (3) that laws regulate both clients' and workers' rights to information (Schwartz, 1989; Watkins, 1989). Despite these concerns, the differences among secrecy, anonymity, and confidentiality are not always clear (Macarov, 1990). In addition, one study found that although social work respondents said they upheld the National Association of Social Workers' *Code of Ethics* concerning confidentiality, they admitted they had never read it (Dubord, 1981).

Generally, it appears to be easy for someone to approach the computer, punch a few keys, and have access to confidential information about clients. Actually, with the use of code words and other devices, computerized records are probably as secure, if not more so, as records kept in file drawers with keys, especially because file drawers are often kept open during the work day for easy access. A number of observers have pointed out that the most common violations of confidentiality take place in casual conversations with colleagues, peers, and support staff, namely secretaries and students (Moore-Kirkland & Irey, 1981; Price, 1980). Computers are not involved.

In situations where nonprofessional staff handle computerized or other records, the question of confidentiality does arise, and the problem of inculcating professional values in nonprofessional staff has been addressed (Chamberlain, Hayes, Kerswell, Martin, & Landsberg, 1982).

Note also that too much stress on confidentiality has been said to contribute to the client's feeling that there is something disgraceful in being a client ("Confidentiality," 1958). Further, confidentiality can come to be viewed as "a sinister device to keep the public from knowing what social work agencies really do" (National Association of Social Workers, 1958). Even that concept of confidentiality that allows using the information obtained on behalf of the client has been termed a form of paternalism—"interfering with the freedom of the individual for his or her own good" (Reamer, 1983).

In many cases, the objection to computerization under the guise of confidentiality may be a projection of other reasons for resistance. Just as confidentiality has been found to be an excuse to avoid suspected evaluations of agencies and social workers (Macarov & Rothman, 1977; Meller & Macarov, 1986), so the same pretext may be advanced to avoid the retraining and rethinking required by the introduction of computers.

SUMMARY

Despite problems that exist and that will be uncovered, communication technology seems destined to continue to penetrate social welfare agencies and social work practice, as well as social work education. Welfare workers must engage in debate about computer-based information systems, which hold the potential to "radically alter their work and the uses to which it is put" (McCulloch, 1989). Safeguards against the misuse of communication technology and perhaps revisions in ethics and standards for social workers will be needed, but the savings in time, the ability to keep track of masses of information, the advantages for case management, and client acceptability and even demand will ensure that future generations of social work graduates operate in a highly technologized environment.

Social workers will have to distinguish between those areas of service and those activities that are aided by computer technology and those for which it is irrelevant or even counterindicated. They will need to be sure they are exploiting the technology for the client's benefit and not allowing the technological imperative of "because it can be done, it should be done" to determine their mode of practice. Social workers also will have to participate actively in the development of programs, be involved in their application, and be concerned about clients' reactions to such programs.

Finally, computer technology will require major revisions in the curricula of schools of social work and in teaching methods.

REFERENCES

Anthony, P. D. (1978). *The ideology of work*. London: Tavistock.

Arber, D. (1987). Using computers with sufferers of Alzheimer's disease. *Computer Applications in Social Work and Allied Professions, 3*, 6–11.

Aydin, C. E. (1989). Occupational adaptation to computerized medical information systems. *Journal of Health and Social Behavior, 30*, 163–179.

Baran, B. (1985). Office automation and women's work: The technological transformation of the insurance industry. In M. Castells (Ed.), *High tech, space, and society*. Beverly Hills, CA: Sage.

Berg, I. (1971). *Education and jobs: The great training robbery*. Boston: Beacon.

Blennerhassett, E. (1988). Consumers, computing and the public service: An overview of European trends. In B. Glastonbury, W. Mendola, & S. Toole (Eds.), *Information technology and the human services*. New York: John Wiley & Sons.

Bowles, S., & Gintis, H. (1976). *Schooling in capitalist America: Educational reform and the contradictions of economic life*. New York: Basic Books.

Butz, R. A. (1985). Reporting child abuse and confidentiality in counseling. *Social Casework, 66*, 83–90.

Caplow, T. (1954). *The sociology of work*. New York: McGraw-Hill.

Chamberlain, E., Hayes, E., Kerswell, G., Martin D., & Landsberg, A. (1982). Transmitting social work values to non–social work staff: Practice into theory. *Australian Social Work, 35*, 7–31.

Cherrington, D. J. (1980). *The work ethic: Working values and values that work*. New York: Amacon.

Computer use in social services network newsletter. (1988/1989). Arlington: University of Texas.

Confidentiality. (1958, June). *The Social Worker*.

Cummings, T. G., & Molloy, E. S. (1977). *Improving productivity and the quality of work life*. New York: Praeger.

Czaja, S. J., & Barr, R. A. (1989). Technology and the everyday life of older adults. *Annals of the American Academy of Political and Social Science, 503*, 127–137.

Dubord, R. A. (1981). *Confidentiality in social work practice; A comparison of rural and urban social workers in public social services*. Doctoral dissertation, University of Utah, Salt Lake City.

Dulchin, J., & Segal, A. J. (1982). The ambiguity of confidentiality in a psychoanalytic institute. *Psychiatry, 45*, 13–25.

Epstein, G. (1988/1989). Case management information: Local, regional and statewide systems. *Computer Use in Social Services Network Newsletter, 8/9*, 17–18.

Epstein, J. (1988). Information systems and the consumer. In B. Glastonbury, W. Mendola, & S. Toole (Eds.), *Information technology and the human services*. New York: John Wiley & Sons.

Etzioni, A. (1964). *Modern organizations*. Englewood Cliffs, NJ: Prentice Hall.

Experts' consultation on client access to personal social service records. (1987). Egham, Surrey, England: Department of Health and Social Security, London, and European Centre for Social Welfare Training and Research, Vienna.

Field, F. (1977). Making sense of the unemployment figures. In F. Field (Ed.), *The conscript army*. London: Routledge & Kegan Paul.

Finn, J. (1988/1989). Microcomputers in private nonprofit agencies: A survey of utilization trends and training requirements. *Computer Use in Social Services Network Newsletter, 8/9*, 27–32.

Fischer, C. S. (1985). Studying technology and social life. In M. Castells (Ed.), *High tech, space, and society*. Beverly Hills, CA: Sage.

Fraser, T. M. (1983). *Human stress, work and job satisfactions*. Geneva: International Labour Office.

Gans, H. (1967). Income grants and 'dirty' work. *The Public Interest, 6*, 110.

Garson, B. (1975). *All the livelong day: The meaning and demeaning of routine work*. Harmondsworth, England: Penguin.

Geiss, G. R., & Viswanathan, N. (Eds.). (1986). *The human edge: Information technology and helping people*. New York: Haworth.

Ginzberg, E. (1976). *Jobs for Americans*. Englewood Cliffs, NJ: Prentice Hall.

Glenn, B. N., & Feldberg, F. L. (1979). Proleterianizing clerical work: Technology and organizational control in the office. In A. Zimbalist (Ed.), *Case studies on the labor process*. New York: Monthly Labor Review Press.

Goldberg, G. S. (1988). *Women, work and welfare: Canada and the United States compared*. Paper delivered at North American Conference on Employment and Underemployment, Adelphi University, Garden City, NY.

Goldthorpe, J. H., Lockwood, D., Becchofer E., & Platt, J. (1968). *The affluent worker: Industrial attitudes and behaviour*. Cambridge, England: Cambridge University Press.

Gripton, J., Licker, P., & De Groot, L. (1988). Microcomputers in clinical social work. In B. Glastonbury, W. Mendola, & S. Toole (Eds.), *Information technology and the human services*. New York: John Wiley & Sons.

Grundiger, F. (1988/1989). The impact of computer application in the human services: An economist's view. *Computer Use in Social Services Network Newsletter, 8/9*, 9–12.

Gyllenhammer, P., Harman, S., & Yankelovich, D. (1981). *Jobs in the 1980s and 1990s: Executive summary*. New York: Public Agenda Foundation.

Hall, K. (1984). How shall we ever get them back to work? *International Journal of Manpower, 5*, 24–32.

Herzberg, F. (1966). *Work and the nature of man*. Cleveland: World.

Horty, J. F. (1981). Guard psychiatrists' patients rights. *Modern Healthcare, 11*, 133.

Howey, K. R. (1988). Factors affecting the use of information technology and computer systems as work aids for the physically handicapped. In B. Glastonbury, W. Mendola, & S. Toole (Eds.), *Information technology and the human services*. New York: John Wiley & Sons.

Jones, B. (1982). *Sleepers, awake! Technology and the future of work*. London: Oxford.

Kanter, R. M., & Stein, B. A. (Eds.). (1979). *Life in organizations: Workplaces as people experience them*. New York: Basic Books.

Kendrick, J. W. (1979). Productivity trends and the recent slowdown. In W. E. Fellner (Ed.), *Contemporary economic problems*. Washington, DC: American Enterprise Institute.

Kirkland, L. (1982, January 30). In slump, labor 'will play its part.' *New York Times*.

Kirst, M. W. (1983). Foreword. In S. Pogrow, *Education in the computer age*. Beverly Hills, CA: Sage.

Klein, M. J., Greist, J. H., & van Cura, L. J. (1975). Computer psychiatry. *Archives of General Psychiatry, 32*, 837–843.

Kogut, A., & Aron, S. (1980). Toward a full employment policy: An overview. *Journal of Sociology and Social Welfare, 7*, 85–99.

Kornhauser, H. (1965). *Mental health of the industrial worker*. New York: John Wiley & Sons.

Kraft, P. (1979). The industrialization of computer programming: From programming to 'software revolution.' In A. Zimbalist (Ed.), *Case studies on the labor process*. New York: Monthly Labor Review Press.

Kranzberg, M., & Gies, J. (1975). *By the sweat of thy brow*. New York: Putnam.

Kulick, J., Kulick, C., & Cohen, P. (1980). Effectiveness of computer-based college training: A meta-analysis of findings. *Review of Educational Research, 50*, 525–544.

Kuman, K. (1984). Unemployment as a problem in the development of industrial societies: The English experience. *Sociological Review, 32*, 184–233.

Kumpke, T. (1986). *Work organization in the post-industrial company*. Paper delivered at the conference on New Technologies and the Future of Work. Maastricht, Holland: European Centre for Work and Society.

Levinson, R. W., & Haynes, K. S. (Eds.). (1984). *Accessing human services: International perspectives*. Beverly Hills, CA: Sage.

Levitan, S. A., & Johnson, C. M. (1983). The survival of work. In J. Barbash (Ed.), *The work ethic: A critical analysis*. Madison, WI: Industrial Relations Research Association.

Levy, C. S. (1976). *Social work ethics*. New York: Human Services Press.

Lewis, A. (1986). *Vocational training: Education as an investment*. Paper delivered at experts' meeting on New Technologies and the Future of Work. Maastricht, Holland: European Centre for Work and Society.

Macarov, D. (1988a). *Quitting time: The end of work*. Bradford, England: MCB Universities Press.

Macarov, D. (1988b). The world of work revisited. In J. S. Eaton (Ed.), *Colleges of choice: The enabling impact of the community college*. New York: ACE/Macmillan.

Macarov, D. (1990). Confidentiality in the human services. In D. Macarov (Ed.), *Computers in the social services: Papers from a consultation* [Special issue]. *International Journal of Sociology and Social Policy, 10*(6/7/8), 65–81.

Macarov, D., & Rothman, B. (1977). Confidentiality: A constraint on research? *Social Work Research and Abstracts, 13*, 11–16.

Maypole, D. (1983). High technology teaching coming to social work education. *Computer Use in Social Services Network Newsletter, 8*, 17.

Mazlish, B. (1961). *The wealth of nations: Representative selections*. New York: Bobbs-Merrill.

McCulloch, A. (1989). Clients, computers and welfare work. *Australian Social Work, 42*, 21–26.

Meller, Y., & Macarov, D. (1986). Social workers' satisfactions: Methodological notes and substantive findings. *Journal of Sociology and Social Welfare, 13*, 740–760.

Ministry of Health. (1988). *How to avoid heart disease*. Jerusalem: Author.

Monnickendam, M., & Morris, A. (1989). Developing an integrated computer case-management system for the Israel defense forces: An evolutionary approach. *Computers in Human Services*.

Moore-Kirkland, J., & Irey, K. V. (1981). A reappraisal of confidentiality. *Social Work, 26*, 319–322.

Morehouse, W., & Dembo, D. (1988). *Joblessness and the pauperization of work in America*. New York: Council on International and Public Affairs.

Moss, P., & Fonda, N. (1980). *Work and the family*. London: Temple Smith.

National Association of Social Workers. (1958). *Confidentiality in social work to individuals*. New York: Author.

Nelson, J. I. (1989). Introduction. *International Journal of Sociology and Social Policy, 9*, 3–4.

New York Times. (1988, March 31). Out of work Michiganders no longer out of luck, p. A18.

Olmsted, B. (1985). 'V-time' pleases employees, helps employers cut costs. *World of Work Report, 10*, 3.

Olson, V. (1983). *White collar waste: Gain the productivity edge*. Englewood Cliffs, NJ: Prentice Hall.

Organization for Economic and Cultural Development. (1981). *Science and technology policies for the 1980s*. Paris: Author.

O'Toole, J. (1977). *Work, learning and the American future*. San Francisco: Jossey-Bass.

Pogrow, S. (1983). *Education in the computer age*. Beverly Hills, CA: Sage.

Price, T. B. (1980). *The ethics of confidentiality: An exploration of Utah social workers' involvement with confidentiality and perceptions of common violations and misuse.* Unpublished doctoral dissertation, University of Denver, CO.

Random House dictionary of the English language. (1966). New York: Random House.

Reamer, F. G. (1983). The concept of paternalism in social work. *Social Service Review, 52,* 254–257.

Remus, W. E. (1986). Toward intelligent decision support systems: An artificially intelligent statistician. *MIS Quarterly, 10,* 403–418.

Resnick, H. (1988). 'Busted,' computerized therapeutic game: Description, development and preliminary evaluation. In B. Glastonbury, W. Mendola, & S. Toole (Eds.), *Information technology and the human services.* New York: John Wiley & Sons.

Richardson, J., & Henning, R. (1984). Policy responses to unemployment: Symbolic or placebo responses? In J. Richardson & R. Henning (Eds.), *Unemployment: Policy responses of western democracies.* London: Sage.

Rosenholm, M.-J. (1990). The client data base in Helsinki. In D. Macarov (Ed.), *Computers in the social services: Papers from a consultation* [Special issue]. *International Journal of Sociology and Social Policy, 10*(6/7/8), 107–116.

Schoech, D., & Arangio, T. (1979). Computers in the human services. *Social Work, 24,* 96–102.

Schommen, N. (1984). Shrinks on the airwaves. *Discover, 5,* 68–70.

Schwartz, G. (1989). Confidentiality revisited. *Social Work, 34,* 223–226.

Shapira, M. (1990). Computerized decision technology improves decision practice in social service: Decision support system in youth probation service. In D. Macarov (Ed.), *Computers in the social services: Papers from a consultation* [Special issue]. *International Journal of Sociology and Social Policy, 10*(6/7/8), 138–153.

Sherer, M. (1990). Computerized simulation game for treating street corner youth. In D. Macarov (Ed.), *Computers in the social services: Papers from a consultation* [Special issue]. *International Journal of Sociology and Social Policy, 10*(6/7/8), 181–201.

Shostak, A. B. (1980). *Blue-collar stress.* Reading, MA: Addison-Wesley.

Starkshell, R., & Rivlin, E. (1987). *An interactive computer program for choosing birth control methods.* Paper delivered at seminar on Use of Computers in Direct Practice of Social Work, Paul Baerwald School of Social Work, The Hebrew University, Jerusalem.

Sutermeister, R. A. (1976). *People and productivity.* New York: McGraw-Hill.

Thompson, S. B. N., & Coleman, M. J. (1988). Making the therapist's prognosis of stroke a more scientific process. In B. Glastonbury, W. Mendola, & S. Toole (Eds.), *Information technology and the human services.* New York: John Wiley & Sons.

United Nations. (1988). *Statistical yearbook 1985/86.* New York: Author.

U.S. Department of Agriculture. (1976). *The secret of affluence.* Washington, DC: Author.

Visser, A., & Monasso, J. (1988). Informatics in schools of social work and social services. In B. Glastonbury, W. Mendola, & S. Toole (Eds.), *Information technology and the human services*. New York: John Wiley & Sons.

Walbank, M. (1980). Effort in motivated work behaviour. In K. D. Duncan, M. M. Gruneberg, & D. Wallis (Eds.), *Changes in working life*. Chichester, England: John Wiley & Sons.

Watkins, S. A. (1989). Confidentiality and privileged communication: Legal dilemmas for family therapists. *Social Work, 34*, 133–136.

Weber, M. (1952). *The Protestant ethic and the spirit of capitalism*. New York: Scribners.

Weizenbaum, J. (1976). *Computer power and human reason: From judgment to calculation*. San Francisco: Freeman.

Wilson, J. O. (1980). *After affluence: Economics to meet human needs*. New York: Harper & Row.

Wilson, M. (1960). *American science and invention*. New York: Bonanza.

Wilson, S. L. (1988). Direct use with clients: Automated assessment, treatment, and decision making. In B. Glastonbury, W. Mendola, & S. Toole (Eds.), *Information technology and the human services*. New York: John Wiley & Sons.

Work in America. (1973). Cambridge, MA: MIT Press.

World of Work Report. (1985a, October).

World of Work Report. (1985b, December).

Yankelovich, D., & Immerwahr, J. (1983). *Putting the work ethic to work*. New York: Public Agenda Foundation.

Zimbalist, A. (Ed.) (1979). *Case studies on the labor process*. New York: Monthly Labor Review Press.

6

Social Work and Privatization

In addition to revisions in social work practice and education that are based on changes that seem inevitable, other changing factors that could affect social work are less predictable. These changes may not occur, or may not take place at the pace expected, necessitating some caution when projecting them into the future. One of these possibilities is the privatization of former government activities in social welfare.

A BRIEF OVERVIEW

Governmental and voluntary social welfare have operated side by side since the beginnings of organized philanthropy, with the emphasis shifting from one to the other at various times, in different places, and for different services. Although the church and voluntary agencies carried out much of the social work in England in the 17th century, the Elizabethan Poor Laws of that time established workhouses and almshouses, which were essentially local government institutions. Similarly, one of the first subsidy programs for the working poor was instituted by the local government in Speenhamland, England, whereas the earliest Charity Organization Societies there were purely voluntary (Macarov, 1978).

Until the 1930s, most social welfare activities in the United States were carried out by voluntary groups such as labor unions, fraternal orders, ethnic associations, religious groups, community centers and settlement houses, and so on. The Great Depression of the 1930s resulted in passage of the Social Security Act, which established the government as the central force in social welfare, at least where financial payments were concerned. These changes were carried further—and beyond the financial area—in the 1960s, by President Lyndon Johnson, with the "Great Society" and "War on Poverty" programs.

Relatively recently, a third sector has grown up: social welfare activities for profit. This, too, did not come into being at any one time. There have always been private for-profit hospitals—for example, homes for elderly people, and child care arrangements. Lately, however, there has been an explosive growth in this sector.

Today, in many countries throughout the world, governmental agencies, institutions, and services are being turned over to public, voluntary, and membership organizations and to private for-profit auspices. This phenomenon is sometimes called a shift from the public to the private sectors (Jackson, 1989), a new welfare "mix" (*Experts' Consultation on Planning the Welfare Mix*, 1986), "loadshedding" (Bendick, 1985), "corporatization" (Stoesz & Karger, 1990), and "dumping" (Karger & Stoesz, 1989). It is referred to as the weakening or dissolution of the welfare state.

Because of the mounting difficulty of maintaining existing social security programs, mandated private pension arrangements are attracting considerable attention in many countries. The United Kingdom, for example, now permits residents to opt out of the governmental pension plan and participate in private pension plans to reduce government expenditures (U.S. Department of Health and Human Services, 1988).

The term "privatization" is the rubric under which many such changes are identified (Starr, 1985), although the activity may, in specific cases, more properly be called denationalization, decentralization, or transfer from public to private ownership. Hatry (1983) listed contracting out, franchises, grants and subsidies, vouchers, volunteers, self-help, use of regulatory and taxing authority, demarketing/reducing demand, obtaining temporary help from private firms, using fees to adjust demand, and formation of public-private ventures as privatizing activities. Perhaps the greatest impetus to privatization in the United States, however, is the reduction of government funding for certain services and/or the refusal of the government to provide services for new or growing needs, thus necessitating and facilitating the emergence of alternative auspices.

For social workers, the move toward divestiture by the government of social welfare activities and concerns can be viewed on two levels—transfer to nonprofit groups and transfer to for-profit organizations. Insofar as social welfare and social work activities are moved from governmental to nongovernmental, nonprofit auspices (churches, voluntary groups, membership organizations), the changes will be noted primarily in three areas. First, the lack of resources available to nongovernmental groups will necessitate their engaging in fund-raising activities, which may involve social workers or impinge on their activities. Second, the nongovernmental agencies will use a different management/administrative structure, including a different de-cision-making process. Third, the client groups served may be different. Movement of service provision from a government agency to a vol-untary group changes the nature of some problems social workers face, such as dealing with a volunteer board (Macarov, 1970), but does not necessarily affect questions of accountability, confidential-ity, or the like. The ultimate goal of effective service to clients will remain primary in voluntary, nonprofit groups, although this goal may be affected somewhat by the personalities in, and public relations needs of, the sponsoring organization.

When the move is to for-profit groups, however, the "bottom line" of making a profit is the criterion for success, and all activities are ultimately controlled by this need. As Nelson (1989) remarked, "Mar-ket economic norms will take root and exert substantial impact on the way services are administered and delivered." Whether this need for profit necessarily results in poor service or bad practice is part of the debate on privatization.

ROOTS OF PRIVATIZATION

Ideology

Privatization has both ideological and economic roots (Brenton, 1985). It is based on the ideology of minimum government—that governments should be involved in the provision of services only when voluntary organizations and the private market cannot be. Privatization also should serve as the ultimate safety net for those who fall through the provisions of the marketplace, voluntary groups, friends, and relatives (Harris & Seldon, 1987). Conversely, as President Calvin Coolidge said in 1925, "The business of America is business," from which it follows that the provision of social welfare services also should be a business.

This is in contradistinction to the ideology underlying the welfare state, which is that the "general welfare," as noted in the Constitution, is a governmental responsibility. Therefore, it is the government's role to intercede in the market to ameliorate inequities and to provide a degree of social and economic security to individuals who are unable to participate fully in the labor market (Karger & Stoesz, 1989) through provision of social welfare programs that are democratic and univer-sal.

There can be no debate concerning the correctness of the ideolog-ical root of privatization, just as there can be no debate concerning the correctness of any ideology. One may agree or not agree with the ideology; one may want to see it put into practice or oppose it; one may welcome its results or decry them. However, because ideologies are not based upon facts, data, experiences, or experiments, they therefore are neither correct nor incorrect. They reflect states of mind, the way one thinks things ideally should be. It is ideology, as espoused by Prime Minister Margaret Thatcher, which has led to the move toward privatization in Great Britain and has included selling the former governmental monopolistic services of the communication system (Telecom) and the fuel-distribution system (BritOil), with the electric supply being prepared for privatization in the mid-1990s.

In the United States, President Ronald Reagan vigorously espoused the same ideology and therefore the same goal—privatization—although more through reduced spending for services than through outright sales. However, there has also been some of the latter, outside the area of services, mainly in the opening up for exploitation or the selling off of government-owned land, among other things.

It should be noted that the ideology of keeping the government out of business is controlling when the economy or the business is successful or profitable, but when difficulties arise, government intervention often is solicited. In Great Britain, for example, a hurricane struck immediately after Telecom was sold to private investors, and telephone and telegraph wires were down all over southern Britain. Telecom did not spurn government intervention, but instead asked that the army be sent in to clear away fallen trees and repair wires. Similarly, the ideology of no government interference in business did not keep the Chrysler Corporation from accepting massive U.S. government help when faced with bankruptcy, nor has it deterred the "bailing out" of bankrupt savings and loan associations.

Similarly, for-profit social welfare agencies depend primarily upon third-party (government) payments for their continuance and success. There would be very few such agencies if they depended solely, or even mainly, upon the individuals who could pay for their services, as is evidenced by the fact that voluntary agencies receive only 12 percent of their revenue from fees paid for their services (Karger & Stoesz, 1989).

Economics

Saving Money. The second root of the move from governmental to nongovernmental auspices is an economic one, which also has two aspects. One is the desire on the part of governments to save money, to balance the budget, or to reduce the deficit by divesting themselves of costly activities. This is particularly cogent when one recognizes that social services, and especially entitlement programs, amount to a very substantial portion of government expenditures. Between 1950 and 1979, government expenditures for social welfare in the United States increased from $23.5 billion to $428.3 billion (McMillan & Bixby, 1980).

Paying private vendors to provide services does not always result in savings, as the experience of the early days of Medicare indicate. The massive cost overruns encountered were not the result of unexpectedly large numbers of clients taking advantage of the service, but rather of the greed of many medical institutions and practitioners.

Getting rid of costly programs will certainly have an effect on government budgeting and financing, although the cost to society as a whole may be as great or greater in other ways than government provision of services. In addition, the savings often is not total, because many of the voluntary groups and even private groups receive some type of government subsidy.

Efficiency and Effectiveness.   The other economic root of privatization is the belief that nongovernmental, and certainly for-profit, auspices are both more efficient and more effective than those of government (Savas, 1987). They are said to be more innovative, more participatory, and more cost-effective (Brenton, 1985). However, the evidence of such is far from conclusive (Kramer, 1981). For one thing, judging efficiency requires controlling for effectiveness, which is notoriously difficult in the services, especially the human services (Knapp, 1988).

A study of homes for the aged done in Great Britain in 1985, for example, found that small homes were more efficient when privately run, whereas large institutions were less costly under government auspices. The difficulty of such comparisons is illustrated by the fact that the savings in the small homes came about from the very low wages paid, the lack of unionization of employees, and the fact that many mom-and-pop operations did not include pay for the proprietors, who usually each worked 70 hours a week and sometimes as many as 93 hours (Judge & Knapp, 1985).

It is not yet possible to come to general empirically based conclusions concerning the relative efficiency and effectiveness of governmental versus nongovernmental, or for-profit versus nonprofit, services, but scattered reports indicate that the purported benefits of privatization are not inevitable. For example, a 1986 study compared the efficiencies of for-profit and nonprofit hospitals, concluding that for-profit hospitals were costlier even though nonprofit institutions were no less efficient (Carroll, Conant, & Easton, 1987). A number of other studies that compared nonprofit and for-profit hospitals came to the same conclusion (Karger & Stoesz, 1989). In many cases, the higher costs are not evident purely in the fees charged, but arise from such practices as keeping patients in the hospital longer than necessary, performing very expensive tests when not indicated, and using consultants and specialists at the patient's expense, all of which are familiar practices to those knowledgeable about the for-profit medical sector.

Similarly, the extent to which private schools offer a higher standard of education is open to dispute (Papadakis & Taylor-Gooby, 1987). Additionally, a study of state and voluntary welfare activities during the 1981–1982 recession found that they were equally satisfactory in terms of program quality, targeting, and costs, but that the voluntary programs were implemented faster (Bendick, 1985).

Lack of agreement concerning the efficiency and effectiveness of privatization is illustrated by the statement that, "The public welfare services are seriously deficient . . . in management, quality of service, accountability, and efficiency. Private provision does not necessarily tackle these issues any better" (Papadakis & Taylor-Gooby, 1987). Morris (1987) summed up the skepticism concerning lower costs in private services: "Investor-owned services are only more efficient and aggressive in securing reimbursement from private or public sources, not more efficient in service delivery."

ASPECTS OF PRIVATIZATION

In addition to the questions of whether private (especially for-profit) agencies represent a savings to the government and whether they are either more efficient or more effective, or both or neither, there are other aspects of privatization to be considered. Privatization also can cause the loss of other values, the commercialization of services, the creation of oligarchies, and the creation of a two-tiered system of social services (Karger & Stoesz, 1989).

The Profit Motive

It has been pointed out that the original establishment of governmental services had objectives in mind other than purely providing needed services—objectives that might be damaged by privatization. These include redistribution of income and services, innovations (Jackson, 1989), reduction of social inequalities, and social integration (Papadakis & Taylor-Gooby, 1987). The savings achieved by privatization may damage these nonmonetary aims of government services.

There are also said to be other dangers in privately run welfare programs. Mendelson (1975) argued that the dominance of profit-seeking interests at various levels of the nursing home industry leads to an increase in elder abuse. Further, as some services become unprofitable, they are abandoned by for-profit agencies, leaving geographical areas without services. This has happened in a number of small towns, where private hospitals have closed down for not being profitable, leaving the towns with no hospitals within a reasonable distance. In many cases, the values of altruism, humanitarianism, volunteering, and service to everyone in need give way to the profit motive.

Low Government Involvement

Even the purported greater inventiveness of private agencies has been questioned, with the result to date of a verdict of "not proven" (Kramer, 1981). Similarly, the desirable participation by staff, clients, and the public that is said to inhere in voluntary groups often boils down to control by a self-perpetuating board or one elected by a small segment of the population, in contrast to elected government officials who are chosen by the entire electorate (Brenton, 1985). It is also charged that in the pursuit of privatization, governmental functions are off-loaded without consideration for the capabilities of alternative systems. This has been termed "returning people to community care within a community that doesn't care" (Sir Alec Dickson, personal communication, 1989).

Unethical Practices

Privatization includes use of both nonprofit and for-profit agencies as substitutes for governmental services, but experience to date is that the main consequence has been a very rapid development of the commercial sector in most welfare states (Johnson, 1989). Between 1978 and 1982 alone, the number of nonprofit home health agencies in the United States grew by 89 percent, but the number of for-profit agencies grew by 540 percent (Estes & Bergthold, 1989).

This growth has been occasioned by the fact that under private auspices, some social welfare services are very profitable. When cost overruns regarding Medicare caused Congress to institute the Diagnosis Related Group plan in 1983, fewer Medicare patients were admitted to hospitals, but nevertheless hospital surpluses attributable to Medicare increased.

The profitability of some areas of social welfare has led to the commercialization of need. Although the establishment of a service usually leads to an increase in need for the service (Macarov, 1978), for-profit agencies sometimes actively play on the fears and needs of clients and charge accordingly. Karger and Stoesz (1989) showed that during the initial AIDS panic, physicians charged $300 for a test that actually cost 82 cents.

Advertisements for homes and treatment for mentally ill people, handicapped people, and others reach out to people for whom these facilities are not always the most suitable. Agencies begin to be chosen by clients on the basis of who has the most attractive advertisements (prepared by professional advertising agencies), and the ethics that keep professional social work practitioners from advertising do not seem to be shared by for-profit agencies. Even social workers in private practice sometimes seek doctoral degrees with the expressed motivation that it will bring them more clients.

Proponents of privatization hope competition between providers will result in better care and lower prices, as in Adam Smith's original economic theory. However, experience indicates that, just as Smith did not foresee cartels and monopolies as interfering in laissez-faire economics, so for-profit agencies soon form associations for a number of ostensible reasons—standards, ethics, advertising, public relations, the sharing of knowledge, and so forth—that very quickly become informal cartels, setting prices and conditions—a situation not unknown among voluntary organizations (Savas, 1987). They also tend to take over other, similar agencies, thus engaging in that which Karger and Stoesz (1989) termed oligopolization. Eventually, a few large corporations end up controlling the major part of the helping system. This imbalance has already led to the "medical-industrial complex" (Relman, 1980), and at least where elder care and child care are concerned, one can already foresee the "social welfare–industrial complex."

Another feared consequence of the growth of privatization is the "creaming" of the more affluent clients by the for-profit agencies, resulting in the emergence of a two-tiered system, with better services for those who can pay for them and poorer services for poorer clients (Estes & Bergthold, 1989; Chamberlin, 1989). This system is termed "preferential selection" by Karger and Stoesz (1989), and it results from the practice of choosing clients with less serious problems, or with more ability to pay, over those with time- and resource-consuming problems and less ability to pay. When for-profit agencies deliberately turn such clients over to another agency, such as a voluntary or nonprofit service, it is called "dumping."

PRIVATIZATION OVERSEAS: A CASE STUDY

Many of the problems inherent in either allowing or requiring nongovernmental bodies to provide needed services are exemplified in the implementation of the Nursing Care Law, which became effective in Israel in 1987. Over 90 percent of Israelis have medical coverage, which includes skilled nursing service but not care in the home. This coverage is provided by various voluntary programs that are somewhat equivalent to health maintenance organizations (HMOs) in the United States. Under the Nursing Care Law, the National Insurance Institute (the functional equivalent of the American Social Security Administration) pays for home care workers in cases where medical conditions create such need. Americans will recognize this as a variation on the Catastrophic Health Care Act of 1988, since repealed.

Before the enactment of the Nursing Care Law, most home care workers were furnished through a national voluntary group or were employed directly by people needing the service. With the passage of the law, hundreds of for-profit firms have come into existence, with fierce competition among them and between them and the voluntary group to be designated as service providers for individual cases by the government or the various HMO equivalents that furnish such service.

This competition includes making personal contacts with the staffs of government or HMO departments; using influence or, when the possibility exists, nepotism; using misleading advertising; employing public relations campaigns; publishing "surveys" of client satisfaction; and offering subtle and not-so-subtle methods of corruption, such as gifts to staff members of the designating agency.

Because the payment rate to the providers is fixed by the government, additional profits can be made only by reducing costs, which often is done by reducing the home care workers' salaries and/or social benefits. The amount of training and supervision given the home care worker is another area where costs can be cut, with predictable results. It is also possible for clients to pay the service providers an addition to the government rate, or to add to the home care worker's salary, in order to continue with unbroken service or with the same worker, thereby beginning a gray market and the two-tiered system.

Service evaluation in general is made difficult by the very large number of private concerns—neither the government nor the HMO can evaluate the quality of care provided by one agency as compared on an empirical basis with another. Further, the quality of the service may vary from time to time or be dependent on the idiosyncratic personality of the home care worker. Nor does the "consumers' choice" operate, because the service provider is usually designated by the National Insurance Institute or the HMO, rarely by the client. Because the service is provided on a third-party payment basis, it also is difficult to control even quantitative aspects, such as the number of hours the home care worker actually spends in the home, whether he or she actually shows up, whether the client still needs the service, or even whether the client is still alive (there is a court case pending against a private provider agency that collected fees from the National Insurance Institute for clients who had died).

Consequently, the social worker and the nurse must designate agencies to care for clients based on minimal background information about the agencies and their home care workers. (Nurses and social workers work together in Israel to assess client needs and determine the amount of help the National Insurance Institute and the HMOs will provide their clients/patients.) This leads to decisions that are intuitive at best, often capricious, and potentially open to corruption. Further, the major for-profit service providers in Israel have already formed an "association" of home care agencies, and some are growing into national chains.

The Israeli experience offers no reason to believe that for-profit agencies are either more efficient or more effective than nonprofit ones. In addition, the Israeli situation demonstrates that private groups are subject to all of the negative consequences mentioned previously.

THE FUTURE OF PRIVATIZATION

The continuation of privatization is not as certain as the other trends described in this book. The current situation could change with a different administration in Washington; with a swing in public sentiment; with widely publicized resistance of clients and social workers; or with clear and demonstrated incapacity, greed, or mismanagement on the part of nongovernmental agencies. The Labour Party in Great Britain is already calling for the renationalization of certain privatized services (*Time*, 1989). However, such changes do not come about easily or quickly. Even if current privatization efforts were to weaken or cease, the results could not be reversed in the near future.

Yet, despite questions and concerns about the privatization of social welfare services—many of them from social workers themselves—both the ideological underpinnings and the purported government savings have currently overridden such objections. Between 1982 and 1988, government funds for social welfare services in the United States were cut 42 percent (Johnson, 1989). Indeed, the repeal of the Catastrophic Health Care Act was partially due to the government's unwillingness to assume responsibility for more of its costs. If the law were reinstated, in almost any form, the Israeli experience indicates that it would become a growth industry for private long-term-care providers.

With enormous budget deficits now facing the United States, and little chance of these deficits being reduced substantially through further taxation, the only alternative open to the government is to continue to try to reduce expenses. With social welfare costs one of the major items in the budget, further cuts that will lead to more privatization seem to be a highly probable outcome.

IMPLICATIONS FOR SOCIAL WORKERS

For many social workers, privatization will mean working for a private enterprise, rather than for a public agency. The classic problem of the professional social worker in the nonprofessional bureaucracy (Kazmerski & Macarov, 1976; Levin, 1975) may be enlarged and emphasized as workers find they are expected to implement policies that result in the highest profit. There may be worker-employer clashes regarding emphasis on efficiency versus effectiveness, as well as debates on ethics, standards, and professional values. In cases of unprofessional practice in the agency, social workers will face the dilemma of whether to "blow the whistle" or attempt to make changes from within the agency. In these cases, social workers will need strong support from their professional associations to ensure that they can continue to demand and represent the philosophies on which social work was founded. Social workers also will need to develop objective tools to use in assessing the agencies to whom they refer clients, or from whom they purchase services.

With all of the benefits or difficulties that privatization may bring, social workers still will be needed. As Cooper (1987) said, "Unless another profession is invented . . . social workers will be needed to protect and promote the individual and group interests of people experiencing social difficulties," whether in government, voluntary, or private agencies.

The role of social workers inside and outside private services will be to demand clear standards, ethics, and procedures from service providers. There should be published regulations, readily available to the public, and governmental supervision that is penetrating, continuous, and enforceable. The areas where professional judgment is needed should be clearly outlined, and there should be sanctions for agencies that do not abide by such guidelines. Finally, social workers will need to be both open-minded and research-minded to determine under which auspices a particular service is best carried out: government, voluntary nonprofit, or private business.

REFERENCES

Bendick, M. (1985). Privatizing the delivery of social welfare service. In *Working paper 6: Privatization*. Washington, DC: National Council on Social Welfare.

Brenton, M. (1985). Privatisation and voluntary sector social services. In C. Jones & M. Brenton (Eds.), *Yearbook of social policy research*. London: Routledge & Kegan Paul.

Carroll, B. J., Conant, R. M., & Easton, T. A. (1987). *Private means, public ends: Private business in social service delivery*. New York: Praeger.

Chamberlin, J. R. (1989). Efficiency vs. equity. *Institute for Social Research Newsletter, 16*, 9–10.

Cooper, J. (1987). The future of social work: A pragmatic view. In M. Coney, R. Babcock, J. Clarke, A. Cochran, P. Graham, & M. Wison (Eds.), *The state or the market: Politics and welfare in contemporary Britain*. London: Sage.

Estes, C. L., & Bergthold, L. A. (1989). The unravelling of the non-profit service sector in the United States. *International Journal of Sociology and Social Policy, 9*, 18–33.

Experts consultation on planning the welfare mix. (1986). Vienna: European Centre for Social Welfare Training and Research.

Harris, R., & Seldon, A. (1987). *Welfare without the state: A quarter-century of suppressed public debate*. London: Institute of Economic Affairs.

Hatry, H. (1983). *A review of private approaches for the delivery of public services*. Washington, DC: The Urban Institute.

Jackson, J. E. (1989). Choosing institutions. *Institute for Social Research Newsletter, 16*, 7–9.

Johnson, N. (1989). The privatization of welfare. *Social Policy and Administration, 23,* 17–30.

Judge, K., & Knapp, M. (1985). Efficiency in the production of welfare: The public and private sectors compared. In R. Klein & M. O'Higgins (Eds.), *The future of welfare.* Oxford: Basil Blackwell.

Karger, H. J., & Stoesz, D. (1989). *The future of American social welfare.* New York: Longmans.

Kazmerski, K. J., & Macarov, D. (1976). *Administration in the social work curriculum: Report of a survey.* New York: Council on Social Work Education.

Knapp, M. (1988). *Contracting-out, efficiency and evaluation in the production of social services.* Canterbury, England: University of Kent.

Kramer, R. (1981). *Voluntary agencies in the welfare state.* Berkeley: University of California Press.

Levin, H. (1975). *Professional-bureaucratic conflict in social agencies: A further consideration.* National project on education for management. Philadelphia: University of Pennsylvania.

Macarov, D. (1970). The executive vs. the chairman of the board. In H. A. Schatz (Ed.), *A casebook in social welfare administration.* New York: Council on Social Work Education.

Macarov, D. (1978). *The design of social welfare.* New York: Holt, Rinehart, & Winston.

McMillan, A., & Bixby, A. K. (1980). Social welfare expenditures, fiscal year 1978. *Social Security Bulletin, 43,* 3–17.

Mendelson, M. A. (1975). *Tender loving greed.* New York: Vintage.

Morris, R. (1987). Re-thinking welfare in the United States: The welfare state in transition. In R. R. Friedmann, N. Gilbert, & M. Sherer (Eds.), *Modern welfare states: A comparative view of trends and prospects.* New York: New York University Press.

Nelson, J. I. (1989). Service for profit. *International Journal of Sociology and Social Policy, 9,* 34–52.

Papadakis, E., & Taylor-Gooby, P. (1987). *The private provision of public welfare.* New York: St. Martin's.

Relman, A. (1980). The new medical-industrial complex. *New England Journal of Medicine, 303,* 404–445.

Savas, E. S. (1987). *Privatization: The key to better government.* Chatham, NJ: Chatham House Press.

Starr, P. (1985). The meaning of privatization. In *Working paper 6: Privatization.* Washington, DC: National Council on Social Welfare.

Stoesz, D., & Karger, H. J. (1990). *The corporatization of the welfare state.* Unpublished manuscript.

Time. (1989). *134* (19).

U.S. Department of Health and Human Services, Social Security Administration. (1988, November). *Publication no. 13-11805.* Washington, DC: Author.

7

What Profession Awaits Us?

In certain respects, the more things change, the more they remain the same, such as the continuation of relative poverty despite new structural arrangements in the economy, or the importance of family ties despite changes in family structure. However, nothing is more certain than change. During the working lives of current social work graduates, many changes will take place in society and therefore in social work.

The areas of social change discussed in this book—aging, family, work, technology, and privatization—are those in which change seems almost certain. The factors underlying current trends are either too deep-rooted to change these areas easily or rapidly, or changes have already occurred, and their repercussions will affect the future. Not all of these sectors will change at the same rate, or to the same extent, but they will change, as will others.

Although each of the areas mentioned in this book was discussed separately, none of the changes within them will take place in isolation. They all interact on various levels in a constant dynamic interchange. Growth in the number of aged people affects families and the world of work, is strengthened and aided by technology, and is one of the causes of the rapid growth of private services. The structure of the family affects the aged, is influenced by work opportunities and outcomes for family members, is affected by technology, and thus either requires or does not require private services. Technology affects the aged, families, and the world of work, making privatization either more or less necessary. Finally, the privatization of services affects the elderly, influences families, is part of the world of work, and either displaces or is displaced by technology.

170

Within this group of changes, the role of social workers will be affected on a number of levels. How social workers deal directly with clients and with collaterals, the working conditions of social workers themselves, and their political/social action endeavors could all be different. All of these, of course, will necessitate changes in education for social work, particularly in the area of continuing education.

THE AGED

Direct Practice

In the future, relatively little social work activity will involve direct practice with the aged themselves—their needs will be met, insofar as they are met, by nonprofessionals and paraprofessionals, most of whom will be employees of private for-profit agencies. Many of the home care tasks undertaken by these workers will not require social work training. However, social workers will be greatly needed as supervisors of such direct-practice workers and volunteers. If for-profit agencies dominate the home care field, the employment of social workers may depend upon whether or not laws or regulations mandate social work supervision as a condition for receiving third-party payments. In the absence of such requirements, the for-profit agencies probably will forego the expense of professional social workers. In such a case, the recruitment, training, supervision, and administration of nonprofessionals will fall either to other nonprofessionals or to professionals in other fields.

It would be unfortunate for the clients and for society if this were to happen. Only social work training equips a caregiver to exercise a holistic approach, being concerned with psychological, physical, emotional, and social components, as well as taking into consideration the real-life situation of the client, the resources available, regulations and laws, and societal attitudes. It is also unrealistic to expect that the values that social work espouses, including independence, confidentiality, respect for differences, and nonexploitation of clients will guide non–social workers to the same extent. Unless social workers become the supervisors of home care workers, clients may not receive the benefits of these values.

Working with Collaterals

On the other hand, dealing with the families, relatives, and friends of the aged will require social work training. The many conflicting emotions that arise concerning responsibilities toward parents or other relatives; the strains that may occur in families as a result; and the financial problems that may ensue all require that caregivers have professional training. Nor is emotional support the sole or primary need in many cases. Social workers will be needed to deal with legal matters, ranging from guardianships through reverse mortgages to abuse of the elderly; administrative problems, such as transferring from home to institution, or from one institution to another; needs of medical patients, such as those arising in Alzheimer's disease or osteoporosis; and technical factors, such as home security systems.

The fact that social workers do not seem to like to work with the elderly may be mitigated by the fact that in these cases they will be working with younger people—that is, family members. Insofar as this involves emotional support and counseling—activities that many social workers seem to prefer—this may be an added attraction. In any case, many of the social work jobs available will be in connection with the elderly, and for purely economic reasons, the number of social workers dealing with the aged will almost certainly grow.

This situation will require radical shifts in the curricula of many schools of social work. Information about elderly people cannot be left for the last few sessions of the "Human Growth and Development" course, nor can the physiology of aging be the main focus. Teaching about family, legal, situational, and personal areas must be widened and stressed. Also, supervision, management, and administration will need to be taught, perhaps at the bachelor's level as well as the master's degree level.

FAMILIES

Three major areas dominate considerations of the future of social work with families. One has to do with the implications of increasing numbers of women—among them, wives, mothers, and mothers of small children—entering the labor force and what impact this has on family relationships, child care, and elder care. The second concerns the needs of grandparents and great-grandparents who remain within the family structure. The third element has to do with the implications of marriage, divorce, and remarriage—sometimes in a repeated pattern.

Working Women

As more women begin working, marriage counselors will deal increasingly with the strains that working will cause some couples and families. Care of elderly people will become particularly problematic. On the other hand, child care probably will not involve social workers to an extent greater than at present, as much of it will be considered part of the educational sector and will be dealt with accordingly. Most child care services will probably be offered under for-profit auspices, and social workers will have few roles to play in such agencies. However, the exceptional cases, including neglected children, abused children, institutionalized children, and children suffering from emotional problems, will continue to need social work attention.

Grandparents

The increasing longevity of grandparents and great-grandparents involves both the problems of aging as such, and the structure of the family. Logically, the growing number of grandparents should relieve the problem of child care, by providing baby sitters for working parents. However, experience indicates that few grandparents see their roles as full-time permanent baby sitters. Indeed, the question of the proper role of grandparents within the family structure requires societal reconceptualization. In the meantime, social workers will find themselves dealing with this problem as a composite of aging and family areas.

This means that social work education cannot really teach helpfully about the aged without doing so in the context of family relationships; nor can it teach family functioning without placing a great deal of stress on the possibilities and problems inherent in families with long-living grandparents, whether they live in, live out, or are institutionalized.

Serial Marriages

Finally, because of the increasing number of serial marriages, social workers will have to change their concepts of what constitutes a family and normative family relationships. Of particular concern will be the immediate postdivorce period and the postmarriage period and their effects on children.

Because divorces and remarriages result in families with children from several marriages, the situation of children will require much study. What constitutes normative relationships, legal relationships, and rights and responsibilities will require reconceptualization. Counseling services for both parents and children will grow in importance, because of need and because this is one of the areas for which social workers indicate preferences—both in their desire to be counselors and in their desire to work with families and children.

WORK

In the future, social work activities in the areas of employment and unemployment will deal with helping people affected by the increasing difficulty of finding full-time, permanent, satisfying work. In addition to early retirees (both voluntary and involuntary), there will be clients who can find only part-time work, despite their desire and need for full-time employment; temporary workers who work for short periods and then are unemployed; the long-term unemployed; and the working poor—clients whose work does not pay enough to meet their financial needs.

In addition to trying to help people find work, social workers will need to deal with the effects of unemployment on clients, including changes in self- and others' images, family strains, and the need to make satisfying use of the leisure time resulting from unemployment. This work will require a shift in conceptualization from unemployment as a temporary phenomenon to be dealt with on a crisis basis, to unemployment as almost a normative aspect of life for some people or groups.

For many people, work will take on new dimensions as they shift from what were industrial settings to service jobs and as technology deskills many jobs previously requiring knowledge and skills. Lack of satisfaction at and from work will grow, and social workers will be required to deal with work-related problems to a larger extent than they do today.

In addition to the problems created in care of elderly people, children, and families by the entry of an increasing number of women into the labor force, the problems of women in the workplace will take on more prominence—problems such as sexual harassment, lack of equal opportunities or equal pay, relegation to part-time and temporary work, and the assumption that women are "naturally" better suited to some jobs. Changes in the nature and amount of work will require a great deal more knowledge about and activity in this area on the part of social workers.

TECHNOLOGY

Although technology will impinge on almost every area of work and nonwork, and therefore on the situations dealt with by social workers, it is the use of technology in social work activities themselves that will affect social workers most directly. Information storage, retrieval, and dissemination will be faster, more complete, and more usable. Case management, especially for clients with complicated problems involving many agencies and people, will be greatly simplified.

However, it is in the area of direct practice that the most dramatic changes probably will take place. The growth of computer-aided decision making can almost be taken for granted. This growth will be followed by, and perhaps exceeded by, interactive programs allowing clients to use computers to give and get information, to clarify alternatives, and to make decisions.

Social workers must understand the uses and misuses of computer technology. They will be required to operate computers in the interests of speedy and complete service to their clients. They will need to protect their clients from any dehumanizing effects of computer use, standardization of services, and possible breaches of confidentiality. Social work agency staff will need to keep abreast of new, relevant computer programs and conduct training and retraining courses as new technology becomes available or is acquired.

Schools of social work not only will have to move beyond "computer literacy" to a deeper understanding of what computers can and cannot do, but also will have to acquire libraries of programs for use with different client groups, concerning a variety of problems and using many methodologies. They will need to use these very much as textbooks and audiovisual devices are used today.

PRIVATIZATION

Whether the ideology underlying privatization changes in the future will have little effect on the results in this area. As the needs of children, the elderly, families, and others grow to the extent predicted, the demand for caregivers of various kinds will outstrip the number of social workers available, and providers of private services will move into the vacuum.

As social workers begin to work for private agencies in increasing numbers, the area of potential conflict between professional values and for-profit requirements will grow. Social work educators not only will have to emphasize principles and values even more than they do today, they also will have to help graduates understand their proper roles in conflict situations and methods of handling them. Professional associations of social workers will have to offer visible, clear, and immediate support to social workers in such situations. For their own protection, social workers may have to become more active in labor unions. Simultaneously, social workers and their associations will have to demand clear, enforceable standards—preferably backed by law—for private caregiving organizations.

CONCLUSION

The five trends discussed in this book that will change the activities of social workers in the future will not take place at the same pace. Some of them will occur more quickly and others will happen over a longer period. Consequently, it is unrealistic to believe that schools of social work can prepare graduates for dealing with these situations (which in some cases exist in relatively small proportions today) to the neglect of current needs.

Two questions thus arise. One is the classic question of whether there is a body of basic knowledge, attitudes, and skills that enables a social work graduate to practice today and that also will serve as a useful, practical foundation for the changes tomorrow's practice will necessitate. If so, then current curricula should be examined as to whether they provide the basis for dealing with the kinds of changes expected in the future.

Even given a useful educational base, social workers still will need retraining and continuing education to deal with changes as they occur. Thus, the second question asks how continuing education can be structured to enable social workers to equip themselves for new situations and whether social workers will avail themselves of this education.

Education usually lags behind practice. Curriculum changes are made because practice has changed; rarely does practice change because of changes in education. This creates an unfortunate cultural lag during which social workers use irrelevant or outmoded theories, concepts, and activities until the new situation is recognized and education for social work responds. This situation could be eased, if not avoided, if social work training consisted of a judicious mixture of present needs and preparation for future changes.

In view of the changes that are almost certain to take place in society during the working lives of present-day social work graduates, social work educators are faced with the formidable task of preparing students to recognize, deal with, act responsibly within, and perhaps influence such future changes.

Of course, it is always possible that some of these changes will not take place, or at least not in the amount or at the speed indicated. Nevertheless, it is better to have a plan that is not needed than to have a need for which there is no plan.

Index

A

Abuse, of elderly people, 33–35, 48
Acquired immune deficiency syndrome (AIDS)
  impact on sexual attitudes, 6
  need to deal with problems resulting from, 2
Adolescents
  effect of divorce on, 67
  helping elderly people, 39
Adoption, effect of new methods of producing biological offspring on, 73–74
Adult children
  as caregivers for elderly parents, 40–41
  death of, 29
  elderly people living with, 35–36
  living with parents, 20, 71
Age Discrimination in Employment Act, 16
AIDS. *See* Acquired immune deficiency syndrome
Alcohol problems, among elderly people, 34–35
Alzheimer's disease
  burdens on family of patient having, 223
  problems resulting from, 2
American Association of Retired Persons, 16, 39–40
Analogies, to predict future, 12

B

Bridge, B., 115

C

Campling, J., 115
Caregivers for elderly people
  overview of, 40–41
  paraprofessionals as, 44
  social workers as, 41–42, 47–48
  volunteers as, 42–43
  women as, 27–28, 95
Case management, 143
Catastrophic Health Act of 1988, 165, 167
Change
  economic, 10
  physical, 11
  resistance to, 146–148
  technological, 6, 8–10, 26, 28.
    See also Technological change
Child care
  changes in views of, 5
  nonfamily, 61–63
  professional view of, 60–61
  well-being of child in, 60
Childless couples, 73

Attitudes, toward elderly people, 48
Australia, methods of dealing with unemployment in, 107, 109

177

About the Author

David Macarov acquired a B. Sc. at the University of Pittsburgh in 1951, an M. Sc. at Case Western Reserve University in 1954, and a Ph.D. from the Florence Heller School for Advanced Studies in Social Welfare at Brandeis University in 1968. He has been teaching at the Paul Baerwald School of Social Work at the Hebrew University in Jerusalem since 1959, retiring as a professor emeritus.

Born in Savannah, Georgia, and growing up in Atlanta, he served in the American Air Force in China, Burma, and India during World War II and in the Israel Air Force during the War of Independence. He has resided in Jerusalem since 1947.

Professor Macarov is the author of *Incentives to Work, The Short Course in Development Training, The Design of Social Welfare, Work and Welfare: The Unholy Alliance, Worker Productivity: Myths and Reality,* and *Quitting Time,* as well as co-editor of *Social Welfare in Socialist Countries.* He was the founding director of the Joseph S. Schwartz Program for Training Community Center Directors and founder of The Society for the Reduction of Human Labor. He is a Life-Fellow of the International Fellowship for Social and Economic Development and advisory editor for a number of international journals.